I NEVER KNEW THAT ABOUT
DEVON & CORNWALL

BY THE SAME AUTHOR

I Never Knew That About the Lake District
I Never Knew That About England's Country Churches
I Never Knew That About New York
I Never Knew That About Royal Britain
I Never Knew That About Scotland
I Never Knew That About Coastal England
I Never Knew That About Yorkshire
I Never Knew That About the River Thames
I Never Knew That About England
I Never Knew That About England Illustrated
I Never Knew That About London
I Never Knew That About London Illustrated
I Never Knew That About Ireland
I Never Knew That About Wales
I Never Knew That About The English
I Never Knew That About The Irish
I Never Knew That About The Scottish
I Never Knew That About Britain: The Quiz Book
London By Tube
Walk Through History – Victorian London

I NEVER KNEW THAT ABOUT
DEVON & CORNWALL

CHRISTOPHER WINN

ILLUSTRATIONS BY
MAI OSAWA

EBURY
PRESS

EBURY PRESS

UK | USA | Canada | Ireland | Australia
India | New Zealand | South Africa

Ebury Press is part of the Penguin Random House group of companies
whose addresses can be found at global.penguinrandomhouse.com

Penguin Random House UK
One Embassy Gardens, 8 Viaduct Gardens, London SW11 7BW

penguin.co.uk

First published by Ebury Press in 2026
1

Copyright © Christopher Winn 2026
Illustrations © Mai Osawa
The moral right of the author has been asserted.

Penguin Random House values and supports copyright. Copyright fuels creativity, encourages diverse voices, promotes freedom of expression and supports a vibrant culture. Thank you for purchasing an authorised edition of this book and for respecting intellectual property laws by not reproducing, scanning or distributing any part of it by any means without permission. You are supporting authors and enabling Penguin Random House to continue to publish books for everyone. No part of this book may be used or reproduced in any manner for the purpose of training artificial intelligence technologies or systems. In accordance with Article 4(3) of the DSM Directive 2019/790, Penguin Random House expressly reserves this work from the text and data mining exception.

Set in 10.5/12.3pt Adobe Garamond Pro
Typeset by Six Red Marbles UK, Thetford, Norfolk

Printed and bound in Great Britain by Clays Ltd, Elcograf S.p.A.

The authorised representative in the EEA is Penguin Random House Ireland, Morrison Chambers, 32 Nassau Street, Dublin D02 YH68

A CIP catalogue record for this book is available from the British Library

ISBN 9781529980660

Penguin Random House is committed to a sustainable future for our business, our readers and our planet. This book is made from Forest Stewardship Council® certified paper.

For

Rupert and Sarah
Thank you for all your kindness and generosity

Mai
Thank you for your beautiful illustrations

CONTENTS

Preface ix
Devon and Cornwall xi

Exeter 1

East Devon 15

North Devon 41

Dartmoor and West Devon 65

South Devon 93

Plymouth 123

North Cornwall 149

West Cornwall 179

South Cornwall 205

Mid Cornwall 227

Gazetteer 251
Index of People 256
Index of Places 264
Acknowledgements 274

PREFACE

Devon and Cornwall combine to make up England's most popular holiday destination, drawn by the lure of golden beaches, clifftop walks, cream teas and unspoiled fishing villages. Go west of Exeter and the pace of life slows, the influence of London fades, the air becomes fresh with adventure and the smell of the sea.

Devon is England's third largest traditional county, with an acre and a half for every word in Shakespeare. Cornwall, half Devon's size, is England's westernmost and southernmost county.

According to legend, Britain was founded in Devon by Brutus of Troy when he landed at what is now Totnes. In Celtic times Devon and Cornwall were both part of the Brittonic kingdom of Dumnonia. In Saxon times the kingdom of Kernow, a Celtic land of saints and legendary kings, emerged in the far west. In AD 926 Athelstan, the Saxon King of Wessex, drove the Britons out of Devon and into Cornwall, later fixing the River Tamar as the border. Devon became part of Wessex and eventually England while Cornwall remained a separate kingdom with its own language, and today proudly maintains its place amongst the Celtic nations.

Devon and Cornwall are very different in landscape, with Devon generally soft and red and rolling, Cornwall rockbound, wild and wind swept. Devon's Dartmoor is grand, gold-green and romantic, Cornwall's Bodmin bleak, brown and treeless but imbued with mystery and unexpected havens of loveliness.

Both are maritime counties that look to the sea. Devon is the only English county with two separate coastlines, while Cornwall has the longest coastline of any English county. They are the only two of England's counties that face the open Atlantic with nothing between them and America. Atlantic waves make Cornwall the surfing capital of England and it was from Cornwall that the first transatlantic radio signals were transmitted.

Preface

Devon men explored the oceans, opened up the world for England, and defeated the Spanish Armada, giving England mastery of the seas for 300 years. A Devon man first sailed around the world in an English ship, another took possession of England's first territory overseas, and yet another established England's oldest colony.

Cornishmen have traded with the world for 4,000 years or more and worked the richest tin and copper mining area in the world. Fired by the desire to mitigate the hazards of mining, Cornishmen invented the steam pump, the safety lamp and the safety fuse, the breeches buoy, the lift, the steam locomotive, limelight and transparent soap.

Devon and Cornwall – Go West.

DEVON AND CORNWALL

Since neither Devon nor Cornwall have any particularly recognisable regions or distinct sub-divisions (such as in other English counties, like the Yorkshire Ridings), I have divided chapters into the points of the compass as follows.

Devon

North Devon being the north coast, Exmoor and north of Dartmoor between the Cornish border (River Tamar) and the River Exe.

East Devon being east of the River Exe, which rises on Exmoor and flows more or less due south through Devon to Exeter.

South Devon being the south coast and south of Dartmoor between the Cornish border (River Tamar) and the River Exe.

Dartmoor and West Devon being Dartmoor, which extends west almost to the Cornish border and therefore includes West Devon. I have also included the towns that lie just off Dartmoor but are considered gateways to the moor: Okehampton for the north moor, Tavistock for the west moor, Ashburton for the south and east moor.

Devon's two cities, Exeter and Plymouth, each have their own chapter.

Cornwall

North Cornwall being the north coast between St Ives and the Devon border.

West Cornwall being west of a line drawn from St Ives to Helston.

South Cornwall being the south coast between Helston and the Devon border.

Mid Cornwall being the area lying between the north and south coasts from Truro to the Devon border.

EXMOOR

PART OF SOMERSET

• Barnstaple

• Bideford

NORTH DEVON

River Exe

• Tiverton

EAST DEVON

• Okehampton

• Honiton

River Tamar

WEST DEVON

• Exeter

DARTMOOR

• Sidmouth

• Tavistock

• Ashburton

PART OF CORNWALL

SOUTH DEVON

• Plymouth • Totnes

• Dartmouth

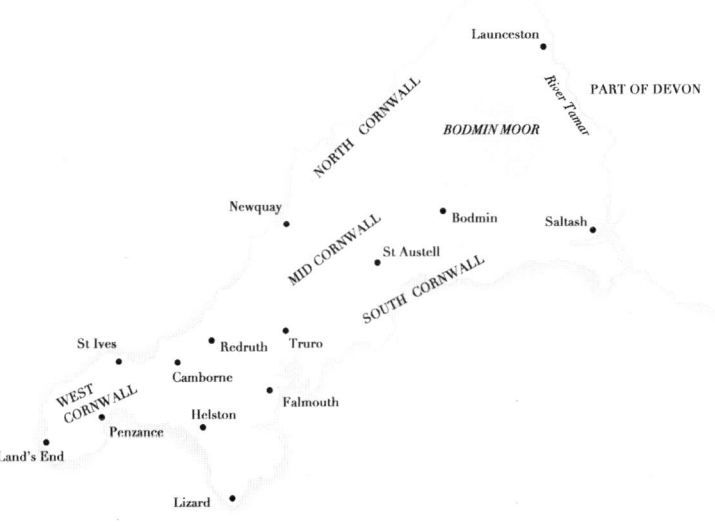

EXETER

Semper Fidelis

Motto bestowed on Exeter by Charles II for
the city's loyalty after the Restoration

Exeter Cathedral

Exeter, Devon's county town, has always been a city, one of England's oldest and loveliest, and was for a long time ENGLAND'S MOST WESTERLY CITY, until Truro usurped that accolade in 1877.

Exeter was founded at the lowest bridgeable point of the Exe by the Romans in around AD 50–55 as Isca Dumnoniorum, a fort that served as the base for the Second Augustan Legion at what was then the southwestern end of the Fosse Way. Exeter's High Street always has and still does follow the dead straight line of the Fosse Way.

After the Romans withdrew, Saxons, Danes and Normans all occupied the city in their time and even though much was destroyed when Exeter was badly bombed in 1942 during World War Two, something from each of these periods survives. A walk through Exeter brings constant surprises as history and ancient red sandstone buildings pop up unexpectedly around every corner.

Roman Exeter

In the 1970s THE LARGEST ROMAN BATH WITH THE MOST ADVANCED HEATING SYSTEM EVER FOUND IN BRITAIN was uncovered outside the west door of the cathedral, suggesting that the Roman settlement at Exeter was larger and more important than first realised. It is thought to date from the 1st century and amongst the finds were fragments from THE EARLIEST FIGURED MOSAIC EVER FOUND IN BRITAIN. In AD 200 the Romans built a red sandstone wall around the centre of the town, which was added to by Saxon, Norman and medieval builders who all followed the course of the Roman walls. A good stretch of wall, including THE ONLY LENGTH OF SAXON CITY WALL IN ENGLAND MADE OF STONE, runs through NORTHERNHAY GARDENS which were laid out in 1612 in the quarry from which the stone for the castle was mined. This is THE OLDEST PUBLIC OPEN SPACE IN BRITAIN. Next to Northernhay Gardens are ROUGEMONT GARDENS, occupying the site of the castle moat. The two are separated by the city wall in the corner of which stands ATHELSTAN'S TOWER, a mostly Norman defensive tower rebuilt using stone from the Saxon fortifications of King Athelstan.

Saxon Exeter

In 926 the Saxon king ATHELSTAN, grandson of Alfred the Great, swept into Exeter and drove out the Britons who were there, chasing them into Cornwall and fixing the River Tamar as their boundary. Athelstan also established a mint and changed the name of the town from Monkton to Exancaester, from where we get the modern name Exeter. He restored the Roman wall and built a castle on the highest point in the town using recycled Roman stone. This was destroyed by the Danes in 1003, although the ruined Athelstan's Tower, which had formed a prominent feature of the Saxon fortifications, was later rebuilt by the Normans.

Norman Exeter

In 1068, two years after the Battle of Hastings, William the Conqueror laid siege to Exeter. He was looking for King Harold Godwinson's mother GYTHA, who was living in Exeter where she had an extensive estate. Thanks to the city walls, Exeter, THE LAST TOWN

IN ENGLAND TO HOLD OUT AGAINST THE CONQUEROR, was able to keep William at bay at the East Gate just long enough for Gytha to slip out the West Gate and escape to Denmark where her family were. To stamp his authority on the city, William built ROUGEMONT CASTLE at the northern corner of the Roman walls on Exeter's highest point, the Red Mound, the red sandstone hill from which the castle takes its name. All that is left of Rougemont today is the massive ROUGEMONT CASTLE GATEHOUSE; built in 1068 and incorporating Saxon architectural features such as triangular windows, it is amongst THE OLDEST STANDING CASTLE BUILDINGS IN BRITAIN. On the wall nearby is a plaque stating that in 1685 ALICE MOLLAND was tried in Rougemont Castle and hanged at Heavitree outside the eastern city walls, THE LAST PERSON IN ENGLAND TO BE EXECUTED FOR WITCHCRAFT.

St Nicholas Priory

ST NICHOLAS PRIORY was established in Exeter in 1087 by Benedictine monks sent from Battle Abbey by William the Conqueror, who handed over to them the properties he had confiscated from Harold's mother Gytha. For over 400 years the monks were an integral part of life in Exeter, offering worship, education and hospitality to townsfolk, pilgrims and travellers. With the Dissolution of the Monasteries the religious parts of the priory were demolished but the north and west domestic ranges were turned into a large Tudor town dwelling. Today the priory buildings accommodate a museum furnished as an Elizabethan house and used as an event venue. St Nicholas Priory, renowned for its superb Norman vaulted undercroft and its guest hall with superb oak ceiling, is THE OLDEST INTACT BUILDING IN EXETER.

Churches

It's easy to overlook the mere churches in a city blessed with the loveliest cathedral in England, but the Normans left us a few worthy of mention.

A bit like a pop-up stall, the little CHURCH OF ST PANCRAS sits incongruously slap bang in the middle of the modern Guildhall Shopping Centre on what is in fact THE EARLIEST CHRISTIAN SITE IN EXETER. The simple two cell design shows the church to be of Anglo-Saxon origin and it has some Norman

St Olave's Church

work but the present building dates mainly from the 13th century.

St Olave's Church, which stands in front of St Nicholas Priory in Fore Street, was founded by King Harold's mother Gytha in the mid-11th century before the Conquest. Most of the church was rebuilt in the 14th century but the tall square tower built, uniquely, into the Sanctuary, is possibly from the original church and therefore even older than the Norman Priory behind it. It was the priests of St Olave's who helped Gytha escape to the west when William the Conqueror laid siege to the city.

St Mary Arches Church, in a mundane setting just off the High Street, looks ordinary from the outside but the stunningly gorgeous Norman interior is unique in Devon: four bay arcades of simple round arches held up by massive round pillars topped with carved square capitals. Norman England at its best. What a shame the church is only open occasionally.

The Church of St Mary Steps stands near the site of the city's old West Gate, now demolished, at the bottom of Stepcote Hill, a flight of more than 100 steps that once formed the main route into Exeter – across the Old Exe Bridge, through the West Gate and up Stepcote Hill. In 1688, having landed on the Devon coast at Brixham, William of Orange rode up Stepcote Hill with a large force of men and horses to be proclaimed in Exeter Cathedral, before marching on to London to claim the Crown from James II. It must have been quite a sight. St Mary Steps Church was founded in 1150 and is famous for its clock of 1619 whereby Matthew the Miller, a local 17th-century miller whose habits were so regular that the folk of Exeter could keep time by him, heralds the hour by leaning forward in his chair to strike a large bell, while his pike-wielding sons strike smaller bells every quarter hour.

The House That Moved

Medieval Exeter

The House That Moved

Opposite the church is THE HOUSE THAT MOVED, a medieval timber-framed merchant's house that was jacked up on rollers in 1961 and, in a move that took four days and gained international attention, was relocated 100 yards across the road, intact, all to make way for a road improvement scheme. The house dates from c.1430, making it ONE OF THE OLDEST TIMBER-FRAMED HOUSES IN DEVON AND, INDEED, ENGLAND.

Old Exe Bridge

The same road improvement scheme left the impressive remains of Exeter's first stone bridge across the Exe marooned in the middle of a traffic island. The OLD EXE BRIDGE was built in 1190, making it THE OLDEST SURVIVING SUBSTANTIAL BRIDGE IN ENGLAND. Eight of the original eighteen arches of the bridge survive, along with the ruins of a bridge chapel dedicated to St Edmund, making the Old Exe Bridge THE OLDEST SURVIVING BRIDGE IN BRITAIN STILL WITH A CHAPEL ON IT. The bridge stayed in service for almost 600 years until replaced in 1778 and it is a thrilling experience to walk along Britain's oldest bridge in the footsteps of the medieval monks and merchants who came this way over the centuries.

St Thomas

Across the river was another chapel, this time dedicated to St Thomas Becket, the martyred Archbishop of Canterbury. The chapel was constantly flooded and washed away and was eventually moved inland from the river, being rebuilt several times into the present rather beautiful red sandstone ST THOMAS CHURCH. Inside is a 14th-century wooden lectern brought from Exeter Cathedral in 1840, THE OLDEST SURVIVING CATHEDRAL LECTERN IN BRITAIN. In 1549 the Vicar of St Thomas, ROBERT WELSHE, was hanged from the top of the church tower for helping lead the Prayer Book Rebellion, an uprising by West Country Catholics against the imposition of the English Prayer Book. In early 1884 General Gordon came to see his grandfather's grave in St Thomas but got no further than the north porch when he received a telegram calling him away to Khartoum, from whence he never returned.

Exeter Guildhall

There was a Guild recorded in Exeter in Saxon times, around AD 1000, and it is thought that there was some sort of guildhall where the present hall stands in the High Street. It is known for certain that there was a guildhall there in the 14th century, and under the Council Chamber there is a cellar dating from the early 14th century known as the '*pytt of the Guyldhall*'. The Council Chamber itself was constructed in 1470, the huge carved oak door to the chamber in 1593 and the impressive frontage, which projects out over the pavement supported on granite pillars, was built in 1594. The hall is still used for civic functions and is believed to be THE OLDEST MUNICIPAL BUILDING IN ENGLAND STILL IN CIVIC USE, while it also contains THE OLDEST CIVIC SEAL IN BRITAIN, dating from 1175.

Wynards Almshouses

WYNARDS ALMSHOUSES were founded in 1435 by WILLIAM WYNARD, Recorder of Exeter, possibly on the proceeds of piracy, which was rife amongst the great and the good of Exeter, and elsewhere in Devon and Cornwall, at the time. The almshouses were built around a courtyard to house a priest and 12 poor or infirm men and they still stand close to the quayside but are now private dwellings. William Wynard endowed his house in South Street, near the cathedral, to provide funds to maintain the almshouses. The house became the Blue Boar Inn and is now the Georgian WHITE HART HOTEL which, being near what was the South Gate, once did a roaring trade as a coaching inn. The Monty Python production team stayed there in 1974 while filming the last series of *Monty Python's Flying Circus*, as did snooker player Steve Davis and singer Chesney Hawkes in 2010.

Tuckers Hall

By the 15th century Exeter had become rich on wool, the third richest city outside London, and in 1471 the COMPANY OF WEAVERS, FULLERS [TUCKERS] AND SHEARMEN, who at the time administered 80 per cent of Exeter's workforce, built themselves a grand headquarters known as TUCKERS HALL, equipped with a magnificent barrel-roofed banqueting hall. The entrance was built at street level but now requires ten steps to reach, showing how far the level of the street has been lowered. The Hall is open several days a week.

Quayside

From prehistoric times until the end of the 14th century, Exeter was a busy port with cargoes unloaded on a handy ridge of sandstone beside the river. In 1381, after a dispute between ISABELLA DE FORTIBUS, COUNTESS OF DEVON, and the city, the Countess built a weir, known as the Countess Weir, across the Exe downstream to power her mills, which restricted the size of ships that could reach Exeter. Then, 25 years later, her cousin HUGH COURTENAY, 9TH EARL OF DEVON, blocked the river completely so that ships could only reach as far as Topsham. Here, the Earl could charge tolls for unloading and to transport goods upriver to Exeter. Topsham became the second busiest port in England for a time and the Earl prospered, although the building of the Exeter Ship Canal and the arrival of the railway in 1861 finally put paid to that particular enterprise.

Exeter Ship Canal

In 1566, in order to bypass the weirs, the city sponsored the construction of the EXETER SHIP CANAL, running just over three miles and extending beyond the Countess Wier. It was THE FIRST CANAL TO BE BUILT IN BRITAIN SINCE THE ROMANS and THE FIRST EVER TO USE LOCKS. The canal was constantly lengthened and improved through the years until Exeter was once again able to thrive as a port. The Roman quayside was enlarged to handle the resulting trade and in 1680 ENGLAND's FIRST PURPOSE-BUILT CUSTOM HOUSE was erected on the quayside and kept in continued use until 1989. The Custom House is now a visitor attraction and museum while the quayside has become a popular recreation area with shops and restaurants.

Cathedral Close

The CATHEDRAL CLOSE, laid out on the site of the Roman Basilica and Bath House, is a peaceful, traffic-free oasis and green space off the

High Street. Once completely walled off behind seven gates, the close is today linked to the High Street and the outside world by narrow alleyways and is lined with a variety of interesting old buildings.

Hidden away in the south-west corner of the cathedral close where the Roman praetorium stood is St Petrock's Church. Squeezed between shops and offices, it often goes unnoticed, although the tower facing the High Street has a peculiar octagonal cap put there in 1736. The present building dates from the 12th century but has been rebuilt, refurbished, repurposed and even reorientated by the Victorians and is now mainly used as a charity centre.

Equally tucked away in the north-west corner is St Martin's Church, consecrated in 1065 but now mostly 15th-century with a strange, immensely tall, square tower with a polygonal staircase attached.

Mol's Coffee House

Next to St Martin's Church is the flamboyantly picturesque Mol's Coffee House, with its ornate gable, shapely Tudor and Dutch windows, black-painted timbers, white walls and outsize set of royal arms of Elizabeth I. It was built in the early 16th century to house

some of the cathedral's priests and after the Dissolution was leased to a John Dyer, who used the house to negotiate payment from the government for ships to take on the Spanish Armada. Legend says that Sir Francis Drake met with his fellow sea captains Hawkins, Raleigh and Grenville on the first floor, but this may just be clever marketing by later leaseholders ...

In 1596 Mol's became the city's first Custom House, then an apothecary's shop, a shoe shop and a haberdasher's. In 1726 the building was leased to a Mary Wildy, also known as Mol, who set it up as a coffee shop. This was subsequently run exclusively by women until forced to close in 1837 after a dispute with the church authorities about opening hours. Since then, Mol's has been an art gallery, a printer's, a jeweller's and a stationer's. Mol's Coffee Shop is currently undergoing redevelopment after narrowly escaping the 2016 fire that gutted next-door ROYAL CLARENCE HOTEL, THE FIRST PROPERTY IN BRITAIN TO BE CALLED A HOTEL.

Exeter Cathedral

While not majestic like Lincoln, powerful like Durham or grand like Canterbury, EXETER CATHEDRAL is pretty much perfect, a sublime

example of English Decorated Gothic in weathered, creamy local stone. UNIQUELY FOR AN ENGLISH CATHEDRAL, Exeter has no central or west towers. Instead, two rugged square Norman towers, one containing THE SECOND LARGEST PEAL OF BELLS IN THE WORLD after Liverpool Cathedral, and each carved with a hundred arches, flank the graceful, buttressed nave halfway along, north and south, like paddle wheels on a steamboat. The west face of the cathedral is covered in statues of angels and prophets and kings, forming THE LARGEST SURVIVING DISPLAY OF MEDIEVAL SCULPTURE IN BRITAIN. But what makes Exeter Cathedral lovely beyond words is inside. Stand with your back to the west door and look east down THE LONGEST UNBROKEN STRETCH OF GOTHIC VAULTING IN THE WORLD, 315 feet (96 metres) of sheer beauty. When dappled in the evening sunlight, as it shines in through the great west window, the cathedral becomes a row of palm trees waving in the wind. Surely a glimpse of Heaven.

Exeter's Saxon Minster became the city's new cathedral when the bishopric of Devon and Cornwall was transferred from Crediton to Exeter in 1050, since Exeter was better defended. In 1112 William Warelwast, a nephew of William the Conqueror, was made Bishop of Exeter by Henry I and began work on a new cathedral to replace the Minster. All that remains from this Norman cathedral are the two transept towers, and in 1270 it was decided not to carry on in the Norman style but to build something in the new and more fashionable, elegant Decorated Gothic style. The cathedral as we know it today was completed in 1400 and has been little altered since then.

Cathedral Treasures
Although the choir stalls have been replaced five times since the cathedral was built, most recently by George Gilbert Scott in the 1870s, the misericords from the original medieval stalls were

installed in the new choir stalls each time. Exeter's fifty medieval misericords are THE OLDEST COMPLETE SET OF MISERICORDS IN ENGLAND, with 48 of them carved in the 13th century, one in the 14th and one in the 15th century. Amongst the carvings under the seats is THE EARLIEST KNOWN DEPICTION IN ENGLAND OF AN ELEPHANT, possibly based on the elephant given by Louis IX of France to Henry III in 1255 and kept in the Tower of London.

High up on the north side of the nave is the MINSTREL'S GALLERY, a balcony decorated with carved and brightly painted angels playing musical instruments. Constructed in c.1360, the gallery is UNIQUE IN ENGLISH CATHEDRALS.

Both the GREAT WEST WINDOW and the GREAT EAST WINDOW contain rare, early 14th-century stained glass.

Also from the early 14th century is the BISHOP'S THRONE. Made from Devonshire oak, it is 53 feet (16 metres) tall, THE TALLEST MEDIEVAL BISHOP'S THRONE IN THE WORLD, and is considered to be the most exquisite example of medieval woodwork in Europe. In 1688, on his way to claim the crown in London after landing at Brixham, William of Orange occupied the Bishop's Throne while his declaration of peaceful intent was read out.

WELL, I NEVER KNEW THIS ABOUT

EXETER

When last I was at Exeter,
The mayor in courtesy showed me the castle
And called it Rougemont, at which name I started ...

From *Richard III* by William Shakespeare

WHEN RICHARD III visited Exeter in 1483, he was shown the castle and was much impressed by its strength and strategic location. When informed that it was called Rougemont, he misheard it as Richmond and became agitated because of a prophecy that said he would '*not long survive the sight of Richmond*'. Two years later, this proved only too true when he faced Henry Tudor, the Earl of Richmond, at Bosworth Field, and became the last English king to die in battle.

The TURK'S HEAD PUB next to Exeter's Guildhall has been serving for over 700 years and is one of Devon's oldest pubs. It was said to be a favourite of CHARLES DICKENS and it was at the Turk's Head that Dickens found inspiration for the character of Joe the 'Fat Boy' from *The Pickwick Papers*.

Running under the centre of Exeter are a series of underground passages, the earliest dating from the 13th century, that were built to bring clean drinking water into the city. Guided tours are run through the passages, THE ONLY SUCH UNDERGROUND PASSAGES OPEN TO THE PUBLIC IN BRITAIN.

The EXETER ASTRONOMICAL CLOCK in Exeter Cathedral, showing the Earth at the centre of the universe, was built in 1484 and is one of four such clocks in the west of England along with those at Wimborne Minster in Dorset, Ottery St Mary in Devon and Wells in Somerset.

On 16 June 1644, during the Civil War, Charles I's youngest child, PRINCESS HENRIETTA, was born in Exeter in Bedford House. This stood to the north of the cathedral and was the home of the Royalist supporter the Earl of Bedford. Exeter was then in Royalist hands and Charles had sent his wife Henrietta Maria to Exeter from Oxford believing that she would be safer there. Princess Henrietta was baptised in Exeter Cathedral on 21 July and met her father Charles I for the first and only time when he visited Exeter on 26 July 1644. Princess Henrietta went on to marry the Duke of Orleans, younger brother of the French king Louis XIV, but died at the tragically young age of 26.

EAST DEVON

And while old Otter's steeple rings ...

From an ode to his birthplace by Samuel Taylor Coleridge

Otter St Mary Church

Tiverton

A DELIGHTFUL SMALL market town full of narrow streets lined with old houses, TIVERTON began life as a Saxon settlement set above the meeting of the River Loman and the River Exe. There were two fords, one across the Loman and one across the Exe, hence the early name of Twyfordtown which eventually became Tiverton.

By the 16th century Tiverton had grown into Devon's foremost cloth manufacturing centre and owes its present prosperity to JOHN HEATHCOAT, a Nottingham lace maker who set up shop in Tiverton in 1816. Heathcoat invented a machine for making lace that threatened the livelihood of the Nottingham workers, and he was chased out of the Midlands by Luddites who invaded his factory in Loughborough and destroyed the machine. So he bought a disused woollen mill on the west bank of the Exe at Tiverton and converted it into a lace factory, installing a new and improved version of his machine, and re-employing many of the workers from his Midlands factory who had walked the 200 miles down to Tiverton with their families in hope of work with their former employer. The factory expanded rapidly along with the town as Heathcoat put up terraced houses and schools for his workers. Today Heathcoat Fabrics remains a mainstay of the town, still occupying the same site as the original lace factory, albeit in more modern factory buildings, and manufacturing all kinds of knitted and woven fabrics.

Tiverton Castle

In 1106 RICHARD DE REDVERS, made the first Norman Earl of Devon by Henry I, built a motte and bailey castle on a defensive site above the Exe which was enlarged and rebuilt in stone by the COURTENAYS, who inherited the castle at the end of the 13th century, and later the Earldom through a cousin. In 1495 William Courtenay, one of the early Courtenay Earls of Devon, married KATHERINE PLANTAGENET, sixth daughter of Edward IV, who came to live at Tiverton Castle. She died there in 1527, and her funeral was held next door in St Peter's Church where she is buried.

At the start of the Civil War the castle was held by the Royalists but in 1645, during a siege by Parliamentary troops led by Sir Thomas Fairfax, a lucky shot from a new long-range cannon sited on

a hill half a mile away hit one of the chains holding up the castle's drawbridge, which promptly fell open, allowing Fairfax's troops to rush in and overwhelm the defenders. They proceeded to dismantle the defensive structures of the castle, leaving only the impressive battlemented gatehouse, some sections of ruined wall and a round corner tower. The castle then passed through a number of hands until early in the 18th century it was inherited by the CAREW FAMILY, Devon landed gentry who converted the castle into a comfortable private home.

In 1960 the house was purchased by screenwriter IVAR CAMPBELL, formerly of Knowstone Manor (see panel on page 18), and was later passed on to his nephew, the current owner. The castle is open for visitors during the summer months.

> ## KNOWSTONE MANOR
>
> Before purchasing Tiverton Castle in 1960, screenwriter IVAR CAMPBELL lived in an infamous house in the village of Knowstone some 12 miles north-west of Tiverton. KNOWSTONE MANOR was built in the late 1930s, reportedly as a luxurious country retreat for ADOLF HITLER had he succeeded in conquering England. During the war, despite having ten bedrooms, a galleried hall and a ballroom, the house was lived in by just one man, a German bachelor, and his housekeeper. Thought to have been financed with funds from the Third Reich, the substantial house stood alone in 1,600 acres and from the air resembled a swastika. At the centre was a glass dome filled with lights that, again, could only be seen from the air and was supposedly to be used as a signal for German aircraft. Knowstone Manor was put up for sale in 1945 not long after Hitler's death and was described in the *Country Life* advert as '*probably the most spacious modern country house of moderate size built in recent years. The residence is one of great architectural distinction, easily accessible but in the heart of unspoilt country*'. Alas, the house burned down in the 1960s and was replaced by a rather less exciting modern farmhouse.

St Peter's Church

ST PETER'S CHURCH stands right beside the castle, on the site of a wooden Saxon church that was replaced in stone in 1073. Only a small doorway in the north wall, once used by the de Redvers Earls of Devon to enter the church from the castle, survives from the Norman church, which was almost entirely rebuilt in the 15th century. Of national interest are the embattled south porch and Greenway Chapel, constructed of pale Beer stone in 1517 on behalf of JOHN GREENWAY, Tiverton's most prominent cloth merchant. Both are beautifully decorated outside with exquisite carvings of ships and other nautical symbols reflecting the source of Greenway's wealth. They are amongst THE BEST CARVINGS TO BE FOUND IN ANY ENGLISH CHURCH, described by English Heritage as '*a tour de force of late Perpendicular decoration*'.

A particularly fine carving of the Assumption of the Virgin above the inner doorway of the porch shows Greenway and his wife kneeling piously alongside the Latin initials I.G. ('I' is the Latin equivalent of 'J'.)

Inside the church on either side of the sanctuary are the chest tombs of two other Tiverton cloth merchants who contributed to the church, John Waldron (d.1579) and George Slee (d.1613). All three merchants built sets of almshouses that still stand in the town and continue to provide housing today. Waldron's almshouse also includes a chapel, with a decorated porch and a bell that was cast in Cleves in Germany in 1539, the year before Anne of Cleves briefly became Henry VIII's fourth queen. It is THE OLDEST DATED BELL IN DEVON.

The church organ of St Peter's was made in 1696 by Christian Schmidt and his uncle Bernard, who also built the organ in St Paul's Cathedral, and was restored in the 18th and 19th centuries. The carvings on the organ case are by Grinling Gibbons. It was on this organ that THE FIRST EVER PERFORMANCE OF MENDELSSOHN'S WEDDING MARCH WAS PLAYED on 2 June 1847 at the wedding of Tom Daniel and Dorothy Carew, arranged and played by Samuel Reay.

Blundell's

Another Tiverton cloth merchant, PETER BLUNDELL, who died in 1601, bequeathed money and land for a school for local children which was duly founded in Tiverton in 1604. The school was relocated to the edge of the town in 1882 but the original school buildings, which were far grander than any other school buildings in the West Country, are now cared for by the National Trust and are open to visitors.

R.D. BLACKMORE (1825–1900) attended Old Blundell's and set the fight scene between John Ridd and Robin Snell from his novel *Lorna Doone* on the triangular lawn in front of the school buildings.

An annual tradition, still honoured at Blundell's, is a cross-country race called the Russell, first run in 1887 and named in honour of Blundell's Old Boy, the sporting parson JOHN 'JACK' RUSSELL (1795–1883).

Others who were educated at Blundell's include JOHN WYNDHAM (1903–69), author of *The Day of the Triffids* and racing driver BEN COLLINS (b.1975) who was the original Stig from *Top Gear* and stunt driver on the James Bond films *Casino Royale*, *Quantum of Solace* and *Skyfall*.

St George's Church

Tiverton's CHURCH OF ST GEORGE, designed by John James, completed in 1733 and largely left alone by the Victorians, is considered to be THE FINEST GEORGIAN CHURCH IN DEVON and one of the finest in England. Buried in the churchyard are SAMUEL WESLEY, older brother of the Methodist founder John Wesley and Master of Blundell's from 1733 until his death in 1739, and the 18th-century playwright HANNAH COWLEY (1743–1809) who was mentored by David Garrick and whose best-known play, a romantic comedy called *The Belle's Stratagem*, provided a favourite role for Ellen Terry and is still often revived.

Opposite St George's is Tiverton's TOWN HALL of 1864, a flamboyant mix of French Venetian and Victorian Baroque architecture and considered the most striking town hall in Devon outside of Plymouth and Exeter.

Knightshayes Court

The gloriously Victorian KNIGHTSHAYES COURT, two miles north of Tiverton, was commissioned in 1868 by SIR JOHN HEATHCOAT-AMORY, grandson of the John Heathcoat who set up the Tiverton lace factory in 1816. The house was designed by WILLIAM BURGES, renowned for his exuberant architectural style, and who at the same time was remodelling Cardiff Castle for the Marquess of Bute. Knightshayes is THE ONLY SMALL COUNTRY HOUSE BURGES EVER DESIGNED FROM SCRATCH. Burges could never be accused of restraint and the exterior of Knightshayes is festooned with his trademark gargoyles and sculptures of fantastical beasts, but he wasn't allowed to complete his full riotously Gothic vision for the interior rooms which proved too excessive – and expensive – for Heathcoat-Amory, who preferred his decor a little more sober. To mask his disappointment, Burges rather let himself loose on the stable block which is almost as extravagant as the main house.

Knightshayes sits on a small hill overlooking Tiverton – or more pertinently, the Heathcoat lace mill – which allowed Sir John to keep an eye on things from his rather splendid garden, designed by leading English landscape gardener EDWARD KEMP. The Heathcoat-Amory family continued to live at Knightshayes until 1972, when it was handed over to the National Trust.

Bickleigh

One of two Bickleighs in Devon (the other is on the southern edge of Dartmoor near Plymouth), this BICKLEIGH lies in the Exe valley south of Tiverton and is one of the prettiest villages in a county of pretty villages, blessed with a very attractive 17th-century stone bridge across the Exe. Although there's not much of it, Bickleigh has a lot going on and most of this happens around the bridge. On the east side of the river, BICKLEIGH MILL is a working 18th-century watermill converted into a recreational and shopping attraction. Next to it, occupying Bickleigh's beautifully restored Victorian railway station, is the DEVON RAILWAY CENTRE offering model and miniature railways and rides on a narrow-gauge railway.

Fisherman's Cot

Across the bridge is the extravagantly thatched FISHERMAN'S COT, built in 1933 as a fishing lodge for Bickleigh Castle and now a picturesque inn. Local legend has it that PAUL SIMON, of Simon and Garfunkel, stayed at the inn in the 1960s while appearing in Exeter. His room overlooked the weir below the bridge and one evening after rain the river became turbulent and flooded its banks, inspiring Simon to write his famous song *Bridge Over Troubled Water*. Many years later, Art Garfunkel denied the story but the inhabitants of Bickleigh know what they know ...

Bickleigh Castle

Lying a little to the south of the village in a picturesque spot on the west bank of the Exe, BICKLEIGH CASTLE is all that is left of a 15th-century fortified manor house built on the site of a Saxon house by the COURTENAYS, and then lived in by the CAREWS, who owned the estate until 1924. The Carews were Royalists and in 1644, during the Civil War, gave sanctuary to a heavily pregnant HENRIETTA MARIA, Charles I's wife, who was on her way to Exeter to give birth to the king's youngest child PRINCESS HENRIETTA. For this act of hospitality Bickleigh Court, as it was then known, was demolished by

Cromwell's men, leaving just the magnificent three-storey gatehouse and a jumble of buildings set around the courtyard behind it, including a section of the old manor house now called the Old Court House. The top part of one of the gatehouse towers blew down in a storm in 2024 and is currently being rebuilt using the original bricks.

Norman Chapel

Across the road from the gatehouse is a rare and beautiful 12th-century thatched single cell chapel, built on the site of a Saxon church that grew out of a 5th-century Saxon meeting house. It is believed that in 1050 EDWARD THE CONFESSOR came to the Saxon manor house at Bickleigh to chair a meeting to discuss the apportioning of land in Devon.

In the 13th century a new parish church dedicated to St Mary the Virgin was built across the river and the splendid Norman font from the old chapel, amongst the best in Devon, was removed to the new church where it can still be seen. St Mary's is also noted for its fine 13th-century church tower and for several impressive Carew family monuments.

Exmouth

EXMOUTH, which lies on the east bank of the Exe estuary nine miles downriver from Exeter, is DEVON'S OLDEST SEASIDE RESORT and began to develop as such towards the end of the 18th century when the Napoleonic Wars stopped people travelling on the Continent. People of means came to Exmouth for the sea air and the town's smartest street, THE BEACON, a terrace of red brick and stucco Georgian houses with fine sea views, was built for them in 1792.

Exmouth expanded rapidly with the arrival of the trains and the day trippers in 1861 and soon began to subsume the surrounding villages. Today the bulk of the town is Victorian. A vestige of the old Exmouth survives in North Street on the northern outskirts, where PRIMROSE COTTAGE is celebrated as THE ONLY THATCHED HOUSE LEFT IN EXMOUTH TOWN CENTRE.

Notable Exmouth Residents

Thanks to SIR JOHN COLLETON, 3rd Baronet, EXMOUTH WAS THE FIRST TOWN IN BRITAIN TO GROW MAGNOLIAS. Born in Exmouth in 1669, Sir John Colleton emigrated to South Carolina to run the family estate that had been set up there by his grandfather. He retired to Exmouth in 1729, bringing the magnolia with him, and planted it in the garden of his home, the Manor of Rill, which stood on the road to Exeter north of Exmouth. The magnolia evolved into the magnificent *Magnolia grandiflora* 'Exmouth' variety from which the local nurserymen were allowed to take cuttings to produce more plants that could be sold around the country. Sir John Colleton's magnolia is incorporated into Exmouth's coat of arms and the town's Magnolia Walk and the Magnolia Centre are named for it.

LADY FRANCES 'FANNY' NELSON, the estranged wife of Admiral Lord Horatio Nelson, lived in a house on the Beacon, now called NELSON HOUSE, from 1803 until 1829 with her son by her first marriage, JOSIAH NISBET. She and Josiah are buried next to each other not far away in the churchyard of ST MARGARET AND ST ANDREW AT LITTLEHAM, the village from which Exmouth developed, which now lies on the eastern outskirts of the town.

LADY BYRON and her daughter ADA moved to Exmouth not long after her separation from her husband, the poet Lord Byron, in 1816 and took up residence in a house on the Beacon now called BYRON COURT. Concerned about Ada's health and worried that she might inherit her father's wild moods, Lady Byron encouraged Ada to study mathematics, a subject that she herself excelled at. Ada would later find fame as THE WORLD'S FIRST COMPUTER PROGRAMMER when she wrote algorithms for Charles Babbage's Analytical Engine, forerunner of the modern computer. An early computer programming language was named ADA in her honour.

ADMIRAL OF THE FLEET SIR FAIRFAX MORESBY (1786–1877) joined the Royal Navy at the age of 13, and in 1821 he was sent to take command of Mauritius Station with orders to stamp out the East African slave trade. To this end he drew up the Moresby Treaty with the Sultan of Oman prohibiting the sale of slaves to British India and Christians of any nationality, praised by William Wilberforce as a huge advance in the anti-slavery cause. Moresby retired to Exmouth and lived from 1861 until his death in 1877 at 1 EXECLIFF, a fine Georgian house sandwiched between Gothic towers in Trefusis Terrace which runs on east from the Beacon.

GENERAL GORDON OF KHARTOUM should be on this list, but he was killed in action before he could move into MIRIMAR, the house that he was having built in Douglas Avenue on the eastern outskirts of Exmouth. The grey brick house, spookily Victorian with tall gables, dormer windows and turrets, is still there, hemmed in by modern blocks of flats, and was eventually lived in by Gordon's sister Augusta.

A La Ronde

Set on a hill above Exmouth is the unique A LA RONDE, a quirky hexadecagonal (16-sided) 'round' house built in 1796 for reclusive spinsters JANE PARMINTER, daughter of a Barnstaple wine merchant, and her cousin Mary after their return from a Grand Tour of Europe. The design is based on the 6th-century Byzantine Basilica of San Vitale in Ravenna, Northern Italy. At the centre of the house is the sea-green OCTAGON ROOM with eight doors leading off it, and above it the incredible SHELL GALLERY decorated with more than 25,000 seashells.

Jane and Mary lived a quiet life at A La Ronde until their deaths, Jane in 1811 and Mary in 1849. They are both buried in a chapel they had built in the grounds called POINT-IN-VIEW.

A La Ronde, which is now owned by the National Trust, is thought to have been the inspiration for Bill Weasley's Shell Cottage in the films *Harry Potter and the Deathly Hallows Part 1* and *Part 2*.

Plymtree

ST JOHN THE BAPTIST CHURCH in the pretty village of PLYMTREE near Cullompton possesses THE FINEST MEDIEVAL ROOD SCREEN IN DEVON – and Devon possesses the finest rood screens in Britain. Above the superb fan vaulting is an exquisitely carved cornice covered in gilt, while below is a colourful, remarkably well-preserved gallery of painted figures, ONE OF

THE MOST COMPLETE SERIES OF SUCH PAINTINGS IN ANY CHURCH IN ENGLAND. The screen dates from around 1470 and is thought to have come from a nearby abbey, donated to the church by Isabel, the widow of Humphrey Stafford, Earl of Devon.

At the back of the church is a striking 16th-century Flemish alabaster panel depicting the Resurrection, once part of an altarpiece.

A niche in the west face of the church tower contains a rare and wonderfully fluid pre-Reformation statue of the Madonna and Child, so immaculately restored in 1989 that it won the John Betjeman Award from the Society for the Protection of Ancient Buildings (SPAB).

In the churchyard is one of the Great Trees of East Devon, a yew tree believed to be over 1,100 years old and thought to have given Plymtree its name.

Famous Rectors of Plymtree

RICHARD SMART, Rector of Plymtree in the 15th century, wrote a carol featuring a character called 'Sir Christemas' who urges his listeners to celebrate the Birth of Christ with drink and good cheer, THE FIRST RECORDED MENTION ANYWHERE OF THE ENGLISH PATRIARCHAL PERSONIFICATION OF CHRISTMAS now known as Father Christmas.

Plymtree's rector in the 17th century was NICHOLAS MONK, brother of General Monk, the Parliamentarian military commander in the Civil War who was then instrumental in the Restoration of Charles II in 1660. Nicholas was apparently the person who, more than anyone, persuaded General Monk to support the Restoration.

Ancient Houses around Plymtree

A little north-east of Plymtree is FORDMOOR FARM which still retains its 17th-century brick front, possibly THE EARLIEST BRICK-BUILT HOUSE IN DEVON.

On the western edge of the village is PLYMTREE MANOR, a quite ravishing red brick William and Mary house built in 1710 for the HARWARD family. The most famous member of the Harwards was the REVEREND CHARLES HARWARD, who was born in the manor in 1723 and died there in 1802. A keen sportsman and farmer much given to swearing, he became chaplain at the court of George III and then Dean of Chichester, where he was described by his contemporary the diarist John Marsh as *'a man much fitter to be at the head of a regiment than of a Chapter'*. Apparently, he would spit at any choirboy who fell asleep during the service.

WOODBEER COURT lies about two miles north-east of Plymtree and was a large 15th century house that has been converted into a farmhouse but little changed.

Budleigh Salterton

Sedate BUDLEIGH SALTERTON is the setting for Millais's painting *The Boyhood of Raleigh* and the sea wall seen in the picture is still there in front of the pink pebbled beach. Sir Walter Raleigh was born c.1552 at a thatched farmhouse nearby called HAYES BARTON and his family had a pew in All Saints Church in East Budleigh.

Sir Walter Raleigh
1552–1618

SIR WALTER RALEIGH, showman, writer, poet, adventurer and explorer, was born at Hayes Barton, a picturesque farmhouse hidden down a quiet lane a couple of miles north of Budleigh Salterton. His wit, looks and self-confident charm made him a favourite at the court of Queen Elizabeth I, and it was entirely in keeping when he took off his expensive cloak and laid it down in front of the Queen at Greenwich, so that she wouldn't have to walk through a muddy puddle.

After sailing to look for the Northwest Passage with his half-brother Humphrey Gilbert, Raleigh was sent to Ireland to put down a rebellion, which he did by

harshly executing those who surrendered, but nonetheless earned the admiration and gratitude of the Queen who subsequently granted him lands in Ireland.

In 1585 Raleigh was knighted and in the same year made Lord Warden of the Stanneries in Devon and Cornwall, instigating mining reforms that made him genuinely popular with his fellow Devonians.

The New World

The previous year, in 1584, the Queen had granted Raleigh a charter to establish a settlement in the New World as a base from which to launch raids on Spanish treasure ships, and in 1585 Raleigh sent a military expedition to set up a colony in Virginia under the leadership of his cousin Richard Grenville. They landed on an island called Roanoke off the coast of what is now North Carolina, but this turned out to be a bad choice. The land was unproductive, the men squabbled, and the local Native Americans resented them. The colony did not take and the would-be colonists had to be rescued and brought back to England by Sir Francis Drake. The venture did achieve something however – the colonists brought back with them two new crops that would become hugely consequential: potatoes and tobacco. They had also given a name to the new territory they had explored – Virginia, in honour of their Virgin Queen Elizabeth.

In 1587 Raleigh tried again and sent a second expedition to establish a colony on Roanoke Island, this time better armed and better prepared. Once the colony was established and fortified the governor, John White, returned to England for further supplies but was delayed by the threat of the Spanish Armada. When he did return to Roanoke three years later, the colonists had disappeared, leaving nothing behind but some strange carvings on a tree. Nothing was ever seen of them again and Roanoke become known as the Lost Colony.

Although Raleigh's attempts to found a colony did not succeed, they planted the seeds of colonisation and for that reason Raleigh can claim to be one of the founders of the British Empire and thus partly responsible for the spread of the English language to all four corners of the world. Raleigh had wanted to lead the expeditions himself but was prevented from doing so by the Queen, who liked having him around and had come to rely on him, making him her Captain of the Guard. However, Raleigh eventually incurred the Queen's wrath by secretly marrying one of her ladies-in-waiting, Elizabeth Throckmorton, and was banished from Court.

When James I came to the throne in 1603 Raleigh, an avowed Protestant, let it be known that he suspected the King wanted a return to Catholicism. Raleigh was arrested at the Old Exeter Inn in Ashburton (see page 82), charged with conspiring against the King and sent to the Tower of London. His cell in the Bloody Tower can be seen there, recreated as it was in Raleigh's time.

Released and given permission to send an expedition to Venezuela to search for El Dorado, the legendary 'City of Gold', Raleigh attacked a Spanish colony in violation of the conditions of his pardon and was brought back to London. In 1618, on the demands of the Spanish ambassador, Raleigh was beheaded in Old Palace Yard in the Palace of Westminster. Before he was led to the block, Raleigh was granted a smoke of his beloved Virginia tobacco, beginning the tradition of granting the condemned man a last cigarette.

Roanoke Island is now a part of North Carolina, whose state capital is named Raleigh in honour of Sir Walter Raleigh.

Ottery St Mary

The quiet little town of OTTERY ST MARY is justifiably proud of its magnificent parish church, the grandest church in all Devon after Exeter Cathedral. Indeed, St Mary's was clearly designed to be a miniature of the latter, with the unusual layout of its two towers flanking the nave mirroring that of Exeter Cathedral. One of the towers has a short lead-covered

timber spire topped with THE OLDEST FUNCTIONING WEATHERCOCK IN THE WORLD. Dating from 1340, the weathercock was equipped with tubes to whistle in the wind but was silenced a few years ago after residents complained that the noise stopped them sleeping at night if there was a high wind.

First consecrated in 1260, the church was refashioned and enlarged in around 1342 by JOHN GRANDISSON, THE BISHOP OF EXETER, who built the present nave, chancel, aisles and Lady chapel and established a college of 40 members at St Mary's. With the Dissolution, St Mary's became the parish church.

After 500 years the interior was restored by the Victorian Gothic Revival architect WILLIAM BUTTERFIELD and then in 1977 the painted roof, for which St Mary's is famous, was repainted in vivid, some might say garish, colours, drawing criticism from some and praise from others. The bosses of the crossing roof gleam with gold leaf while the central 'founders' boss sports a tiny sculpture of a robed Bishop Grandisson himself.

In the south transept is Bishop Grandisson's astronomical clock, one of four such clocks from the 14th century in England, which puts the Earth at the centre of the universe and, if it was built at the same time as the church in 1342, could be THE OLDEST WORKING CLOCK IN THE WORLD. Bishop Grandisson also gave the church its rare carved wooden lectern whereby the Bible is rested on the outstretched wings of an eagle. There are thought to be only 21 such eagle lecterns in the world.

The only 'modern' addition to Grandisson's church is the DORSET AISLE, built in 1520 and funded by CECILY BONVILLE whose first husband was the Marquess of Dorset. The aisle's glorious fan vaulting is considered THE FINEST FAN VAULTING OF ANY PARISH CHURCH IN ENGLAND.

Dotted around the walls of the church inside and out are 21 consecration crosses, placed there during the consecration ceremony in 1260 as a symbol of the dedication of the church to God. Ottery St Mary has THE MOST COMPLETE SET OF CONSECRATION CROSSES IN ENGLAND, and the collection is unique in that they contain figures.

Outside on the churchyard wall there is a stone plaque commemorating the poet SAMUEL TAYLOR COLERIDGE, who was born in 1772 in the Old School House, since demolished. Samuel was the youngest of the 13 children of the REVEREND JOHN COLERIDGE who was headmaster of the King's School in Ottery as well as being vicar of St Mary's.

Next to the church stands THE CHANTER'S HOUSE, dating from the establishment of the college in the 14th century, but altered out of all recognition. The 17th-century version of the house was known as HEATH'S COURT and in 1645 OLIVER CROMWELL stayed the night and used the Grand Parlour to plan his strategy for the Civil War in the West Country with his leading commander General Fairfax. Fairfax stayed on for the next three months, using Heath's Court as the headquarters for his New Model Army. Heath's Court was then encased in red brick by William Butterfield while he was restoring the church next door in 1849–50.

Samuel Coleridge's older brother James bought the Chanter's House in 1796 and it remained in the Coleridge family for more than 200 years, during which time they built up a library of 22,000 books – THE LARGEST PRIVATE LIBRARY IN DEVON AND CORNWALL.

Sidmouth

Today SIDMOUTH HAS THE HIGHEST PROPORTION OF RESIDENTS AGED OVER 90 IN ENGLAND, which just goes to show that those who came to the little fishing village in Regency times in search of health-giving sea air were on to something.

Situated in a glorious setting between two long sweeps of Devon red cliffs, with Beer Head gleaming white in the eastern distance, Sidmouth presents an unspoiled vision of Regency cottage orné, particularly along the sea front where long terraces of cream and white houses with wrought iron balconies and shapely windows gaze out to sea.

Candyfloss and rollercoasters are notable by their absence and if this gives Sidmouth a somewhat staid air, then that is just what folk come looking for – Sidmouth is one of the top ten places to live in Devon according to the women's lifestyle magazine *Muddy Stilettos*. For excitement there is cricket played on one of the oldest cricket grounds in the country, laid out in 1823.

In 1819 EDWARD, DUKE OF KENT, arrived incognito both to escape his creditors and improve his health. He settled in WOOLBROOK COTTAGE, a rather fine Regency Gothic affair near the sea front, with his wife and their seven-month-old daughter, the PRINCESS VICTORIA. It is said that the little girl narrowly escaped death when a stray shot from a boy shooting pigeons in the street came in through a window and grazed her sleeve. The Duke, who went under the name Salisbury just in case, would walk along the beach carrying Victoria and showing her off to visitors *'for she is to be your queen'*, which rather gave the game away. Alas, he himself never saw Victoria become queen but died at Woolbrook Cottage of pneumonia in January 1820, six days before his father George III died. The building still stands, now as the ROYAL GLEN HOTEL.

Honiton

HONITON'S High Street is dead straight, following, as it does, the line of the Roman Fosse Way linking Exeter and Lincoln. At one mile, this is DEVON'S LONGEST ACTUAL HIGH STREET, as opposed to 'main' street (see Combe Martin, page 45).

To the traveller coming down from the Blackdown Hills in the east, Honiton provides a spectacular introduction to Devon, with the Otter Valley spread out before them, the wild expanses of Dartmoor and Exmoor shimmering on the horizon. As Daniel Defoe wrote in 1724, *'coming down the hill and the entrance to Honiton, the view of the county is the most beautiful landscape in the world – a mere picture and I do not remember the like in any one place in England'*.

Honiton was more or less rebuilt after two devastating fires in the 18th century and as a result the High Street is lined with attractive Georgian buildings of every kind. Unhappily located on a busy roundabout at the eastern end of the High Street (and thus overlooked by harassed motorists – I have driven through Honiton countless times and never noticed it) is MARWOOD HOUSE, built in stone in 1619 by the son of Queen Elizabeth's physician THOMAS MARWOOD and concealed from the hoi polloi by a high stone wall. Thomas Marwood, born in Honiton in 1512, was a physician for 73 years and was clearly good at his job for he himself reached the age of 106, living through the discovery of the New World, the Reformation, the awful reign of Mary Tudor, Shakespeare, the Spanish Armada and the Gunpowder Plot. He is buried beneath a black marble tomb near the door of the 15th century ST MICHAEL'S PARISH CHURCH, situated on a hill east of the town and rebuilt in 1911 after a fire.

Sometime before Trafalgar, LORD NELSON stayed the night in Honiton and invited the mother and sister of one of his officers, BLAGDON WESTCOTT, to breakfast at his hotel. The son of a Honiton baker, Westcott had sailed with him and perished at the Battle of the Nile. When Nelson learned that Mrs Westcott had not received the gold medal her son had earned at the battle, Nelson took off his own medal and gave it to her.

Honiton was famous for HONITON LACE, a fine bobbin lace of a style introduced to the area in the 17th century by Flemish refugees. The lace was handmade in their homes by the wives of local workers until machines made the industry obsolete. Honiton lace regained popularity when Queen Victoria ordered her bridal gown to be made of Honiton lace for her marriage in 1840. Although no longer commercially viable, locally made Honiton lace is available for sale in a number of Honiton shops.

Branscombe

The pretty little village of BRANSCOMBE boasts THE OLDEST WORKING THATCHED FORGE IN ENGLAND, the only such forge that is still operational. The present forge dates from the 1700s although there is thought to have been a forge here since Norman times and a stone built into the present forge wall bears the date 1580. Just up the road, hidden from the sea and Viking raiders by a ridge of hills, is ST WINIFRED'S Norman church, one of the oldest and best churches in Devon. It has ONE OF ONLY TWO THREE-DECKER PULPITS IN DEVON and A LINEAR SCRATCH DIAL THAT IS UNIQUE IN ENGLAND (the norm is semi-circular), which uses the shadow cast by a buttress to mark the hours, shown in Roman numerals. Amongst a number of impressive memorials in the church is the Elizabethan altar tomb of Joan Wadham, who died in 1583. She had 14 children by her first husband John Kellawy and six by her second husband Sir John Wadham. One of those six, Nicholas, a lawyer, was the founder of Wadham College, Oxford. Joan features on the memorial twice, kneeling behind a statue of each of her two husbands, A UNIQUE DOUBLE THAT IS FOUND ON NO OTHER FAMILY MONUMENT IN BRITAIN.

At Branscombe beach the cliffs turn starkly from Devon red sandstone to white chalk, for Branscombe sits at the western extent of the chalk that makes up much of southern England. BEER HEAD, a little further east at the far end of the Hooken Cliffs, is 426 feet high and THE SOUTHERNMOST AND WESTERNMOST CHALK HEADLAND IN ENGLAND. In 1790, the Hooken Cliffs were the scene of a dramatic landslide when some 10 acres of cliff slid 250 feet towards the sea, leaving a spectacular jumble of rock pinnacles and trees.

Seaton and Axmouth

SEATON and AXMOUTH face each other across the River Axe and share a long history as a flourishing Roman port – Axmouth stood towards the southern end of Britannia's most important Roman road, the Fosse Way, which linked the south west to Lincoln. It prospered again under the Saxons and the Normans and by the 14th century the port was handling some 15 per cent of England's shipping trade as the most important port in the south west of England. Then the mouth of the River Axe was choked off by landslides and scree and Seaton settled into becoming a Victorian resort town, while Axmouth retired into a dignified slumber of thatched cottages and inns gathered around the ancient church of St Michael, with its richly carved Norman doorway and fine medieval wall paintings.

In the 19th century Seaton and Axmouth were linked by BRITAIN'S FIRST CONCRETE ROAD BRIDGE, a toll bridge which was built across the mouth of the River Axe in 1877. The bridge is still in use for pedestrians but has now been bypassed by a modern road bridge.

THE SEATON TRAMWAY, established in 1970, runs north for three miles from Seaton to Colyford and Colyton along the route of the former Seaton branch line, which joined the main Salisbury–Exeter line two miles further north. It is THE ONLY ELECTRIC TRAMWAY IN THE WORLD TO STILL USE OLD-STYLE TRAMCARS WITH OPEN UPPER DECKS.

Axminster

A XMINSTER, one of England's most ancient towns, is today a quiet market town of narrow winding streets and smart Georgian houses, but its name is known around the world as the home of the finest English carpets. AXMINSTER CARPETS were first made in 1755 at Court House next to the church by cloth weaver THOMAS WHITTY who had been impressed by a carpet imported from Turkey in a London warehouse and wanted to learn how to make something similar but for a cheaper price. After watching a group of French carpet makers in Fulham, he invented and built an ingenious new loom based

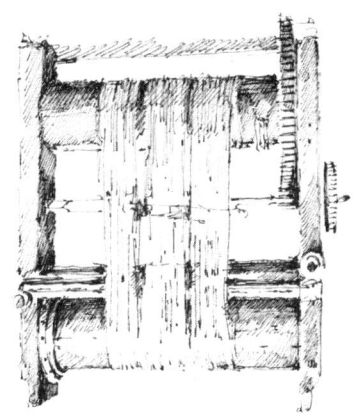

on what he had seen, co-opted his children into becoming his assistants, thus ensuring cheap labour, and got to work on his first Axminster weave carpet.

For the next 80 years, Axminster produced the best hand-knotted carpets in Europe, despite only having a small workshop and few staff. One visitor wrote in 1791, *'I was surprised to find such a paltry place the origin of so much magnificence'*. Rather in the tradition of Italian shoemakers, whenever a new carpet was finished the church bells would ring out and the townsfolk would flock to take a look at it laid out in the church.

Axminster carpets soon became the flooring of choice in England's stately homes. Original Axminsters can still be found in the rooms for which they were made at Blickling Hall in Norfolk, Chatsworth House in Derbyshire, Dumfries House in Ayrshire, Harewood House in Yorkshire, Kingston Lacy in Dorset, Saltram House near Plymouth and in the Music Room at Powderham Castle near Exeter. The biggest and most famous Axminster of them all was made in 1822 for the Sultan of Turkey's Topkapi Palace in Istanbul. It measured 74 feet (23 metres) by 52 feet (16 metres), took 30 men to carry it and cost £1,000 – more than a million pounds at today's value. Alas, the Topkapi Palace is now a museum and the carpet has vanished, its whereabouts a mystery.

In 1789 Axminsters truly came of age when the Axminster factory received a visit from George III and Queen Charlotte, who ordered a number of carpets, thus bestowing the royal seal of approval. Not long afterwards, the Prince Regent also ordered an Axminster for the Royal Pavilion in Brighton.

After Thomas Whitty died in 1792 the business passed to his son and then his grandson, but in 1828 the workshop suffered a disastrous fire from which the company never recovered and in 1835 the business went bankrupt. The looms, designs and remaining stock were sold to Wilton Carpets and carpet weaving disappeared from Axminster for the next 100 years. In 1937 an enterprising young man from a carpet business in Kidderminster called HARRY DUTFIELD brought carpet-making back to Axminster, building a new factory near the station and sourcing wool from a woollen spinning mill in Buckfastleigh. Harry's son and grandson have continued the business and Axminster Carpets, Britain's oldest carpet maker, are still manufacturing in Axminster today, and have supplied carpets for Windsor Castle, after the fire of 1992, Osborne House on the Isle of Wight, King Charles III's Clarence House and even the circular Royal Albert Hall.

Although Thomas Whitty's factory is no more, the beautiful Georgian house with its elegant bow windows where he lived still stands behind the church and is now occupied by a firm of solicitors.

WELL, I NEVER KNEW THIS ABOUT

EAST DEVON

THE BARN AT Foxholes Hill, a clifftop community on the eastern outskirts of Exmouth, was built in 1896 by local architect Edward Prior and is THE EARLIEST EUROPEAN EXAMPLE OF THE ARTS AND CRAFTS 'BUTTERFLY' DESIGN, which is characterised by wings extending at an angle from a central core.

ORCOMBE POINT, a headland two miles east of Exmouth, is the most westerly point of the JURASSIC COAST, THE ONLY PLACE IN THE WORLD WHERE YOU CAN FIND EVIDENCE OF 185 MILLION YEARS OF EVOLUTION.

GEORGE BOONE III, grandfather of the frontiersman and legendary American hero DANIEL BOONE (1734–1820), who trailblazed the Cumberland Gap in the Appalachian Mountains and founded the first settlements in Kentucky (Boonesborough), was christened in the 14th century church at STOKE CANON, four miles north of Exeter.

ST GILES CHURCH IN SIDBURY on the River Sid, a few miles upstream of Sidmouth, is an imposing church with a Norman tower from which 12th-century statues of St Giles and St Peter look down on the village from niches either side of the clock. Inside, the tower crossing has a rib vaulted roof with the ribs resting on carved corbels of lions and a central corbel carved with an Atlas figure, all 12th century. The 500-year-old font is fitted with a lock to prevent witches getting away with the Holy Water, THE ONLY SUCH LOCKED FONT IN DEVON. But St Giles's special treasure is its rare 7TH-CENTURY SAXON CRYPT beneath the chancel, accessed through a trap door in the chancel floor. If you visit the church on the right afternoon, you can clamber down into the small rough-hewn chamber – it is a magical, moving place created by simple faith some 1,300 years ago. Buried in the churchyard is JOAN HICKSON, fondly remembered for playing Agatha Christie's Miss Marple in the TV series.

Just west of Beer are a series of man-made caves, the result of quarrying for BEER STONE since Roman times. Beer stone is a pleasing creamy-coloured limestone that is easy to work, being soft when first mined but hardening when exposed to the air, and it was found to have been used in the construction of Honeyditches, a 2nd-century Roman villa uncovered near Seaton. Beer stone was also used for a number of Norman cathedrals including Exeter, Winchester, St Paul's and Westminster Abbey. The quarries are no longer in use and are open for guided tours in the summer months. Nearby, at the bottom of a steep zig-zag railway track, there is a siding served by a branch line from the BEER HEIGHTS LIGHT RAILWAY, a miniature railway that offers commanding views of Lyme Bay from the cliff tops above Beer.

In 2015 in the Church of Ottery St Mary, SARAH MULLALLY, the first woman Archbishop of Canterbury, at that time the Bishop of Crediton, officiated at the first Church of England ordination service to be led by a woman, ordaining two deacons as priests.

CADHAY HOUSE is a most attractive Tudor manor house that slumbers in meadows a mile north-west of Ottery St Mary. It was built in 1540 by JOHN HAYDON, a local lawyer and first governor of St Mary's church, who became wealthy by dissolving the monasteries of the West Country, built Ottery's first bridge over the river, founded the grammar school and used many of the stones from

the old college in Ottery to build Cadhay. He is buried beneath a splendid altar tomb in St Mary's Church. John Haydon's house was a typical Tudor E plan with central great hall and two wings until Haydon's nephew Robert created a courtyard by enclosing the three ranges with a Long Gallery. The courtyard is Cadhay's most treasured feature, its ornamentation of chequered sandstone and flint unique amongst Devon's courtyard houses. Above the four doors are statues of Henry VIII and his three children – Edward VI, Mary I and Elizabeth I. – hence the name, COURT OF SOVEREIGNS. Below Elizabeth I is the date 1617. Robert's father-in-law was Sir Amias Poulett, Privy Councillor and Keeper of Mary Queen of Scots during her imprisonment while his wife's cousin, William Paulet, was also on the Privy Council for all four Tudor monarchs, hence the statues in the Court of Sovereigns.

THE HONITON HOT PENNIES CEREMONY is one of England's oldest customs, still taking place in the town today. In 1221 Henry III granted Honiton a royal charter to hold a market and to celebrate the town instituted the HONITON FAIR. In order to draw in people from the surrounding countryside, it was declared that nobody could be arrested for debt for the duration of the fair. The local gentry would throw hot chestnuts from their windows for the fairgoers and eventually it was decided that hot pennies would be more appreciated. At noon on the first day of the fair, the Town Crier raises a glove on top of a garlanded pole and proclaims that '*The glove is up. No man may be arrested until the glove is taken down'*. Then the pennies begin to rain down ...

OLD SHUTE HOUSE near Axminster, begun as a hall house in 1380 by Sir William Bonville (c.1132–1408), is considered to be THE MOST IMPORTANT SURVIVING EXAMPLE OF A MEDIEVAL MANOR HOUSE IN ENGLAND. The fireplace in the Great Hall has a span of 24 feet (7 metres) and is said to be THE BIGGEST MEDIEVAL FIREPLACE IN BRITAIN. Old Shute House was the birthplace of Cecily Bonville in 1460 who, as Marchioness of Dorset, financed the sublime Dorset aisle in the Church of Ottery Saint Mary. She became known as the Great Heiress after her father, grandfather and great grandfather, all supporters of the House of York, were killed in the Wars of the Roses and she inherited their estates. Her first marriage was to Thomas Grey, son of Edward IV's wife Elizabeth Woodville, whom the King made Marquess of Dorset, and her second to Elizabeth Woodville's cousin Henry Stafford, 1st Earl of Wiltshire.

NORTH DEVON

When the sun's highest point
Peeps like a star o'er ocean's western edge,
When those far clouds of feathery gold,
Shaded with deepest purple, gleam
Like islands on a dark blue sea ...

From *Queen Mab* by Percy Bysshe Shelley, inspired by his stay at Lynmouth in the summer of 1812

Clovelly

Exmoor

JUST UNDER A third of Exmoor belongs to Devon. Smaller, less bleak and more intimate than Dartmoor, Devon's slice of Exmoor nonetheless has its own wild grandeur, with windswept heights and deep wooded valleys, large tracts of heather moorland, a rugged coastline of towering cliffs and hidden sandy coves, pretty villages, interesting churches and mysterious prehistoric sites. Thanks to its remoteness and lack of light pollution, in 2011 Exmoor was designated THE FIRST INTERNATIONAL DARK SKY RESERVE IN EUROPE. And, of course, Exmoor is the source of the River Exe which, although it actually rises in Somerset, quickly becomes Devon's river as it flows due south through the county's glorious countryside to Devon's capital city of Exeter.

The first village in Devon encountered by the traveller from Somerset is windswept COUNTISBURY, home to one of the finest historic coaching inns in Devon: the Blue Ball Inn. Then comes one of Devon's gems, Lynmouth.

Lynmouth

A steep one-in-four hill takes the coast road down into LYNMOUTH, a pretty former fishing village set where the West Lyn and East Lyn rivers converge before emptying into the sea. Here the South West Coast Path meets the Tarka Trail from Barnstaple, the Two Moors Way linking Exmoor and Dartmoor, and the Coleridge Way from Nether Stowey.

Artists

Lynmouth prospered on herring until the start of the 17th century when the herring went elsewhere, and the village was then largely forgotten, although in 1746 the artist THOMAS GAINSBOROUGH honeymooned in the village with his bride Margaret. He declared Lynmouth to be *'the most delightful place for a landscape painter this country can boast'.*

When the Napoleonic Wars curtailed continental travel and compelled people to explore Britain instead, Lynmouth was rediscovered as a Little Switzerland and was, in addition, given a boost by the poet SHELLEY who brought his new 16-year-old bride Harriet to Devon in 1812, seeking refuge both from family disapproval and from a government determined to stop him writing seditious pamphlets about Ireland which he sealed in bottles and sent out to sea. Indeed, there is a story that at one point, fearful of arrest, Shelley paid a local boatman to row him across to Wales where he would be safe. Nonetheless, despite these alarms Shelley extolled the virtues of Lynmouth to all his friends and was inspired by the beauty of the place to write his first major poem, *Queen Mab*, while staying in what is now Shelley's Hotel, a Georgian cottage with Victorian additions that stands above the spot where the roads into Lynmouth meet.

Floods

In August 1952 a savage storm deposited nine inches of rain on Exmoor overnight and sent torrents of water laden with trees and boulders down both the Lyn valleys into Lynmouth, washing away over 100 buildings and 28 bridges, killing 34 people and making 420 people homeless. The village was rebuilt and the river diverted but the flood is not forgotten. There is a memorial garden where a group of houses once stood on the bank of the East Lyn and a memorial hall near the harbour. The unusual Rhenish-style BEACON TOWER standing on the stone harbour pier is an exact replica of the tower built there in around 1830 by a General Rawdon, both as a beacon to guide boats into the harbour and as somewhere to store salt water for his bathtub, but which was subsequently carried away by the flood. Nobody seems to know who this General Rawdon was, however ... A Devon mystery.

Today Lynmouth is mostly comprised of Victorian hotels and guesthouses but a delightful row of traditional thatched cottages survives down by the harbour.

Beacon Tower

When Lynmouth needed to expand as a result of its newfound popularity in the early 19th century, there was nowhere left to build down by the sea and so it was decided to establish a new hotel in Lynton, 500 feet up on the moor above the harbour and at that time consisting of just a few cottages and a church.

Lynton

Lynton grew rapidly into a smart Victorian resort after the building of its first hotel in 1807. Much of the development was financed by SIR GEORGE NEWNES, publisher of *Tit-Bits* magazine, the forerunner of popular journalism that gave P.G. Wodehouse his first break, and *The Strand Magazine*, for which Sir Arthur Conan Doyle created Sherlock Holmes. After watching some poor donkeys struggling to haul great loads up the hill from Lynmouth to Lynton, Sir George decided there must be a better way to connect the two villages and in 1890 he opened the LYNTON AND LYNMOUTH CLIFF RAILWAY, THE WORLD'S HIGHEST AND STEEPEST WATER-POWERED FUNICULAR RAILWAY at 862 feet long with a rise of 500 feet. Each of the two cars has a 700-gallon water tank which is filled when the car is at the top and discharged when the car is at the bottom. The heavier weight of the top car forces it to descend while the lighter, lower car is hauled up to the top, with the speed controlled by a brakeman in each car.

Valley of the Rocks

On the coast west of Lynton, the VALLEY OF THE ROCKS is a dry valley edged with spectacular jagged pinnacles of rock that rise 800 feet out of the sea, with names such as Ragged Jack, Devil's Cheesewring and Castle Rock. The poet ROBERT SOUTHEY, visiting in 1799, described the valley as *'the*

very bones and skeletons of the earth; rock reclining upon rock, stone piled upon stone, a huge terrific mass' while R.D. BLACKMORE set some of *Lorna Doone* here and based the witch featured in the story on an old woman who lived in MOTHER MELDRUM'S CAVE in the valley in the 19th century. Wild goats gaze down from the heights.

Combe Martin

Eight miles west of Lynton is the GREAT HANGMAN, THE HIGHEST SEA CLIFF IN ENGLAND at 1,044 feet (318 metres). From this unsurpassed viewpoint the path drops down into COMBE MARTIN, where THE LONGEST VILLAGE STREET IN ENGLAND winds its way up a deep valley for two miles from a sandy beach. Halfway along, just before the 13th-century church of St Peter ad Vincula, is the extraordinary PACK O' CARDS INN, built in 1690 as a home by a local squire called George Ley with his winnings from a game of cards. It has four storeys, one for each suit in a deck of cards, with 13 doors and fireplaces on each floor, for the number of cards in a suit, and originally had 52 windows, one for each card in a pack.

Church of St Mary, Molland

For anyone who loves Georgian church interiors the two Exmoor churches of MOLLAND and PARRACOMBE have the best in Devon. Molland's mainly 15th-century CHURCH OF ST MARY sits on a hill below the high moors and looks down on the valley of the River Yeo. It completely escaped restoration by the Victorians, largely because the Throckmortons, Lords of the Manor at the time, were Catholics and had little interest in this small Anglican church on the far edge of their estates. All that survives of Molland's original Norman church is the splendid font, which struggles to be seen amongst the sea of shoulder-high 18th-century box pews that threaten to swamp the leaning, clustered pillars of the central arcade. The lovely three-deck pulpit sports an immense sounding board while the chancel is enclosed by a wooden screen, above which is a plastered tympanum bearing a Royal Coat of Arms and a board of the Ten Commandments. In the north aisle are three fine mural monuments to the COURTENAYS, Lords of the Manor in the 17th and 18th centuries.

Parracombe

PARRACOMBE, slumbering in the beautiful Heddon valley, IS THE LARGEST DEVON VILLAGE ON EXMOOR. First recorded in Saxon times, it is an ancient place watched over from the east by the prehistoric CHAPMAN BARROWS, Bronze Age burial mounds lying at 1,575 feet at the highest point on Exmoor in Devon, along with two Iron Age hillforts and the scant remains of a Norman motte and bailey castle. It can also boast two churches.

St Petrock's

ST PETROCK'S sits on a hillside high above the village, reached by a farm track from the main road. They were going to pull the ancient church down at the end of the 19th

century but a national outcry and a cheque for £10 from John Ruskin saved it for posterity. A new church was built closer to the village, leaving St Petrock's gloriously unrestored. The rugged square tower is 12th-century, with some mysterious carvings on one of the buttresses, the chancel 13th-century and the nave 15th-century, while the interior is an 18th-century Georgian feast, all except for the gated screen separating the nave from the chancel, which is 15th-century. Above it the wall is painted with the Royal Arms, the Creed, the Ten Commandments and the Lord's Prayer. There are benches and box pews with hat pegs and a three-deck oak pulpit. St Petrock's is THE LAST CHURCH IN DEVON TO HAVE USED LIVE MUSICIANS TO ACCOMPANY THE HYMNS. They sat in the raised pews at the back and there is a hole in one of the pews to allow elbow room for the bow of the bass viol.

Verity

Ilfracombe

ILFRACOMBE tumbles down a series of cliffs towards its attractive harbour, one of the few safe refuges along the North Devon coast and active as an important trading port during the 14th to 16th centuries. Like other Devon resorts, it became popular during the Napoleonic Wars and then again with the coming of the railway, boasting numerous extravagant Regency and Victorian hotels and holiday terraces overlooking the mainly Georgian quayside.

The 13th-century Holy Trinity Church looks down from its own hill to the west. The church tower finds itself half inside the north aisle, built around when the church was expanded. There is a Norman font, an Elizabethan pulpit and a magnificent, richly carved and colourful 15th-century wagon roof, regarded as the finest in the West Country. ANNA PARNELL, youngest sister of Irish nationalist Charles Stewart Parnell, is buried in the churchyard. She drowned while swimming off Ilfracombe in 1911.

Perched 100 feet up on Lantern Hill, a rocky outcrop above the harbour entrance, is a 14th-century chapel dedicated to the patron saint of sailors, ST NICHOLAS, which has long been used as a lighthouse to guide sailors safely into harbour. In the days of Henry VIII indulgences were granted to those who kept a lantern burning in the chapel window. No longer a chapel, St Nicholas became an official lighthouse in 1819 and is still operational, very possibly making it BRITAIN'S OLDEST WORKING LIGHTHOUSE.

St Nicholas Chapel, one of Ilfracombe's oldest structures, looks straight down on one of Ilfracombe's newest and most controversial: a 66-and-a-half foot (20 metres) sculpture of a pregnant woman holding aloft a sword. Called *VERITY*, the sculpture was loaned to the town for 20 years in 2012 by its creator DAMIEN HIRST, who lives in nearby Combe Martin. The internal anatomy of the mother is shown along with the foetus.

Never afraid of controversy, Ilfracombe is clearly enamoured of the female form for just across town is the eye-catchingly conical LANDMARK THEATRE, opened in 1997 and known locally as Madonna's Bra – because that is indeed what it looks like.

Ilfracombe has no main beach but straggles along a series of rocky coves with patches of sand, where it is quite easy for swimmers to be cut off by the tide. In 1820 Welsh miners were hired to carve four tunnels though the cliffs from the western edge of the town to give access by horse and carriage to two tidal pools on the beach. In Victorian times the two pools were strictly segregated, one for men and the other for women. It is still possible today to walk through the tunnels on to what are known as the Tunnels Beaches.

Actor PETER SELLERS first trod the stage at Ilfracombe, where his parents managed the GAIETY THEATRE, still there on the Promenade sporting its quaint turreted tower, although now used as a gallery and shopping arcade rather than as a theatre.

Barnstaple

BARNSTAPLE was minting its own coins in the 10th century, and tradition has it that the town received its charter from King Athelstan in AD 930, vying with Malmesbury in Wiltshire to be BRITAIN'S OLDEST BOROUGH. It was an important port in the Middle Ages and a major textile and pottery centre but as the River Taw silted up, so the port declined. The town remains an important agricultural and market centre.

Although much rebuilt, the antiquity of Barnstaple is reflected in its medieval street pattern and a number of attractive old buildings. CASTLE MOUND, a steep flat-topped hillock that rises out of the old cattle market was the motte of Barnstaple's Norman motte and bailey castle. William the Conqueror had the motte raised and wooden fort erected on the top in 1068 to enforce Norman rule over the Saxon burghers of Barnstaple. A stone castle was built later but was never much used and was abandoned in the 14th century before finally falling down altogether during a storm in 1601.

Barnstaple's pride is the 522-foot (159m) LONG BRIDGE, whose 16 arches have straddled the River Taw since the early 13th century. ONE OF THE LARGEST MEDIEVAL BRIDGES IN BRITAIN, it has been refurbished and widened over the years and is still in use for traffic although most vehicles now use the modern bridge upstream.

The twisted lead broach spire of 13th-century ST PETER'S CHURCH, warped by a lightning strike in 1810 but still regarded AS THE BEST SPIRE OF ITS KIND IN ENGLAND, rises from a jumble of narrow winding shopping streets in the town centre, while beside it is St Anne's chapel, built as a chantry chapel in the early 14th century and then converted into a school. Barnstaple-born JOHN GAY (1685–1732), author of *The Beggar's Opera*, was a pupil there. The building is now used as a museum. There are also two delightful sets of almshouses. PENROSE'S ALMSHOUSES, with a splendid colonnaded front, was

Queen Anne's Walk

built in 1627 in memory of a former Mayor of Barnstaple, and the cream-painted HORWOOD ALMSHOUSES, by the church, were endowed in 1659.

QUEEN ANNE'S WALK, a small colonnade that was constructed in 1708 as a Merchant's Exchange, can be found down on the quayside. Here ship owners and merchants would conduct their business and deals would be sealed by touching the TOME STONE, today mounted on a pedestal beneath the huge statue of Queen Anne that stands above the entrance. Five ships departed from the quay here in 1588 to fight the Spanish Armada while, in quieter times, it was Barnstaple cloth and pottery that was sent to the New World.

An archway beneath the 19th-century Grecian Guildhall in the High Street leads to Barnstaple's PANNIER MARKET, named for the pannier baskets carried by horse or donkey from which the market traders sold their produce. The market is still held here three days a week in a splendid market hall of glass and iron latticework built in 1855, although stalls have replaced the panniers.

BUTCHERS ROW, which runs alongside the Pannier Market, is a very pretty arcade of small white and cream-painted Victorian shops, all with green doors.

Dominating the Square at the Barnstaple end of Long Bridge is the tall, distinctive clock tower of the ALBERT CLOCK, built in 1862 in honour of Prince Albert, who had died the year before.

Barnstaple also played a minor role in the Jeremy Thorpe scandal in the 1970s as the home of Norman Scott, the male model who tried to blackmail Thorpe, leader of the Liberal Party, over their homosexual relationship. Andrew Newton, who was hired by Thorpe's friends to intimidate Scott into silence, misheard his instructions over the phone and went to Dunstable in Bedfordshire instead.

Swimbridge

Above the squat 13th-century tower of St James Church in Swimbridge, four miles south-east of Barnstaple, soars a quite lovely, and unexpected, lead broach spire from 1310, one of only three such spires in Devon. The whole ensemble reaches to a height of 90 feet and dominates the village. Inside the church are treasures galore, the finest being a precious rood screen of c.1500, 44 feet wide and 10 feet high, stretching across the middle of the church, every inch of the pillars and the superb fan vaulting decorated with delicate tracery and carvings of grapes and vine leaves and other foliage. A rare 15th-century carved limestone pulpit and a UNIQUE FONT COVER also grace the church, the latter consisting of a crown-shaped canopy above a tall octagonal carved oak cupboard with doors that open to give access to the font.

The pub opposite the church is named THE JACK RUSSELL in honour of JOHN 'JACK' RUSSELL, known as the Sporting Parson, who was vicar here for almost 50 years from 1832 until 1880, and is buried in the churchyard.

Parson John 'Jack' Russell (1795–1883): The Sporting Parson

JOHN 'JACK' RUSSELL was born in Dartmouth and attended Plympton Grammar School (see page 142) and then Blundell's School in Tiverton (see page 19) where he formed a pack of hounds, much to the headmaster's disapproval. In 1814 he went up to Exeter College, Oxford and while he was there he took a fancy to the milkman's dog, a small white terrier with a tan spot over her eyes, ears and tail. He bought her from the milkman, named her TRUMP, crossed her with a local dog and the result was the creation of a line of fox-hunting terriers that became known as Jack Russells: brave, intelligent, sturdy and able to go down fox holes. In 1819 Russell became a curate in South Molton, a small town in the foothills of Exmoor, then moved to nearby Iddesleigh and finally, in 1832, to Swimbridge. Here he got himself a pack of hounds with which he spent much of his time hunting across North Devon, and he quickly became popular with his parishioners for giving short sermons while his groom stood outside the church with his horse ready so that the Sporting Parson could get hunting.

In 1826 Russell had got married in the church at Swimbridge to PENELOPE INCLEDON-BURY who would inherit the 17th-century COLLETON MANOR

and estate a few miles south near Chulmleigh. The house is famous for its 15th-century gatehouse containing a chapel dedicated to a 13th-century Archbishop of Canterbury, EDMUND RICH. He was later canonised as St Edmund of Canterbury and is remembered by the hall he founded at Oxford, ST EDMUND HALL, THE LAST SURVIVING MEDIEVAL ACADEMIC HALL AT OXFORD. The Sporting Parson's lavish and expensive sporting lifestyle, along with, it must be said, his generosity and kindness to his parishioners, by whom he was much loved, was said to have put a strain on his wife's finances and Colleton Manor was left somewhat neglected. It is now a smart farmhouse called Colleton Barton and the gatehouse survives in good condition.

In 1880 Parson Russell took up his last post as the Rector of BLACK TORRINGTON near Okehampton, so called because of the dark waters of the River Torridge on which it lies, before being brought back to rest in the churchyard of his beloved Swimbridge.

Bideford

Bideford has more than played its part in Britain's seafaring story. Bideford men sailed with the great Elizabethan explorers Hawkins, Raleigh and Drake, while in the 16th and 17th centuries Bideford was THE THIRD LARGEST PORT IN BRITAIN, trading across the world, in particular with Spain, the West Indies and North America, and becoming Britain's leading port for the import of tobacco. This was all thanks in large part to the town's sea-faring Lords of the Manor, the Grenvilles (see page 53).

Bideford's lovely tree-lined

quay still bustles today but only with local traffic, such as the ferry to Lundy Island. From the quayside there is a splendid view of Bideford's impressive LONG BRIDGE, built throughout the course of the 15th century on top of an earlier stone bridge that in turn replaced a 13th-century timber bridge of oak. At 677 feet long, it is THE SECOND LONGEST SURVIVING MEDIEVAL BRIDGE IN ENGLAND after Swarkestone Bridge in Derbyshire. Intriguingly, each of the 24 arches has a different span, possibly because each arch was funded by a different individual business or patron.

The Grenvilles

The most famous of these was RICHARD GRENVILLE, born in Bideford's manor house in 1542, son of Roger Grenville who was drowned when Henry VIII's flagship the Mary Rose sank in the Solent in 1545. Richard sailed from Bideford to explore and colonise the New World and in 1585 captained the seven-strong fleet taking English settlers to establish a colony on Roanoke Island sponsored by his cousin Sir Walter Raleigh. On one of his expeditions in 1586, Grenville brought back a native American Indian to Bideford, THE FIRST EVER RECORDED AMERICAN INDIAN TO SET FOOT IN ENGLAND. The fellow was named Raleigh and baptised as such before the massive Norman font in Bideford's parish church of St Mary, still in use today. In 1588 Grenville provisioned five ships at Bideford for the fight against the Spanish Armada, and sitting in Victoria Park at the north end of Bideford's quayside, are nine cannons believed to be captured from one of the Spanish ships.

The Revenge

We have fought such a fight for a day and a night
As may never be fought again!
We have won great glory, my men!

From 'The Revenge, A Ballad of the Fleet' by Alfred, Lord Tennyson

In 1591 Grenville sailed from Bideford in a ship called the *Revenge* to join an English fleet under Admiral Howard that was hoping to waylay Spanish treasure ships off the Azores. The *Revenge* was the ship that had carried Sir Francis Drake into battle against the Spanish Armada and was considered the finest ship in the Elizabethan navy. Confronted by a much larger Spanish fleet than expected, Admiral Howard retired the fleet but Grenville, who had men ashore he would not abandon, refused to withdraw, saying he would rather die than be dishonoured. By the time his men were safely aboard, it was too late. The *Revenge* stood alone in the face of 53 Spanish ships, one small ship against a fleet. Her crew repulsed wave after wave of Spanish boarders, hurling them into the sea, driving back the Spanish warships with ceaseless cannon fire and indomitable spirit. For 15 hours the *Revenge* fought, badly damaging five Spanish galleons before its masts were gone and Grenville collapsed from his wounds. Finally his crew surrendered on the condition that the survivors were allowed to return to England. Grenville died a few days later and the shattered *Revenge* sank not long afterwards in a storm, along with 15 Spanish ships. Grenville's exploits convinced the Spanish that English sailors were fearless and were later glorified in a poem by Alfred, Lord Tennyson called, appropriately enough, 'The Revenge'.

Westward Ho!

At the north end of Bideford's quay is a statue of CHARLES KINGSLEY (1819–75) who was living in Bideford when he wrote his 1855 novel *Westward Ho!*, set in North Devon during the era of the buccaneering Elizabethan explorers like Richard Grenville. In 1925 it became THE FIRST NOVEL TO BE ADAPTED FOR RADIO BY THE BBC.

Such was the popularity of the book that a Victorian resort founded on the coast a mile north of Bideford by the Earl of Portsmouth in 1863 was named after it. The resort began life as the WESTWARD HO!-TEL, THE ONLY HOTEL TO BE NAMED AFTER A BOOK, and when the hotel evolved into a village, WESTWARD HO! became not just THE ONLY VILLAGE IN BRITAIN TO BE NAMED AFTER A BOOK but THE ONLY PLACE IN BRITAIN TO HAVE AN EXCLAMATION MARK AFTER ITS NAME.

Another writer, RUDYARD KIPLING, spent his schooldays in Westward Ho! and set his novel

Stalky & Co on the hill south of the village where Kipling and his friends used to bunk off and smoke cigars. The hill is now known as KIPLING TORS. Westward Ho! has a huge sandy beach, some fine hotels, lots of bungalows and one of the oldest and most famous golf courses in Britain.

Lundy Island

Occupied since prehistoric times, the old pirate hideout of LUNDY ISLAND, which is reached by ferry from Bideford, lies 12 miles off the North Devon coast and at 1,100 acres is THE LARGEST ISLAND IN THE BRISTOL CHANNEL. Because of its unique flora and fauna, Lundy was designated as ENGLAND'S FIRST MARINE NATURE RESERVE AND MARINE CONSERVATION ZONE. The name Lundy comes from the Viking word for puffin and the island is still one of the best places in Britain to see puffins. Today Lundy has 23 holiday properties managed by the LANDMARK TRUST and receives up to 20,000 day trippers every year. There is a resident population of about 28 people who look after the wildlife and the island's many archaeological sites as well as the pub and tourist facilities.

Clovelly

CLOVELLY's whitewashed, flower-bedecked cottages cascade down to the sea in a tumble of loveliness. The cobbled High

Street, 'Up-along' or 'Down-along' depending on which way you are going, is so steep that villagers step out of their front door onto their neighbour's roof. Falling over 400 feet in just half a mile, the street is far too precipitous for cars, meaning that Clovelly is THE ONLY VILLAGE IN ENGLAND WHOSE MAIN STREET IS ENTIRELY TRAFFIC-FREE. Instead, residents and visitors must go by foot while essential supplies such as furniture and groceries are hauled by sledge. Both people and supplies were once carried up and down by labouring donkeys but, as at Lynmouth further up the coast, the Victorians considered this practice to be cruel and put a stop to it, although donkeys are still employed to give rides to children and pose for photographs.

Clovelly was a fishing village as far back as Domesday or before, while the harbour, with its bollards made from captured Spanish cannons, dates from the 16th century when the village began to grow prosperous on herring. It was discovered as a tourist attraction in the mid-19th century thanks to the writings of CHARLES DICKENS in *A Message from the Sea,* and more particularly CHARLES KINGSLEY, who spent his childhood in Clovelly where his father was the rector. Kingsley returned to Clovelly to write *The Water Babies* while staying in a cottage on the High Street now called KINGSLEY'S COTTAGE.

Clovelly has managed to preserve its ancient beauty, partly because the nature of the site means there is no room for modern intrusions, but also in large part thanks to CHRISTINE HAMLYN, who owned the village from 1884 to 1936 and made it her life's work to protect and restore Clovelly's charming old buildings. Many of the cottages, some of which date from Tudor times, bear her initials.

The HAMLYN family acquired Clovelly in 1738 when locally born lawyer ZACHARY HAMLYN bought it off the Cary family who had been Lords of the Manor since the 14th century. The village is today managed by a descendant of the Hamlyns, JOHN ROUS, great-great-nephew of Christine Hamlyn and great-grandson of Prime Minister H.H. Asquith. He lives in CLOVELLY COURT, the much-restored 18th-century great house at the top of the village. Nearby is the Norman ALL SAINTS CHURCH, approached by a long yew avenue and filled with elaborate monuments to the Cary Lords of the Manor.

Clovelly still fishes but its main income today comes from tourism. Boat trips from the harbour take visitors out into Bideford Bay and along the coast while the RED LION HOTEL, overlooking the harbour, provides food and accommodation. Also overlooking the harbour is CRAZY KATE'S COTTAGE, a long narrow house with a veranda which belonged to KATE LYALL who went mad when she watched from that very veranda as her fisherman beau drowned in the harbour. She died in 1736.

The best way to approach Clovelly is from the east via the three-mile-long HOBBY DRIVE, constructed along the cliff top during the Napoleonic Wars for JAMES HAMLYN-WILLIAMS, as a job creation scheme for French prisoners of war and afterwards for unemployed English soldiers returning from the war.

Victorians gave up, turning the Customs House into a hotel in 1886 and the coastguard cottages into private residences along with a shop and museum.

HARTLAND POINT, three miles to the north, marks THE WESTERN LIMIT IN ENGLAND OF THE BRISTOL CHANNEL. From here on west, it is the Atlantic Ocean.

The Kracken

Hartland Quay is home to THE WORLD'S MOST DIFFICULT CRACK BOULDER CLIMB, THE KRAKEN. Crack climbing is a form of free climbing using natural fissures or cracks in the rock. The Kraken is a sea cave with cracks in the roof that was thought to be impossible to navigate until professional rock climber TOM RANDALL made the 40-foot-long horizontal climb in August 2015, acknowledging that it was the hardest climb he had ever done.

Hartland Quay

A harbour was built at HARTLAND in Henry VIII's day but since this spot experiences some of the roughest seas on the English coast, ships were constantly being wrecked in the harbour and the piers destroyed. Eventually the

St Nectan's Church

St Nectan's Church, Stoke

The 128-foot-high tower of ST NECTAN'S CHURCH in Stoke, known as the Cathedral of North Devon, can be seen from Hartland Quay a mile away on the coast. The tower, which was built in 1420 as a landmark for sailors, is THE SECOND TALLEST CHURCH TOWER IN DEVON. The church, begun in 1170 and completed in 1360, possesses a Norman font, a fabulous painted wagon roof and THE BIGGEST AND MOST COMPLETE MEDIEVAL ROOD SCREEN IN DEVON. Created in 1450, the screen has 11 bays, each one unique, and is 45 feet long and 12 feet high with a top as wide as the lane running past outside. In the chancel is an altar tomb thought to have held the relics of St Nectan, a 5th-century saint of Irish descent from Wales. Also in the chancel is a chair in which the Ethiopian Emperor HAILE SELASSIE sat when opening the church fete in 1938. Buried in the churchyard is SIR ALLEN LANE, founder of Penguin Books, the man who published the unexpurgated version of D.H. Lawrence's *Lady Chatterley's Lover* in 1959 (which led to a famous obscenity trial) and the original publisher of the incomparable Pevsner Architectural Guides. Also buried in the churchyard is children's writer MARY NORTON, author of *The Borrowers* and *Bedknobs and Broomsticks*.

Hartland Abbey

St Nectan's church is the work of the monks from nearby HARTLAND ABBEY, THE LAST ABBEY

Hartland Abbey *NORTH DEVON* Weare Giffard

in England to be dissolved by Henry VIII. The abbey was gifted to the Keeper of the King's Wine Cellar, William Abbot, and the estate still remains in the same family, now going by the name of Stucley. It was a member of the Stucley family, archaeologist William Stucley, who saved Stonehenge and Avebury Stone Circle from demolition in the 18th century. The present house on the estate was built in 1779 with a Strawberry Hill Gothic facade, and the interior was designed by Sir Gilbert Scott in 1845. Both house and gardens are open to the public in the summer months.

Hartland Abbey is a popular filming location, used by the BBC adaptation of Jane Austen's *Sense and Sensibility*, Rosamunde Pilcher's *The Shell Seekers*, John Le Carré's *The Night Manager* with Hugh Laurie, Tom Hiddleston and Olivia Colman, *The Guernsey Literary and Potato Peel Pie Society* (2017) with Lily James, the 2019 film of *Rebecca* from the novel by Daphne du Maurier, starring Lily James and Kristen Scott Thomas, the *Game of Thrones* prequel *House of the Dragon* (2021), and the CBBC series of Enid Blyton's *Malory Towers*.

Weare Giffard

The excellently named village of Weare Giffard near Great Torrington gets its name from *'the place of the fishing weir'* on the estate of the family of de Wear, while the Giffard comes from the Giffard family who owned the estate in the 13th century. The hammer-beam roof of the Great Hall of the 15th-century Weare Giffard Hall is amongst the finest in a private house in England. Constructed between 1450 and 1500, every inch of the roof is rich in carvings with each hammer-beam

supported by a carved animal including a pig, a unicorn, a lion, and a bear. There has been a manor house here since Norman times, but the present house was built by the son of Henry VI's Chief Justice and later Lord Chancellor Sir John Fortescue, influential in the development of common law and the constitutional role of the monarchy. There is also a rather splendid 15th-century gatehouse.

WELL, I NEVER KNEW THIS ABOUT

NORTH DEVON

Three miles west of Lynton, a steep track leads down to the rocks and sand of WOODY BAY, named for the dense oak woods that sweep down to the bay and once earmarked for development in a scheme that bankrupted the owner in the 1890s. It is now owned by the National Trust. Woody Bay Station, about two miles inland, is the modern-day base for the Lynton and Barnstaple Railway, built in 1898 by Sir George Newnes. The railway never made a profit, largely because of the steep inclines it had to negotiate, and it closed in 1935 but was rescued and part reopened between Woody Bay and Killington Lane in 2004. At 964 feet above sea level, Woody Bay station is THE HIGHEST RAILWAY STATION IN SOUTHERN ENGLAND.

William Turner (1745–1829), father of the painter J.M.W. Turner, was born in SOUTH MOLTON on the edge of Exmoor, where he worked as a barber and wig maker. He moved to London in 1770, five years before his son was born.

Hidden away in a secluded valley just outside Ilfracombe, CHAMBERCOMBE MANOR dates from the 11th century and is one of THE OLDEST HOUSES STILL OCCUPIED IN BRITAIN. Mentioned in the Domesday Book, it was owned by the Champernon family until the 15th century and eventually passed into the hands of the Duke of Suffolk, father of the ten-day queen Lady Jane Grey, who stayed many times in what is now the Lady Jane Grey Room. Not surprisingly considering its age, the manor is said to be one of the most haunted houses in the country. Today the house is open to the public, both to visit and to stay in, and has rooms on display dating from the Elizabethan to the Victorian periods.

The Art Deco SAUNTON SANDS HOTEL overlooks SAUNTON SANDS, which stretches for three and a half miles south to Crow Point at the mouth of the River Taw and is much favoured by surfers. The beach is backed by BRAUNTON BURROWS, THE LARGEST AREA OF SAND DUNES IN ENGLAND, and is sometimes closed so that military aircraft can practice short take-offs and landings. In 1944 the beach was used by American assault troops to practise the D-Day landings.

Between Saunton Sands and BRAUNTON VILLAGE, which claims to be THE LARGEST VILLAGE IN ENGLAND, lies the GREAT FIELD, BRITAIN'S LARGEST REMAINING AREA OF STRIP FARMING. Just to the south, BRAUNTON MARSH was part of an area designated as the North Devon Heritage Coast in 1992 which paved the way for BRITAIN'S FIRST BIOSPHERE RESERVE to be designated by UNESCO ten years later, covering a large area of North Devon which is managed to maintain a balance between population and environment.

THE TARKA TRAIL, which follows the route taken by HENRY WILLIAMSON'S *Tarka the Otter*, follows a figure of eight centred on Barnstaple. The northern loop goes up the coast to Lynton and back, while the southern loop goes through Bideford to Dartmoor and back and constitutes THE LONGEST CONTINUOUS OFF-ROAD CYCLE PATH IN BRITAIN.

The NORTH DEVON CREMATORIUM IN BICKINGTON, across the river from Barnstaple, is THE LARGEST CREMATORIUM IN ENGLAND.

SIR FRANCIS CHICHESTER (1901–1972), THE FIRST MAN TO SAIL SINGLE-HANDEDLY AROUND THE WORLD, was born in BARNSTAPLE, as were theatre director RICHARD EYRE, in 1943, TV antiques expert TIM WONNACOTT, in 1951 and TV presenter DERMOT MURNAGHAN, in 1957.

All that is left of a medieval gristmill that lay a mile south of Hartland Quay is BLACKPOOL MILL COTTAGE, a simple 15th-century cottage set on a platform above a stream just back from the sea. Although now a B&B it is frequently used as a film location, most recently for the BBC adaptation of *Sense and Sensibility*, the TV film of Rosamunde Pilcher's *The Shell Seekers,* the BBC drama *The Night Manager*, the 2017 film *The Guernsey Literary and Potato Peel Pie Society* and the film of *The Salt Path* by Raynor Winn, starring Jason Isaacs and Gillian Anderson.

HOLSWORTHY'S CHURCH OF ST PETER AND ST PAUL is famous for being one of the only churches in the country with the Devil depicted in a stained-glass window.

HATHERLEIGH, a few miles north of Okehampton, is either the smallest town or largest village in Devon, depending on who you ask.

THE DUKE OF YORK INN, a 15th-century pub in IDDESLEIGH near Okehampton, with fine views of Dartmoor, is where MICHAEL MORPURGO sat in front of the fire talking to World War One veteran WILFRED ELLIS about how horses were used in the war, a conversation that inspired his 1982 novel *War Horse*, since turned into an award-winning play and a film by Steven Spielberg. In 2021 Charles, then Duke of Cornwall, and his wife Camilla, Duchess of Cornwall, visited the pub and met Michael Morpurgo and his wife Clare, daughter of Sir Allen Lane, founder of Penguin Books, who is buried not far away at Hartland. Iddesleigh is celebrated for having THE HIGHEST PROPORTION OF THATCHED BUILDINGS OF ANY VILLAGE IN DEVON.

ST NECTAN'S CHURCH IN WELCOMBE, THE WESTERNMOST

village in Devon, has the oldest rood screen in the county, dating from the early 14th century. Although but a mile from the sea, both the Torridge and the Tamar rivers rise on the high ground near Welcombe, with the Torridge taking a great 58-mile loop inland through Devon before coming back to the sea at Bideford and the Tamar striking due south for 61 miles to form the border between Devon and Cornwall on its way to Plymouth on the south coast.

Crediton is thought to have been the birthplace of St Boniface (c.675–754), the man who is credited with the first Christmas tree. In 909 it was decided that Devon needed its own bishopric and, as the birthplace of the saint, Crediton's 8th-century Saxon Minster was chosen to be Devon's first cathedral with Edwulf as the first Bishop of Crediton. This explains why Crediton parish church is the size of a cathedral, although the present Perpendicular Gothic building was put up in the 15th century on the foundations of the Norman cathedral that replaced the original Saxon Minster. In 1050 the cathedral was removed to Exeter as the city was larger and had better defences, and the Bishop of Crediton then became a suffragan bishop.

DARTMOOR AND WEST DEVON

I have never before, in my long and eclectic career, been gifted with such an abundance of natural beauty as I experienced filming War Horse *on Dartmoor.*

Film director Steven Spielberg

Haytor

DARTMOOR, THE LARGEST AREA OF GRANITE IN BRITAIN, THE HIGHEST REGION IN ENGLAND SOUTH OF THE PENNINES and THE LARGEST AREA OF OPEN COUNTRYSIDE IN THE SOUTH OF ENGLAND, is 368 square miles of mountains, moorland, rivers, woods and valleys. A landscape of exquisite bleakness and beauty tempered by remote villages and ancient sites, it stretches between the towns of Okehampton and Ivybridge, Tavistock and Ashburton. Dartmoor leaves no-one unmoved: when the sun shines, a place of warm corners, golden grass, babbling brooks, endearing ponies and spectacular views; when the mist descends and the wind howls and the rain drives horizontal, a place of madness and nightmares and devilry. Dartmoor's highest point is HIGH WILLHAYS, 2,039 feet (612 metres) above sea level, with YES TOR coming in second at 2,013 feet (619 metres). A tor is an outcrop of bare rock that has been worn by erosion into a variety of distinctive shapes and there are 160 named tors on Dartmoor with hundreds more unnamed.

Haytor

HAYTOR is perhaps the best known of the Dartmoor tors, a distinctive landmark on the eastern edge of the moor visible from miles around. In the 19th century steps were carved into the easternmost of the two outcrops and a handrail fitted to make the climb to the top less precarious. The handrail rusted away while the steps remain, but even so, the climb can be slippery and hazardous, involving a leap across a deep crack in the rocks halfway up. Those who make it to the top are rewarded with one of the finest views in England, east towards the Teign estuary and the sea, south across the red rolling fields of the South Hams, west and north across the vast empty green-gold wilderness of Dartmoor.

Stannary Towns

TIN has been mined on Dartmoor for centuries, the trade regulated and administered from Devon's four stannary towns: Tavistock, Chagford, Ashburton and Plympton. These were towns where the tin was taken to be weighed, stamped, taxed and traded. The word 'stannary' comes from the Latin word for tin, *'stannum'*.

Okehampton

First there was an Iron Age fort set on a steep slope above the Okemont river. Then the Saxons built a church on a small hill to the west, which still stands although heavily restored. Next, in 1068, the Norman knight Baldwin Fitz-Gilbert, who fought with William the Conqueror at the Battle of Hastings and was handed the largest fiefdom in Devon as a reward, built a motte and bailey castle to guard a crossing point on the West Okemont river. The market town of OKEHAMPTON grew up beside the river a little distance away.

Okehampton Castle

OKEHAMPTON CASTLE sits on a high wooded ridge above the West Okemont river and was in its day one of the most powerful castles in Devon. The motte is formed largely of natural rock and is unusual in Devon and Cornwall in having a rectangular keep on the top rather than a circular one. In the 14th century the Courtenay family, later Earls of Devon, converted the castle into a palatial hunting lodge but this was abandoned when the 10th Earl of Devon, Henry Courtenay, was executed on the orders of Henry VIII. The Courtenays then moved to Powderham Castle near Exeter, which remains the seat of

the Earls of Devon to this day. The substantial ruins of Okehampton Castle are most picturesque and have long inspired artists such as J.M.W. Turner.

Meldon Viaduct

Two miles downriver of Okehampton Castle is the slender MELDON VIADUCT, built in 1874 and ONE OF ONLY TWO SURVIVING WROUGHT IRON TRUSS AND TRESTLE RAILWAY BRIDGES IN BRITAIN. The viaduct is 535 feet (163 metres) long and crosses the West Okemont river at a height of 151 feet (46 metres). No longer used by trains, it now forms part of the Granite Way cycle path and commands superb views over north Dartmoor and down to the Meldon Dam.

Meldon Dam

MELDON DAM was opened in 1972 as the last of eight reservoirs built in the Dartmoor National Park. A circular walk around the reservoir takes you across the top of the dam, providing superb views to the north-east up the steep-sided Meldon Gorge to the Meldon Viaduct.

Finch Foundry

Right in the middle of the wonderfully named Sticklepath village stands FINCH FOUNDRY, THE LAST WORKING WATER-POWERED FORGE IN ENGLAND. It began life in the late 18th century as a corn and textile mill until, in 1814, William Finch set the foundry up as a tool factory and sawmill. The foundry continued to be operated by members of the Finch family for the next 150 years, at its peak producing some 400 sharp tools a day of every kind as used by Devon miners and farmers, including shovels and scythes.

In 1960 part of the building collapsed and the foundry was forced to close. It was inherited by Richard Barron, whose mother was a Finch, and it was his idea to turn the foundry into museum of rural industry. Initially funded by charitable trusts and then owned by the North Devon Museums Association, the foundry was taken over by the National Trust in 1994. The foundry drew water from the River Taw via a leat which drove a number of waterwheels to power a tilt hammer, a drop hammer and a shear hammer. All are still in working order and are demonstrated several times a day by National Trust staff.

Tom Pearce's Summerhouse

Tom Pearce, Tom Pearce, lend me your grey mare.
All along, down along, out along lea.
For I want for to go to Widecombe Fair ...

From a traditional English folk song

Behind the foundry is a Quaker burial ground and standing near the entrance is a delightful thatched summerhouse which once stood in the garden of a local miller, TOM PEARCE, who lived in a cottage across the road from the foundry and himself lies in the burial ground. Local legend has it that this was the Tom Pearce who rashly lent his grey mare to Uncle Tom Cobley and all in the famous folk song of Widecombe Fair.

Four Village Trail

STICKLEPATH lay on the main packhorse route from Exeter to Launceston at the bottom of a steep hill, hence '*stickle*' meaning 'steep' in Old English. The packhorse route became the main road from London to Penzance which continued to run through the village until 1987 when the A30 bypass was opened, leaving Sticklepath to slumber once again in peace. It is now one of the four beautiful Devon thatch villages

on north Dartmoor's Four Village Trail which also takes in South Tawton, South Zeal and Belstone.

South Tawton

The centre of SOUTH TAWTON forms one of the most picturesque scenes on Dartmoor with its old, thatched church house – the finest in Devon – set beside an attractive lychgate with the magnificent 15th-century church tower behind, all framed by the branches of a young spreading oak tree. The church house is 15th-century and was the medieval equivalent of a modern church hall, used as a meeting place for the clergy and for fundraising events which would have been charged with strong, locally brewed ale.

South Zeal

The 'new town' of SOUTH ZEAL came into being in 1299 when the Lord of South Tawton was granted the rights to a market, and is a planned village formed of a long street of white-painted thatched cottages with long thin burgage plots behind (see page 144). The street is interrupted by the 15th-century St Mary's Chapel which sits in the middle of the road along with a fine 18-foot-high (5.4 metre) 14th-century granite memorial cross, one of the best in Devon. Nearby is the superb stone-built OXENHAM ARMS, named after local landowners the Oxenhams, of Oxenham Hall at South Tawton. It was formerly a 12th-century Benedictine monastery built around a prehistoric menhir which can still be seen set into the wall of the lounge bar. In Tudor times the monastery was made into a manor house by the Burgoyne family.

Belstone

Unlike the other three villages on the trail, BELSTONE, which sits at almost 1,000 feet (300 metres) above sea level, is built almost entirely of stone, hewed from the granite heights of Dartmoor, which rises up behind the village to an elevation of 1,508 feet (460 metres) at Belstone Tor. On the slopes of the tor is a Bronze Age stone circle and burial chamber known as THE NINE MAIDENS, young girls who were turned to stone for dancing on a Sunday. The infant River Taw, which rises nearby on Dartmoor, flows through the village at the start of its journey to Torridge.

Belstone, which lies at the entrance to one of the most beautiful parts of Dartmoor, was the model for the village of Sittaford in Agatha Christie's *The Sittaford Mystery*, while the name of Belstone was made famous by the 1973 film *The Belstone Fox* based on David Rook's novel *The Ballad of the Belstone Fox*.

Canonteign

The LADY EXMOUTH FALLS, one of a series of waterfalls that make up the Canonteign Falls on the Canonteign estate on the eastern edge of Dartmoor, is THE HIGHEST MAN-MADE WATERFALL IN ENGLAND, with a drop of 230 feet (70 metres). The falls were the idea of Lady Susan, wife of the 3rd Lord Exmouth, to provide employment for miners made redundant by the closure of the local silver and tin mines and were created by diverting an existing leat that provided water for the sawmill and mines to a precipitous rocky outcrop.

The nearby neo-classical Canonteign House was built in 1828 for Captain Pellew, later 2nd Viscount Exmouth, while hidden away down a country lane to the north is one of Devon's most ravishing secret gems, the original Canonteign House, now Canonteign Barton, a 16th-century Tudor manor house with stunning views across the Teign valley. After years of neglect the house was restored in the 1970s and is now run as a luxurious holiday let.

Castle Drogo

Set on a spectacular granite bluff high above the deep wooded valley of the River Teign and visible from miles around, CASTLE DROGO is BRITAIN'S NEWEST CASTLE, completed in 1930, and THE LAST CASTLE TO BE BUILT IN BRITAIN.

Castle Drogo was designed by Edwin Lutyens for JULIUS DREWE, founder in 1883 of Home and Colonial Stores, at one time Britain's largest retail chain. Once the business was up and running Drewe retired and began to plan how to spend his fortune. On discovering that his family could have come from Drewsteignton or 'Drew's town on the River Teign' in Devon and therefore be related to a Norman knight called Drogo, who came over with William the Conqueror and founded Drewsteignton, he bought some land in the vicinity and began to build a castle worthy of his Norman ancestor.

The result is a mix of 13th-century-style castle, with thick

walls, turrets, arrow slits, battlements, a castellated gatehouse and portcullis, and 16th-century-style Tudor mansion with huge mullioned Elizabethan windows looking out over Dartmoor. Running water and electricity are provided by a hydro turbine drawing water from the River Teign, and comfortable rooms were furnished from Drewe's other property, Wadhurst Hall in Sussex.

At the outbreak of World War One in 1914 many of those working on the house went off to the Front, leaving just two local masons behind to carry on with the work. Consequently Castle Drogo took nearly 20 years to build and ended up only a third of the size that Julius Drewe had originally envisaged. This was not all bad, for the loveliest room in the whole castle: a chapel, which occupies the undercroft of what was supposed to be the Great Hall, was not included in the original plans.

Towards the end of those turbulent war years, some of the fire went out of Julius Drewe when his son Adrian was killed at Ypres in 1917. As a memorial to Adrian, Mrs Drewe, Frances, had her son's things laid out in a bedroom in the North Wing, which was given the name Adrian Drewe's Room. Julius Drewe himself died in 1931, having enjoyed his castle for just one year.

Outside there is a terraced formal garden with herbaceous

borders planted with many species you wouldn't expect to see on Dartmoor, such as rhododendrons, magnolias and roses. Ideas for plants and shrubs for the garden and the long, winding driveway leading up to the castle were sought from the famous garden designer GERTRUDE JEKYLL, who Lutyens had long worked with. There is also a croquet lawn upon which visitors may play.

Castle Drogo is a magical place in a sublime setting, one of the more unusual jewels of Dartmoor. I could happily live there, as did the Drewe family until 1974 when the castle was given over to the National Trust, THE FIRST 20TH-CENTURY PROPERTY EVER ACQUIRED BY THE TRUST.

Lydford

I oft have heard of Lydford Law,
How in the morn they hang and draw,
And sit in judgment after ...

From 'Lydford Journey' by William Brown of Tavistock (c.1590–1645)

Beautifully situated on the western edge of Dartmoor, LYDFORD was fortified by Alfred the Great in AD 880 and established as one of Devon's four Saxon towns or 'burhs'. The village sits on an easily defended natural promontory protected on two sides by deep river valleys and on the third by a Saxon earthen rampart. During the reign of Ethelred the Unready, Lydford had its own mint, while under Edward the Confessor it was the most populous place in Devon after Exeter. Vestiges of the Saxon defences remain, as does the Saxon street pattern.

After the Conquest, a small wooden fort surrounded by a deep ditch was built on the tip of the promontory to protect what had become the administrative centre of Dartmoor, and in 1194 King John ordered the building of a stone castle on top of its own mound east of the church, that could be used as a prison and court for those who offended against Dartmoor's stannary laws. Lydford Castle remained Dartmoor's main gaol until Dartmoor

Prison was opened at the beginning of the 19th century. Conditions were cruel and the notorious 'Lydford Law' gained a reputation for harsh justice with offenders condemned without trial and then left to languish in the castle dungeons. In 1510 Richard Strode, MP for Plymouth (see page 123), was incarcerated at Lydford for complaining that tin mining debris was silting up the Dartmoor rivers and hence the harbour at Plymouth; he described the castle as *'the most annoious, contagious and detestable place within this realm'*.

Lydford remained a royal borough until 1239, when it was granted by Henry III to his brother Richard, Earl of Cornwall, and is now owned by the Duchy of Cornwall.

Lydford Gorge

Lydford overlooks LYDFORD GORGE where the River Lyd runs for one and a half miles through THE DEEPEST GORGE IN DEVON AND CORNWALL on its way from Dartmoor to the River Tamar. There are two spectacular features in the gorge, the beautiful 100-foot (30 metres) WHITE LADY WATERFALL and the exhilarating DEVIL'S CAULDRON where the narrow rock channel forces the water through a series of roiling whirlpools.

St Pancras, Widecombe in the Moor

Widecombe in the Moor

Tom Pearce, Tom Pearce, lend me your grey mare.
All along, down along, out along lea.
For I want for to go to Widecombe Fair,
With Bill Brewer, Jan Stewer, Peter Gurney,
Peter Davy, Dan'l Whiddon, Harry Hawke,
Old Uncle Tom Cobley and all,
Old Uncle Tom Cobley and all.

Devon folk have been coming to WIDECOMBE FAIR, held annually in September in the lee of the great church of St Pancras, CATHEDRAL OF THE MOORS, since at least 1850, and probably for centuries before that. Church and village nestle in a deep green vale ringed by desolate moorland hills. From the top of the surrounding heights, the distant view of the landmark Perpendicular-style church tower, 135 feet high to the tips of its pinnacles and rising out of a patch of trees, is one of the most stirring sights in Devon, a beacon promising welcome and refuge from the hardships and terrors of the moor.

The church was first built in the 15th century, constructed from locally mined granite, and it has been enlarged and restored over the years thanks in part to the riches of Dartmoor's tin mines. In 1638, during a great thunderstorm, it was struck by a fireball and badly damaged. Four people attending afternoon service were killed, and over 60 injured.

The interior is bright but fairly bare, like the moors, with just a font to fill the west end, high arcades supported by singular monolithic pillars of granite, and wagon roofs above the nave and aisles. There are some quaintly carved roof bosses including ONE OF THE ONLY SIX ROOF BOSSES IN ENGLAND DEPICTING ST KATHERINE, and another of three hares sharing three ears between them, known as the TINNER'S RABBITS, a symbol of the Holy Trinity adopted by the tin miners of Devon and Cornwall found in a number of Dartmoor churches.

A plaque on the north wall at the west end of the church in

memory of MARY ELFORD (d.1642) includes an anagram of her name, 'Fear my Lord'.

Princetown

In the Bleak Mid-Moor

PRINCETOWN, 1,400 feet above sea level and almost the highest village in England (after Flash in Staffordshire), is bleak, the bleakest place in Devon, set in the middle of the high moor and made bleaker still by the menacing grey Victorian gaol blocks of England's most notorious prison that loom over the town. When the sky is grey and lowering – which is quite often on Dartmoor – the effect is chilling, and the imagination can run riot. It clearly did for Sherlock Holmes author Sir Arthur Conan Doyle, who started to write *The Hound of the Baskervilles* while staying at the Duchy Hotel, now the National Park Visitor Centre, in the middle of the village.

Princetown is named after the Prince of Wales, later George IV, whose Duchy of Cornwall still owns much of Dartmoor, and was brought into existence by the vision of one man, the Prince's Private Secretary and Lord Warden of the Stannaries THOMAS TYRWHITT, who wanted to tame this desolate stretch of moorland and turn it into profitable farmland.

Tyrwhitt began by building himself a comfortable villa, Tor Royal, which still exists today as a B&B. He intended this villa to serve as a farmhouse and attempted to create a small farming community around it, but Tyrwhitt's attempts to grow crops were defeated by the stony moorland terrain and harsh weather. Instead, he came up with the idea of building a prison to house the thousands of captives from the Napoleonic Wars who were being kept on filthy prison hulks in Plymouth Sound and dying off in unacceptable numbers.

Dartmoor Prison

Thomas Tyrwhitt himself laid the foundation stone for DARTMOOR

Prison in March 1806. It took three years to build, using local labour and local stone, with the first 2,500 French prisoners arriving in May 1809. As the prison was laid out in a radial pattern around a central space, the prisoners were not watched over from the centre but by militia posted on the high double circular perimeter walls surrounding the complex.

The prison was designed to hold 5,000 men in open-plan dormitories, 1,000 in each of the five two-storey blocks, but by the end of 1809 it was already overfilled and by the end of 1815 some 6,500 American sailors from the war of 1812 had joined the French in Dartmoor. The cell windows were tiny, there was little fresh air and water was supplied by a culvert to each block from a reservoir beside the main gate. Some 1,200 French prisoners died from fever and disease along with 271 Americans, all of whom are buried in a graveyard just outside the prison walls. Their memorials can still be seen.

In 1816, with the ending of the two wars, the prison closed and fell into disrepair but in 1850, when transportation to Australia or the Colonies was no longer an option, it was re-opened to house some of Britain's most notorious convicts, who were made to work in the local quarries and help rebuild the prison into more or less what we see there today.

During World War One prisoners were removed so that Dartmoor could serve as a Home Office Work Centre for Conscientious Objectors. After the war prisoners returned, amongst them a number of Irish Republican activists including the future Irish president Éamon de Valera.

Dartmoor was thought suitable

for the toughest criminals because it was considered pretty much escape-proof. If an inmate did manage to get beyond the prison walls it was a ten-mile trudge across desolate open moorland with very little cover to the nearest civilisation – all the while being chased by mounted police and bloodhounds. And those who hid in the nearby woods until the hue and cry was over were swiftly caught, as the prison authorities had placed sensors there to detect movement.

Dartmoor's Most Notorious Inmates
JACK THE HAT MCVITIE, hitman and associate of the Kray twins in the 1950s and '60s, so named because he wore a trilby hat to cover his thinning hair. Paid by Ronnie Kray to kill an informer, McVitie failed but kept the money and was consequently murdered by Reggie Kray in 1967.

FRANK MITCHELL, THE MAD AXEMAN, considered Britain's most violent gangster, and so-called because he held a couple hostage with an axe during a prison escape from Broadmoor. Sent to Dartmoor for life for robbery with violence, Mitchell was sprung by the Kray twins in 1966. Sirens were sounded and local people were told to stay inside and lock their doors. The Mad Axeman soon became too hot for even the Krays to handle and consequently was murdered by their top hitman Freddie Foreman, his body thrown into the sea off Newhaven.

JOHN HAIGH, THE ACID BATH MURDERER, accountant who battered his six victims to death or shot them and then dissolved their bodies in drums full of sulphuric acid.

Dartmoor Prison continued to be used for dangerous criminals until 2002, when it became a Category C prison for non-violent offenders. Although the Home Office intend to continue using Dartmoor as a prison, it was forced to close in 2024 due to the discovery of unsafe levels of radioactive gas and the prison's future remains unclear.

Dartmoor Prison Museum
Housed in the old prison dairy not far from the main gate, DARTMOOR PRISON MUSEUM tells the story of Britain's most notorious gaol's 220-year history and is open seven days a week.

St Michael's Church

Princetown's granite CHURCH OF ST MICHAEL was built between 1812 and 1814, begun by prisoners from the Napoleonic Wars and finished by American prisoners from the war of 1812, who were being held in Dartmoor Prison. It is THE ONLY CHURCH IN ENGLAND BUILT BY PRISONERS OF WAR. The church's east window commemorates the Americans who were incarcerated in the prison and was part paid for by the National Society of United States Daughters of 1812. The church is now under the care of the Churches Conservation Trust, and is still consecrated and used for occasional services.

The Hound of the Baskervilles – *Locations*

The most famous of Sir Arthur Conan Doyle's Sherlock Holmes novels, *The Hound of the Baskervilles*, is in part based on the story of a real-life 17th-century squire called RICHARD CABELL who lived at BROOK MANOR near Buckfastleigh on the edge of Dartmoor, and was said to have murdered his wife and sold his soul to the Devil. When he died, huge black fire-breathing hounds with red eyes were apparently seen galloping across the moor, baying fearsomely. The 17th-century Brook Manor still stands, although much restored. One of the doors in the west wing sports a knocker inscribed 'RC 1656'.

Hayford Hall

a dream place, a lovely, heavenly poetic garden, a Paradise, far from nowhere, deep in the trees beneath the moor.

Emily Coleman, author of *The Shutter of Snow* and guest at Hayford Hall in 1932–33

HAYFORD HALL, west of Buckfastleigh on the edge of the high moor not far from Brook Manor, is believed to be the prime candidate for Baskerville Hall. Converted from a 14th-century farmhouse into a country residence in the early 19th century, the hall was rented out in the 1930s to American heiress PEGGY GUGGENHEIM at the suggestion of her boyfriend, literary critic John Holms, who rather liked the idea of following in his namesake's footsteps. While her fellow American heiress Dorothy Elmhirst was setting up an alternative arts community 15 miles away at Dartington Hall, Peggy and John established a boozy bohemian literary community at Hayford, which became affectionately known as 'Hangover Hall'. Female writers, in particular, came to Hayford to write novels based on their life experiences, and the Hayford community during the summers of 1932 and 1933 are recognised for fostering the emergence of female-led modernist literature. The American modernist writer Djuna Barnes, for instance, wrote her highly praised cult classic *Nightwood* while staying at Hayford.

The following year, 1934, saw Hayford Hall echo its alter ego Baskerville Hall as a house of ill-omen when John Holms rode out on to the moor from the hall and fell from his horse, breaking his arm. He died under anaesthetic while undergoing surgery to reset the arm.

Sherlock Holmes author Sir Arthur Conan Doyle stayed at the Duchy Hotel in Princetown while researching locations on Dartmoor for *The Hound of the Baskervilles*. Dartmoor Prison in Princetown is certainly the '*great convict prison*' from which the convicted murderer Selden escapes to roam the moor. You can still see the building that housed the mounted prison warders who hunted for him after he escaped, just inside the gate and visible from the road. Guards armed with rifles continued to patrol on horseback while escorting prisoners to work in the quarries right up until 1971, making Dartmoor THE LAST PRISON IN BRITAIN TO HAVE MOUNTED ARMED GUARDS.

FOX TORE MIRE, a few miles southwest of Princetown, is the model for the treacherous Grimpen Mire into which Stapleton, the villain of the story, flees and is assumed to have drowned in a bog.

down beneath me in a cleft of the hills there was a circle of the old stone huts, and in the middle of them there was one which retained sufficient roof to act as a screen against the weather.

This is how Dr Watson describes Sherlock Holmes's hideout in *The Hound of the Baskervilles* and it is almost certainly inspired by GRIMSPOUND, which lies to the north of Widecombe in the Moor, and is perhaps the best-known prehistoric settlement on Dartmoor. Dating from around 1300 BC in the late Bronze Age, it covers four acres and consists of 24 hut circles surrounded by a low stone wall. Archaeologists argue over whether it was a Druid temple, an Iron Age fort or simply a settlement.

Tavistock

TAVISTOCK, stannary town and capital of west Dartmoor, stands on the River Tavy from which it gets its name. An abbey was founded here in AD 974 and became one of the richest abbeys in Devon and Cornwall until the Dissolution when it was demolished, leaving just the refectory and a gateway surviving in the town centre. The estate was granted to John Russell, later Earl of Bedford. The Russell family, created Marquesses of Tavistock and Dukes of Bedford in 1694, continued to maintain an interest in Tavistock and in 1810 Georgiana, the wife of the 6th Duke of Bedford, had a cottage orné built for her in the village of Milton Abbot on the edge of the moor, five miles from Tavistock. Designed by Jeffry Wyattville and set in 100 acres of gardens by Humphry Repton, Georgiana spent many a summer there in her 'garden paradise of the west'. Endsleigh Cottage is now Hotel Endsleigh.

Sir Francis Drake was born just outside Tavistock at CROWNDALE FARM where his father was a tenant farmer. The 16th-century farm where he first saw the light of day has more or less disappeared, although there are some ruins thought to be remnants of Drake's birthplace.

MORWELLHAM QUAY, five miles west of Tavistock on the River Tamar, was set up by the monks of Tavistock Abbey in the 10th century as a port outlet for the abbey from which goods could be sent to or brought from Plymouth. When tin and copper began to be mined on Dartmoor and brought to the stannary town of Tavistock, the importance of Morwellham grew and in 1817 the Tavistock Canal was opened to bring the ore from Tavistock to the quay and then on to Plymouth. At its peak in the mid-19th century, Morwellham became known as the 'richest copper port in Queen Victoria's Empire', according to the Morwellham Quay official website. The arrival of the railways put an end to Morwellham's use and the site has been beautifully preserved as an outdoor museum of Victorian industrial and rural life.

Ashburton

The ancient stannary town of ASHBURTON, which lies on the southeastern edge of Dartmoor, is one of the few towns in Britain to legally retain a court leet, a type of local court dating from Saxon times, through an Act of Parliament. The court leet appoints a portreeve, an early kind of mayor, to administer and implement the decisions of the court within the town. Other appointed officials include an ale taster, to assess the quality of the town's ale and whether it is being sold in the correct measures, and a bread weigher to assess the freshness of the bread being sold in the town. The court leet meets in the Chapel of St Lawrence, which was built in 1301 as a private chapel for the Bishop of Exeter. He handed it to the town in 1314 for use as a chantry chapel and a grammar school that operated there for over 600 years until 1938.

Ashburton still retains its medieval core around North, East and West Streets, each of which contains a number of notable buildings. The town's granite church in West Street is noted for its 90-foot (27 metres) 15th-century tower, while almost opposite is the OLD EXETER INN where Sir Walter Raleigh was arrested for treason on the orders of James I on 19 July 1603. The inn has been trading on the same spot since 1130 and claims to be THE FIFTH OLDEST PUB IN ENGLAND.

The crooked old building with a medieval arched doorway in North Street, now a shop, was once the Mermaid Inn where in 1646 Oliver Cromwell's Civil War commander, General Fairfax, established his headquarters while routing the Royalists out of the West Country.

A little further along at 10 North Street is Ashburton's most celebrated building, the 17th-century HOUSE OF CARDS, originally a gaming club and decorated with the shapes of the four card suits: hearts, diamonds, clubs and spades punched into the grey slate hanging tiles of the upper storeys.

St Leonard's Church, Sheepstor

White Rajahs

The little 15th-century granite church of St Leonard's, on the southern edge of Dartmoor, lies right beneath the granite tor that gives the village its name. This is quintessential Devon, but there is also a whisper of the romantic east about the place. Hanging on a wall inside the church is a PUA KUMBU, or ceremonial textile, given as a gift from the Malaysian state of Sarawak to the final resting place of SIR JAMES BROOKE, CHARLES BROOKE AND CHARLES VYNER BROOKE, THE THREE LEGENDARY WHITE RAJAHS OF SARAWAK, who are buried in the churchyard.

JAMES BROOKE (1803–68), born of Devon stock, was a British East India Company officer who helped quash an uprising against Sarawak's ruler, the Sultan of Brunei, and in return was granted the title RAJAH OF SARAWAK. Under his rule, which lasted 26 years from 1842 until his death, Sarawak prospered, with Brooke overseeing the suppression of slavery and piracy and developing trade. He was succeeded by his nephew CHARLES BROOKE (1829–1917), who founded schools, parliamentary government and railways, and was in turn succeeded by his own son CHARLES VYNER BROOKE (1874–1963). Sarawak was occupied by the Japanese during World War Two after which, much against the will of Charles Vyner Brooke, it became a British colony. Granted independence in 1963, it is now part of the Federation of Malaysia.

A window in the south wall of St Leonard's church was donated by the Association of the Sarawak Civil Servants in memory of those from Sarawak who died in World War Two, and shows a pitcher plant from Sarawak and a butterfly, *Trogonoptera brookiana* or Rajah Brooke's birdwing, named after James Brooke.

Buckfast Abbey

A small wooden Benedictine monastery was founded at Buckfast, meaning 'stronghold where deer and bucks are held' in 1018 in the reign of King Canute. In 1147 this became a Cistercian abbey and was rebuilt in stone, and for the next 400 years the abbey became prosperous as a wool producer, exporting wool to Italy. After the Dissolution of the Monasteries in 1539 the abbey buildings were stripped for stone and allowed to ruin until nothing was left except the Abbot's Tower and Abbot's Lodging. In 1882 a group of French Benedictine monks purchased the abbey ruins and over the next 25 years built the present abbey on top of the original foundations in the 13th-century Romanesque and Gothic style of the medieval abbey. None of the monks were masons or professional builders but somehow they managed to construct an impressive church of cathedral-like proportions that is now a flourishing tourist attraction. The working monks of today still produce honey and a much-praised tonic wine.

RICHARD CABELL

Perched on a high rock between Buckfast Abbey and Buckfastleigh, only reachable from Buckfastleigh by a flight of 195 steps known as the DEVIL'S STEPS, is the blackened and burned-out ruin of HOLY TRINITY CHURCH. Spooky and isolated down a narrow country lane, only a 13th-century tower and the slim 15th-century spire above it are still standing after the church was set on fire, allegedly by devil worshippers, in 1992. Devil worshippers?

Well, within the churchyard lies the CABELL MAUSOLEUM where the 'monstrously evil' 17th-century local squire RICHARD CABELL is entombed behind iron railings. Cabell lived at Brook Manor just outside Buckfastleigh and reportedly terrorised the neighbourhood while riding out across the moor with his pack of vicious hunting hounds. It was alleged that he murdered his wife and got away with it by selling his soul to the Devil. He died in 1677 and on the night of his internment, a phantom pack of slavering dogs are said to have galloped over the moor to howl over their master's grave. Each year on the anniversary of his death, Cabell would rise from the tomb and lead his hounds across the moor and so the people of Buckfastleigh placed a huge slab on top of the gravestone and enclosed the tomb behind thick walls and iron railings to stop him from getting out. Ever since there have been reports of a strange red glow emanating from behind the railings while demonic beasts prowl around outside trying to get in. Directly below the tomb, in Reed's Cave, a stalactite and a stalagmite have fused to form a sinister shape resembling a man in 17th-century garb known as the 'Little Man'. Such fearsome tales have long attracted body snatchers and devil worshippers, and it is they who are thought to have set the church on fire while holding some sort of satanic ceremony around the altar where the fire started.

Unsurprisingly, the story of Richard Cabell is thought to have provided the inspiration for Sir Arthur Conan Doyle's Sherlock Holmes story *The Hound of the Baskervilles*.

Buckfastleigh

BUCKFASTLEIGH means the 'clearing' or 'pasture' belonging to Buckfast, and the small settlement in this clearing soon grew into a market town and a centre of the woollen textile industry. By the 18th century it developed as a mill town with woollen, corn and paper mills and a tannery powered by the Dart, the Mardle and the Dean Burn. In 1838 there were 700 looms in Buckfastleigh, more than any in other town in Devon. In the centre of the town is Town Mill, the largest of the Buckfastleigh mills, which was built in 1800 and later purchased by the Hamlyn family.

The Valiant Soldier

THE VALIANT SOLDIER in Fore Street was a pub from the early 1800s until 1965, when the brewery withdrew its license and the landlord closed the pub after the last customers departed leaving everything as it was: the optics, the glasses, the furniture, even the change in the till. Today the Valiant Soldier, the pub where time is never served, remains untouched as a unique museum giving an insight into a small-town pub of the 1960s.

Pridhamsleigh Cavern

Across the A38 from Buckfast Abbey is one of Devon's best-kept secrets, PRIDHAMSLEIGH CAVERN, three quarters of a mile long and 180 feet (50 metres) deep and said to be suitable for inexperienced cavers. Close to the cave entrance is the Bishop's Chamber, from which a number of passages lead through to one of the largest underground lakes in Britain. The lake is over 100 feet (30 metres) deep and an opening at about 80 feet (24 metres) leads through to another partially air-filled chamber named after the caver who discovered it, Gerry Pritchard. GERRY'S CHAMBER IS THE BIGGEST CAVE CHAMBER IN DEVON.

Other notable caves in the area include Reed's Cave (see page 85), Baker's Pit and Joint Mitnor Cave, noted for its wealth of fossil remains that include animals such as elephants, hippos, lions and monkeys from the Ipswichian Age, a warm interglacial period of the Ice Age, when summer temperatures in the area were much warmer than those of today.

Brentor, St Michael

England's Highest Church

The views from BRENTOR are arguably THE WIDEST AND MOST SPECTACULAR FROM ANY CHURCHYARD IN ENGLAND. Bodmin Moor and half of Cornwall lie to the west, Exmoor to the north, Whitsand Bay to the south and bleak Dartmoor to the east, a vast panorama of green and gold rising majestically to a tor-strewn skyline, lush and wild all around. Joyous and uplifting on a clear summer's day, romantic and mysterious as the sun is setting, terrifying and yet exhilarating as the mist descends, the wind blows and the driving rain stings your face.

ST MICHAEL DE RUPE sits right on top of a volcanic cone, on the edge of a precipice, at a height of 1,110 feet above sea level, THE HIGHEST WORKING CHURCH IN ENGLAND. Churches on heights are often dedicated to St Michael, the Chief of Angels, with perhaps the most famous being St Michael's Mount off Penzance on the south Cornish coast.

Legend tells us that this St Michael's was built by a rich merchant rescued at sea, who vowed to build a church on the most prominent piece of land he saw on his safe return to Plymouth. Both the church and tor are certainly a distinctive landmark for miles around, in particular for sailors coming into Plymouth Sound – how Drake and Raleigh, Gilbert and Grenville must have been cheered to see its distant embattled tower welcoming them home from their adventures.

The first church was actually put here by Sir Robert Gifford in 1130 – he was indeed a wealthy merchant, so there could be some truth in the story. It is certainly an ancient site, with the remnants of an Iron Age fort scattered around the foot of the tor. During one of the many renovations, skeletons were found under the church floor, laid north to south, indicating that this was a pagan burial site.

The church as we see it today is mainly 13th-century and measures only 37 feet (11 metres) by 15 feet (4.6 metres), making it ONE OF ENGLAND'S TEN SMALLEST CHURCHES. The walls are solid and thick, a fortress against the elements. It is astonishing how quiet it is once inside and how cosy and secure beneath the low roof beams. St Michael himself watches over the church from the modern east window.

There are still services held at St Michael's in the summer. It is a steep climb to get there, even for the casual visitor, but how much more so for the bride at her wedding, the mother carrying her baby to be christened or the coffin bearers at a funeral. Their reward is a matchless view and an unforgettable experience.

Buckland Abbey

BUCKLAND ABBEY, a 13th-century Cistercian house lying in a sheltered valley on the edge of Dartmoor between Tavistock and Plymouth, resounds with stirring memories of two Devon men who conquered the world for England and for their Queen Elizabeth I.

Buckland Abbey was bought from Henry VIII after the Dissolution in 1541 by Sir Richard Grenville as a home for his son Roger. Four years later Roger went down with the Mary Rose in the Solent and Buckland passed to Roger's son Richard, a cousin of Walter Raleigh. The story of Richard Grenville and the *Revenge* are told in the North Devon chapter (see page 54).

In 1581 Sir Francis Drake, enriched by his triumph of becoming the first Englishman to sail around the world, bought Buckland Abbey from Richard Grenville and made it his home.

Buckland Abbey

SIR FRANCIS DRAKE
(1540–96)

Sir Francis Drake was the greatest of all the Elizabethan pirate sailors. Born at Crowndale Farm on the River Tavy just south of Tavistock, he grew up staunchly opposed to Catholicism and became an implacable foe of Spain after being double-crossed by the Spanish on a trip to Mexico. He built up a huge fortune plundering Spanish treasure ships off South and Central America and while Queen Elizabeth could not sanction his actions, she certainly didn't disapprove of the booty he won for her. Almost single-handedly, Drake wrestled supremacy of the seas away from Spain, draining her of wealth and influence. His capture of a Spanish ship carrying secret papers about Spain's East India trade was a vital spur to the setting up of Britain's own East India Company.

In 1577 he was secretly commissioned by Queen Elizabeth to persecute the Spanish colonies on the west coast of America and, as well as successfully achieving that task, he ended up becoming THE FIRST ENGLISHMAN TO SAIL AROUND THE WORLD in his ship, the *Golden Hind*. Drake came back with enough money to pay off the national debt, and buy Buckland Abbey.

Drake was not yet finished with Spain, however. King Philip II of Spain, who regarded himself as the rightful King of England through his marriage to Queen Elizabeth's late sister Mary I, began preparing a battle fleet to invade England and so, in 1588, Drake sailed into Cadiz harbour in southern Spain and sank 24 Spanish warships, much to the annoyance of King Philip. As Drake put it, '*we have singed the King of Spain's beard*'.

When the Spanish Armada did finally appear off the English coast in 1588, Drake was playing bowls on Plymouth Hoe and insisted on finishing the game, thus creating a legend. The story of Drake's game of bowls on Plymouth Hoe is told in the Plymouth chapter (see page 126).

Suffice to say Drake and his fellow navy officers prevailed over the Armada. Interestingly, Drake's flagship was the *Revenge*, which would later suffer a glorious fate in the hands of the previous owner of Buckland Abbey, Richard Grenville.

In 1595 after a few quiet years at Buckland Abbey enjoying his second marriage, Drake went back to sea to once more harry Spanish possession in the Caribbean. He became ill while sailing along the coast of Panama and died in his cabin. He was buried in a lead coffin off Porto Bello on 18 January 1596.

Buckland Abbey remained in the Drake family until the 1940s when it was handed over to the National Trust. The abbey's most priceless treasure is a replica of Drake's Drum, which he took with him around the world and was returned to Buckland Abbey on his death. The actual drum is too fragile to be put on display and is kept in a climate-controlled facility. It is said that if the drum is sounded, Drake will rise again to save his beloved England from her foes.

WELL, I NEVER KNEW THIS ABOUT

DARTMOOR AND WEST DEVON

Castle Drogo overlooks FINGLE BRIDGE, a 17th-century packhorse bridge that crosses the River Teign at one of Dartmoor's most popular beauty spots. It is sometimes known as the Fisherman's Bridge, since '*fingle*' means 'catch' in Old English, suggesting that the river here is good for fishing.

EVELYN WAUGH wrote his most famous novel *Brideshead Revisited* during his stay at the EASTON COURT HOTEL IN CHAGFORD in 1944 while on unpaid leave from the Army having broken his leg while parachute training. The hotel was sold in 2014 and is now a private home.

The hard-to-find thatched village of LUSTLEIGH, lost down impossibly narrow lanes in a thickly wooded valley of north-east Dartmoor, is regularly voted Britain's prettiest village.

On Sharpitor, at the southeastern end of Lustleigh Cleave, one of Dartmoor's best viewpoints, sits the NUTCRACKER ROCK which once, if gently rocked, could crack open a nut placed under it. Alas, vandals dislodged the rock in 1950 and so this entertaining activity can no longer be enjoyed.

The 13th-century clapper bridge at POSTBRIDGE, a hamlet in the heart of Dartmoor, is possibly the most photographed feature on Dartmoor. The bridge was built for packhorses taking tin to the stannary town of Tavistock.

DARTMOOR BREWERY near Princetown stands at 1,430 feet (436 metres) above sea level and is ENGLAND'S HIGHEST BREWERY.

SHEEPS TOR, one of the largest in area of the 170 named tors on Dartmoor, overlooks the village to which it gives its name as well as BURRATOR RESERVOIR, the first reservoir to be built on Dartmoor to supply Plymouth.

A little way out of the village of Sheepstor is the MARCHANT'S

CROSS, at least 700 years old and at 8 feet (2.4 metres) in height, THE TALLEST ANCIENT CROSS ON DARTMOOR. Travellers would stop here to pray for a safe crossing of the perilous Dartmoor.

Ashburton was famous in the 18th century for ASHBURTON POP, a popular locally brewed sparkling beer. The recipe was unfortunately lost when the brewer died.

ASHBURTON'S CARNIVAL, first held in the mid-1880s to raise funds for a hospital, is believed to be THE OLDEST FAIR IN DEVON.

ASHBURTON was THE FIRST TOWN IN BRITAIN TO ELECT A MONSTER RAVING LOONY PARTY CANDIDATE TO PUBLIC OFFICE. Alan Hope, a local publican, was elected to Ashburton Town Council in 1989 and later became mayor of Ashburton.

BUCKFASTLEIGH stands at one end of the South Devon Railway, formerly the DART VALLEY RAILWAY, the longest established heritage steam railway in the West Country. The line follows the Dart for seven miles to Totnes along a branch line of the Great Western Railway built in 1872, using a variety of vintage steam trains and carriages.

Having 13 letters, BUCKFASTLEIGH IS THE SECOND LONGEST PLACE NAME IN ENGLAND with no repeated letters, exceeded only by Bricklehampton in Worcestershire with 14 letters.

SOUTH DEVON

Here I sit and here I rest
And this town shall be called Totnes

Brutus, Prince of Troy, legendary founder of Britain

Burgh Island

Burgh Island

BURGH ISLAND is separated from Bigbury-on-Sea on the mainland by South Devon's largest sandy beach, 250 yards of firm sand which is covered at high tide. When cut off by the sea, which rushes in from both sides of the beach, access to the island is by sea tractor, an ungainly looking machine with huge wheels and an elevated deck that keeps driver and passengers clear of the water. It is an exhilarating way to arrive at the island's elegant white Art Deco hotel, which was built in 1929 by filmmaker ARCHIBALD NETTLEFOLD – heir to the Guest, Keen and Nettlefold (GKN) company – and is considered one of the finest examples of Art Deco design in Britain. In the 1930s the captain's cabin of Britain's last wooden flagship, HMS *Ganges*, was reconstructed inside the hotel for use as a dining room.

During its heyday in the 1930s, the Burgh Island Hotel attracted many rich and famous guests including Lord Mountbatten, the last Viceroy of India; Edward VIII and Mrs Simpson; Winston Churchill; actress Gertrude Lawrence; aviator Amy Johnson; and R.J. Mitchell, designer of the Spitfire. Noel Coward visited intending to stay for three days and ended up staying for three weeks and later, in 1963, the Beatles stayed there while appearing in Plymouth.

Agatha Christie loved Burgh Island and wrote two books while in residence at the hotel. In *And Then There Were None*, THE

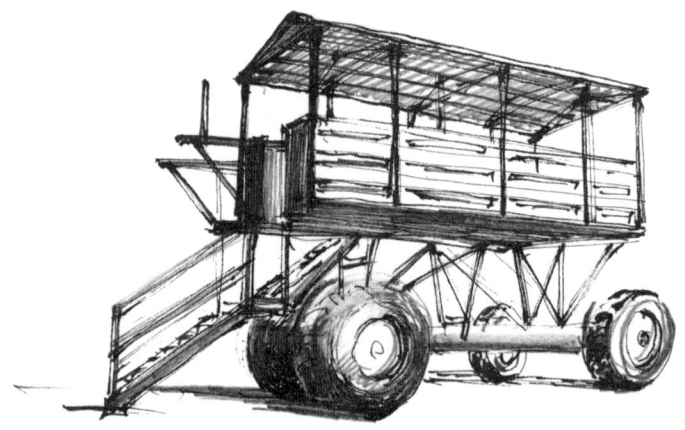

WORLD'S BEST-SELLING MYSTERY AND SIXTH BEST-SELLING NOVEL OF ALL TIME, Burgh Island appears as Soldier Island, home of the mysterious millionaire who lures a variety of guests on to the island and kills them off one by one. In *Evil Under the Sun* Hercule Poirot has to solve a murder case while holidaying at a secluded Devon hotel, based on the Burgh Island Hotel.

A small, ruined chapel at the island's summit was once used as a huer's hut where observers would make a 'hue and cry' to alert fishermen when they spotted a shoal of pilchards. Pilchard fishing is recalled by the presence on the island of the 14th-century PILCHARD INN, one of Britain's oldest pubs.

Slapton Sands

SLAPTON SANDS should perhaps be called Slapton Shingles, since it is a three-mile-long shingle bar that runs north–south between Torcross at the southern end and Strete Gate at the northern end. Enclosed inland by the bar is Slapton Ley, THE LARGEST FRESHWATER LAKE IN THE SOUTH WEST at one and a half miles long. The lake sits at the centre of a nature reserve and is home to a huge variety of wildfowl. It is also THE ONLY PLACE IN BRITAIN WHERE THE FLOWERING PLANT STRAPWORT GROWS.

On a fine day, when the sun shines and the sea is blue, Slapton Sands is a calm and beautiful place to be. However, a rusty Sherman tank retrieved from the sea in 1984 and now standing in the car park at Torcross stands as a monument to one of the most tragic events of the Second World War. On the night of 28 April 1944, eight landing craft full of American soldiers and equipment left Plymouth to rendezvous in Lyme Bay prior to storming Slapton Sands as part of Exercise Tiger, a rehearsal for storming Utah Beach in Normandy as part of the D-Day landings. German torpedo boats attacked the landing craft and sank two of them, pitching hundreds of men into the sea. The other landing craft scattered, leaving the men floating in the cold water and many of them drowned, weighed down by their heavy kit. The disaster was caused by a simple administrative error. Orders given to the landing craft contained a typing error which meant that the American craft and the British Naval HQ on shore were on different radio frequencies. The German boats were spotted on radar by a British destroyer but because of the radio mix-up the British were unable to warn the landing craft and up to 1,000 men died, with bodies being washed up on the shores of Lyme Bay for days afterwards. More men lost their lives that night than died during the actual storming of Utah Beach on D-Day.

River Dart

The RIVER DART is one of Devon's most beautiful rivers and a trip up the Dart from Dartmouth to its tidal limit at Totnes is a must – passing, as it does, through the most idyllic scenery, beginning at that most unspoiled of ancient towns, Dartmouth.

Dartmouth

Dartmouth's safe natural harbour has been there for a long time and has seen the comings and goings of Phoenicians, Romans, Saxons, Normans and Elizabethan explorers. In 1091 William II left from Dartmouth to wrest Normandy from his brother Robert. In 1147 Dartmouth served as the assembly point for the Crusaders from Flanders, France, Frisia and England who made up the Second Crusade, and in 1190 the vast fleet for Richard the Lionheart's Third Crusade assembled in what is now called Warfleet Creek in recognition of the many fleets of war that gathered there, including some 400 American ships before D-Day.

In the Middle Ages Dartmouth was one of England's greatest ports, exporting Devon wool and cloth and receiving wine from Bordeaux. Guarding the entrance to the Dart estuary and the harbour are two artillery forts, DARTMOUTH CASTLE on the west bank and KINGSWEAR CASTLE on the east bank. They were both built at the end of the 15th century, during the reign of Henry VII, and are THE FIRST

castles in Britain to be specifically designed for artillery. Dartmouth Castle shares its rocky bluff with the oldest of Dartmouth's three churches, St Petrox, whose 12th-century tower used to show a beacon to light the way into the harbour. Castle and church together make a dramatic spectacle. Kingswear Castle is now owned by the Landmark Trust and can be let for holidays.

Dartmouth's original wharf is now a picturesque, cobbled waterfront lane called Bayard's Cove. This is backed with pretty 17th- and 18th-century cottages and has the remains of a small Tudor fort at its southern end, much used for filming, most prominently for the popular 1970s television series *The Onedin Line*.

Stone stairways climb away from the harbour through the numerous black and white houses that overhang the tangle of narrow streets making up the town centre. The oldest building in Dartmouth is the Cherub Inn on Higher Street which dates from 1380. Down by the inner harbour, which is known as the Boat Float and more or less acts as the town square, is the early 17th-century Butterwalk, its crooked first-floor wooden facades held up from the pavement by granite columns. Charles II held court in one of the rooms looking down on the street.

The 14th century church of St Saviour, close by the waterfront, boasts a beautifully painted 15th-century wooden rood screen considered amongst the best in the country and a quite magnificent 14th-century wooden door covered in intricate ironwork showing the leaves and branches of a tree and various beasts. The ironwork, added later to strengthen the door, is dated 1631. Buried in the church is its founder John Hawley (c.1350–1408), a merchant and seaman who was elected Mayor of Dartmouth 14 times and is said to be the inspiration for the *'schipman ... from Dertemouthe'* in Chaucer's *Canterbury Tales*.

Dominating the town from the north is the impressive Britannia Royal Naval College, where Royal Navy officers have been trained at Dartmouth since 1863 when the hulk of HMS *Britannia*, a wooden ship of the line, was towed from Portsmouth and moored on the Dart to serve as a training base. The present campus building was designed by Sir Aston Webb and opened in 1905. Amongst those

who attended the college are George V, George VI, the Duke of Edinburgh, Charles III and Prince William. The Queen and Prince Philip had their first encounter at Dartmouth, after meeting previously as children, in 1939 when Prince Philip of Greece, as he was then, was a cadet there.

People of Dartmouth

In the visitor centre in the Royal Avenue Gardens beside the Boat Float, you can see 'The Engine That Changed The World', THE WORLD'S OLDEST WORKING STEAM ENGINE, built by a son of Dartmouth, THOMAS NEWCOMEN, in 1720. Newcomen was born in Dartmouth in 1663 and became an ironmonger and blacksmith. Many of his friends worked in the Devon tin mines which were constantly under threat from flooding so, along with his friend and neighbour THOMAS SAVERY, Newcomen devised a steam driven beam engine to pump the mines clear of water. Although crude and not very efficient, NEWCOMEN'S BEAM ENGINE, THE WORLD'S FIRST WORKING STEAM ENGINE, saved Britain's mining industry and made it possible to retrieve the raw materials that fuelled the Industrial Revolution.

PARSON JACK RUSSELL, born in Dartmouth in 1793, was a flamboyant churchman who loved the chase and developed a strain of terrier adapted for hunting, brave, intelligent and able to go down fox holes. Jack Russell terriers, all of them descended from Parson Russell's white fox terrier called TRUMP, are now popular all over the world, not just for hunting but as pets.

FLORA THOMPSON wrote her best-selling novel *Lark Rise to Candleford* while living in Dartmouth, her home for nearly 20 years from 1927. She is buried in Dartmouth's Longcross Cemetery.

CHRISTOPHER MILNE, son of A.A. Milne and known to the

Greenway

world as Christopher Robin from the *Winnie the Pooh* stories, owned and ran the Harbour Bookshop in Dartmouth for over 40 years.

Greenway

GREENWAY, a late Georgian house that was once the beloved holiday home of the most popular crime writer of all time, DAME AGATHA CHRISTIE, sits high up above the River Dart on the east bank, about a mile upriver from Dartmouth, close by the ferry to Dittisham. The original Greenway was a Tudor mansion built in the late 16th century by the seafaring Gilbert family. SIR HUMPHREY GILBERT, the man who took possession of Newfoundland for Elizabeth I in 1583, was born there in 1539 and grew up there, while his half-brother SIR WALTER RALEIGH also lived there for a while. Greenway is one of the places thought to be where a servant threw a bucket of water over Raleigh, thinking his master was on fire, when all Raleigh was doing was trying to have a quiet smoke – the servant had never seen tobacco before! The present gardens were laid out in the 18th century, possibly by HUMPHRY REPTON, but they were originally created with the help of prisoners of war from a battleship of the Spanish Armada that had been captured by Sir Francis Drake and was moored off Dartmouth. The crew were put to work by the Gilberts on levelling the ground at Greenway.

Agatha Christie, who was born in Torquay in 1890, bought Greenway in 1938 and the house featured in many of her novels under a variety of guises, including Nasse House in *Dead Man's Folly*, published in 1956. Apparently, it was while sitting in Greenway's boathouse down by the River Dart that Agatha got the idea for that story and she does indeed have a murder victim found in the boathouse.

Greenway was later home to Agatha Christie's daughter Rosalind and is now run by the National Trust with the house and gardens open most days.

Totnes

According to legend, TOTNES is where Britain began. Brutus, grandson of Aeneas, Prince of Troy, travelled across Europe to find a new home after the sack of Troy, inspired by a prophecy of the goddess Diana (see page 100).

Totnes Castle

He sailed up the Dart and landed at the highest navigable point on the river, naming the spot Totnes and calling this new land Britain (Bruton) after himself. Should you doubt this tale, on the right-hand side a little way up Fore Street, leading uphill from the river, you can find the BRUTUS STONE, the very stone upon which Brutus first set foot in Britain. And, since all subsequent British monarchs are said to descend from Brutus, by tradition the Mayor of Totnes stands on the Brutus Stone to proclaim a new monarch.

DIANA'S PROPHECY

Brute, past the realms of Gaul, beneath the sunset,
Lieth an island, girt about by ocean,
Guarded by ocean, erst the haunt of giants,
Desert of late, and meet for this thy people,
Seek it! For there is thine abode for ever,
There by thy sons again shall troy be builded;
There of they blood shall kings be born, hereafter
Sovereign in every land the wide world over.

From Geoffrey of Monmouth's *History of the Kings of Britain*

Whether Trojan or not, Totnes was certainly a fortified Saxon settlement, recorded as such in 907, and with its own mint. After the Conquest, Totnes was given to a Breton supporter of the Conqueror, JUHEL OF TOTNES, who built a castle and priory to guard the strategic river crossing point.

Today, ancient and legendary, Totnes is one of Britain's most beautiful towns and boasts MORE LISTED BUILDINGS PER HEAD THAT ANY OTHER TOWN IN BRITAIN. Not much more than a single narrow street leading uphill from the river to the castle, but what a street it is, lined with 16th- and 17th-century merchant's houses and colourful Georgian facades.

It all begins on The Plains, once tidal marshland, by the fine three-arch bridge across the Dart, built in 1828 by Devon-born CHARLES FOWLER, architect of London's Covent Garden Market. Here is a granite obelisk to surveyor and explorer WILLIAM WILLS, born in Totnes in 1834. As second in command of the Burke and Wills expedition in 1860 he became THE FIRST EUROPEAN TO CROSS AUSTRALIA FROM SOUTH TO NORTH but died on the return journey.

Opposite the bridge, the 16th-century TOWN HILL houses a Victorian mill wheel and information centre and the Totnes Image Bank. At the entrance to Fore Street stands the 17th-century coaching inn the ROYAL SEVEN STARS where author DANIEL DEFOE stayed in 1720, describing it as *'the great inn next to the bridge'* while Totnes was *'a very good town'*.

Further up on the right is handsome red brick THE MANSION, the grandest Georgian house in Totnes, built in 1797 by merchant GILES WELSFORD. Home to the King Edward VI Grammar School between 1887 and the 1960s, the Mansion is now run as a community centre.

> Perhaps the most distinguished pupil of the King Edward VI Grammar School was the mathematician CHARLES BABBAGE, originator of the programmable computer, who was born, possibly in Totnes, in 1791. Although there is a degree of uncertainty over his birthplace (it might have also been Teignmouth or London) his family had Devon roots: his grandfather Benjamin Babbage was Mayor of Totnes in 1754 and there is a room dedicated to him in Totnes Museum.
>
> Babbage was a prolific inventor, best known perhaps for his Difference Engine, the forerunner to the digital computer, for which Ada Lovelace, daughter of Lord Byron, developed a number of programmes. Babbage also set up the postal system for the uniform rate Penny Post, championed the broad gauge for railways as used by Brunel's Great Western Railway and invented the cowcatcher attached to the front of trains to clear obstacles from the track (as seen on American and Canadian trains). Although neither Babbage's Analytical Engine nor his Difference Engines were ever actually built in his lifetime, an engine constructed from his design for the Difference Engine No. 2 by the Science Museum in 1991 proved that his computer would have worked.

Just below the Eastgate arch is one of the best examples of a half-timbered Elizabethan merchant's house, not just in Totnes but in the whole country. Built in around 1575 for merchant Waltert Kellond, it is now the home of the Totnes Museum.

The EAST GATE, remodelled in Gothic style in 1837, marks the entrance to the original Saxon town and is where Fore Street becomes the High Street. From here steps climb up to what is left of the old town walls which lead round behind the church to the GUILDHALL, built in 1553 on the ruins of the old priory of 1088. Over time the Guildhall has served as a magistrate's court, school and prison. In 1646, during the Civil War, Oliver Cromwell held a meeting in the Guildhall with his army

commander General Fairfax and the very table at which they sat is still used in the Council Chamber today.

The huge red sandstone CHURCH OF ST MARY next door to the Guildhall dates from the mid-15th century and is one of the finest churches in a county of fine churches. It is renowned for its stone rood screen which runs right across the church and is regarded as THE FINEST STONE SCREEN IN ENGLAND. The tower, 120 feet high, is a landmark for miles around.

Across the High Street from the church is the house of pilchard merchant and mayor NICOLAS BALL. Dated 1585, the house is unusual in its modern design and in that it is made of stone rather than timber framing. Ball's widow married the diplomat and scholar Thomas Bodley and used her first husband's fortune to help found the great Bodleian Library in Oxford.

Totnes Guildhall

Further up the High Street, a row of Tudor merchants' houses rest on pillars above the pavement along the BUTTERWALK, a covered arcade built to protect stalls selling dairy products from the weather.

The motte and bailey castle at the top of the High Street was built around 1087 and the ruins sit atop THE LARGEST PRESERVED NORMAN MOTTE IN ENGLAND. The unusual round keep was rebuilt in the 1320s and remains one of the best of its kind in England. There are stupendous views from the battlements of the keep over Totnes and the surrounding countryside.

Dartington

A village of international renown, DARTINGTON, two miles north-west of Totnes, is an extraordinary place, an intriguing mix of medieval and modern, with its various elements – church, school, inn, cottages and hall – scattered over a wide area, but all deferring to the Great Hall on the hill.

The estate was first mentioned in 833 when the 'Homestead of the Meadow by the River Dart' came into the hands of the Saxon Lady Beornwynn of Shaftesbury. After the Conquest, the Norman Fitz Martin family took over and enclosed a 100-acre deer park within a nine-foot-high wall in around 1325, much of which is still standing.

St Mary's Old Church

At the same time, the family built a church, next to the manor house, beside a yew tree that was already over 800 years old. The yew tree flourishes to this day but only the tower of St Mary's church survives, the main body having been pulled down in 1878. Many of the people of Dartington regard this yew tree and this old church of St Mary as the spiritual heart of Dartington and there is a small chapel in the base of the tower used for private prayer.

The Cott Inn

Dartington lay on an important trade route and around this time a wealthy merchant called Johannes Cott set up an inn beside an old packhorse bridge across the Bidwell Brook, on the edge of the park at what is now Shinners Bridge. The beautiful thatched COTT INN, licensed since 1320, is still serving, one of the oldest inns in the country, and boasts THE LONGEST THATCHED ROOF IN ENGLAND.

Dartington Hall

In 1384 Richard II gave the estate to his half-brother JOHN HOLAND, 1ST DUKE OF EXETER, who built the magnificent GREAT HALL, THE FINEST EXAMPLE OF A DOMESTIC MEDIEVAL HALL SURVIVING IN ENGLAND. The Hall boasted an early example of a hammer-beam roof, pre-dating that of Westminster Hall, while the central boss of the vault in the three-storey porch shows the White Hart badge of Richard II, which dates the building to no later than 1399 when Richard was deposed. Holand also built a range of domestic buildings radiating out from the hall and grouped around a massive double courtyard, which for 200 years was THE LARGEST

COURTYARD EVER BUILT FOR A PRIVATE RESIDENCE IN ENGLAND. Except for the south range, the courtyard and buildings survive almost unchanged to this day.

The Champernownes
In 1559 Dartington was bought by SIR ARTHUR CHAMPERNOWNE, Vice-Admiral of the West under Elizabeth I, who transformed the Hall into an Elizabethan mansion. His family would own the estate for the next 366 years and Sir Arthur and many of his descendants are buried beneath splendid monuments in the tower of Old St Mary's next to the Hall. The Champernownes gradually ran out of money and by the start of the 20th century, the Hall and outbuildings had fallen into disrepair.

The Elmhirsts
In 1925 the Dartington estate was purchased by LEONARD AND DOROTHY ELMHIRST with the aim of creating a model self-supporting estate, a centre for music and arts and crafts, and a laboratory for a new approach to sustainable farming and forestry. Dorothy was an American heiress, a member of the Whitney dynasty of inventors and industrialists. Using her fortune, the Elmhirsts restored the medieval Great Hall, rebuilt the hammer-beam roof using local timbers, and renovated the medieval outbuildings. A number of commercial enterprises were established including a builders, a cider press, textile mill and sawmill and in 1931 a new co-educational school was opened, Dartington Hall School (see page 107).

> ## DARTINGTON HALL SCHOOL
>
> Run on what we would now call 'progressive' principles, Dartington Hall School educated the children of 'free thinkers' such as BERTRAND RUSSELL, and pupils who would go on to become prominent in the arts or politics, including:
>
> LORD YOUNG OF DARTINGTON (1915–2002) Social activist who drafted the Labour manifesto for the 1945 general election (which included the setting up of the NHS) and founded *Which?* magazine and the Open University. Father of Free Speech Union founder Toby Young (Lord Young of Acton).
>
> SUSAN WILLIAMS-ELLIS (1918–2007) Pottery designer and founder of PORTMEIRION POTTERY. Daughter of Clough Williams-Ellis, founder of Portmeirion.
>
> Brothers LUCIEN FREUD (1922–2011), the artist, and CLEMENT FREUD (1924–2009), a writer, broadcaster, chef and politician, grandsons of psychoanalyst Sigmund Freud.
>
> KIRSTY LANG (b.1962) Journalist and broadcaster.
>
> CHARLOTTE COLEMAN (1968–2001) Actress best known for her role as Scarlett in *Four Weddings and a Funeral*.
>
> The school closed in 1987 due to financial difficulties along with rumours of sex and drugs and a scandal involving the headmaster and his wife appearing in a pornographic magazine.

Modern Dartington

A series of houses in different modernistic styles were constructed for the estate workers and students, including HIGH CROSS HOUSE, designed in 1931 by the Swiss architect William Lescaze for William Curry, the headmaster of Dartington Hall School, now seen as THE FIRST AND BEST INTERNATIONAL MODERNIST HOUSE IN ENGLAND.

High Cross House

Dartington Arts

In 1935 the Elmhirsts set up the Dartington Trust to run the estate and over the next decades they invited international artists and craftsmen to set up various enterprises at Dartington. BERNARD LEACH, one of the most respected potters of the 20th century, known for his fusion of Eastern and Western traditions, established DARTINGTON POTTERY, still sold at Dartington although now based at Grayshott in Hampshire.

In 1953 the DARTINGTON INTERNATIONAL SUMMER SCHOOL was established, giving amateur musicians the opportunity to learn from and perform in the Great Hall with internationally renowned artists such as Arthur Rubinstein, Igor Stravinsky and Benjamin Britten.

In 1961 DARTINGTON COLLEGE OF ARTS opened, combining a number of the courses already operating at Dartington and offering specialist degree courses in theatre, music, arts and crafts. It gained an international reputation as a centre for artists from all over the world. One of its more celebrated students was Plymouth-born GEORGE PASSMORE of Gilbert and George. The college closed in 2010 and was re-established at Falmouth University.

In 1967 DARTINGTON GLASS (now Dartington Crystal) was established in Torrington, North Devon, and has become THE LEADING MANUFACTURER OF GLASSWARE IN BRITAIN.

In 1990 the SCHUMACHER COLLEGE was founded at Dartington, offering courses centred around ecology and sustainability and attracting teachers such as James Lovelock, famous for his Gaia hypothesis, as well as students from around the world. The college closed suddenly in 2024 due to lack of money.

Today Dartington Hall continues to be very much a public space, offering live music, theatre and cinema, B&B accommodation in the medieval ranges, a pub, a hostel and wedding and conference facilities.

Dartington Hall Gardens

Laid out informally in the 1930s by acclaimed American landscape designer BEATRIX FARRAND, who designed the White House gardens for President Woodrow Wilson, the Dartington Hall gardens cover 29 acres of trees, shrubs and flowers and include unexpected vistas, modern sculptures, such as Henry Moore's *Memorial Figure*, and a former tilting yard with grass tiers of natural seating around three sides where open-air performances are held.

Born in Dartington

ROBERT FROUDE (1771 1859) Rector of Dartington for over 60 years and Archdeacon of Totnes for 40 of those years. Robert and his wife Margaret had eight children, of whom only three sons survived to adulthood, each of them going on to find renown in different fields.

RICHARD FROUDE (1803–36) Eldest of three surviving sons of Robert Froude. Richard Froude was one of the leaders of the Oxford Movement, founded by a group of high-church Anglicans from Oxford University who wanted to reintroduce the ancient traditions of Christianity to the Anglican faith, leading to the development of Anglo-Catholicism. He died of tuberculosis at the young age of 33.

WILLIAM FROUDE (1810–79) Initially a railway engineer who worked with Isambard Kingdom Brunel on the design of the Great Eastern Railway, William Froude became a naval architect and the first man to formulate laws to predict how the hull shape of a ship affects how efficiently the ship moves through the water, a formula known as THE FROUDE NUMBER. He designed and built THE WORLD'S FIRST SHIP TESTING TANK in Torquay to study different hull designs and in 1877 INVENTED THE HYDRAULIC DYNAMOMETER used to measure the power of large naval engines. In 1881 his son Richard joined forces with civil engineer Hammersley Heenan to found Heenan & Froude, which continues to design and manufacture engine testing equipment to this day under the name Froude Ltd. The WILLIAM FROUDE MEDAL, named in his honour, is the Royal Institution of

Naval Architect's highest honour and is awarded annually to an individual who has made a significant contribution to naval architecture and shipbuilding.

JAMES FROUDE (1818–94)
The youngest of eight children, James Froude was only three years old when his mother and five siblings died of consumption and, after dallying with a career in the Church, he became disillusioned with religion and turned to writing about history. He eventually became the most widely read historian of his day, known in particular for his *History of England from the Fall of Wolsey to the Defeat of the Spanish Armada* and his biography of Thomas Carlyle.

Torbay

TORBAY consists of three resort towns – Brixham, Paighton and Torquay – as well as the village of Goodrington, all lining the coast of the east-facing Tor Bay. Thanks to mild weather, sandy beaches and picturesque coastline, the area has long been fashioned the English Riviera.

Brixham

BRIXHAM is the oldest of the three towns lining Tor Bay and in the Middle Ages it was one of Britain's most important fishing ports. In the 18th century the fishermen of Brixham developed the trawl net and THE BRIXHAM FLEET BECAME THE FIRST TRAWLING FLEET IN THE WORLD.

Today, colourful old cottages tumble down towards the harbour where there is a life-size replica of the *Golden Hind*, the ship in which Sir Francis Drake became the first Englishman to sail around the world from 1577 to 1580. In 1588 Drake sailed into Brixham with the *Capitana*, the first prize he had captured from the Spanish Armada.

One hundred years later in 1688, WILLIAM OF ORANGE landed on Brixham Quay to begin his march to London to take over the throne of England at the start of the Glorious Revolution. As he set foot on English soil he claimed, *'The liberty of England and the Protestant religion I will maintain'*. There is a statue of him looking rather cross, or perhaps seasick, on the waterfront where he stepped ashore.

A little way from the harbour is the 19th-century church of All Saints where HENRY FRANCIS LYTE (1793–1847) was minister for 25 years. He lived at Berry Head House, now a hotel, high above the town, and one night in 1847, the last year of his life, when he was dying of tuberculosis, he sat alone and weary in his garden. As he watched the darkness of the evening creeping up towards him from the bay, the words of what would become one of the most beloved hymns of all time, 'Abide with Me', came to him and brought him comfort, just as they have to millions of people all over the world ever since. Soldiers sang 'Abide with Me' in the trenches in World War One, Nurse Edith Cavell sang it as she faced execution as a spy by the Germans, Gandhi is said to have sung it while incarcerated and it was played by the band of the *Titanic* as the ship sank beneath the waves.

> *Hold thou Thy Cross, before my closing eyes*
> *Shine through the gloom and point me to the skies*
> *Heaven's morning breaks and Earth's vain shadows flee*
> *Help of the helpless, O Abide with Me*

Paignton

PAIGNTON began life as a small fishing village gathered around a wooden Saxon church. This was replaced in 1100 and the subsequent Norman church was itself rebuilt in 1250. The church is noted for the 15th-century KIRKHAM CHANTRY, a richly carved stone screen consisting of a doorway flanked by two canopied tombs. Nearby is the 14th-century KIRKHAM HOUSE, probably built as a residence for a priest in charge of the Kirkham Chantry.

The Reredos behind the High Altar in Paignton's St Michael's Church commemorates Paignton-born SAMUEL CHAPIN who was baptised and married in the church before emigrating to America in the 1630s and helping to found Springfield, Massachusetts. Amongst his many notable descendants are presidents Grover Cleveland and William Howard Taft, publisher of the first American dictionary Noah Webster, founder of Kelloggs W.K. Kellogg, banker J.P. Morgan, financier Warren Buffet, astronaut Alan Shepherd, aviator Amelia Earhart, author of *Uncle Tom's Cabin* Harriet Beecher Stowe, poet T.S. Eliot, Playboy founder Hugh Hefner, singers Harry Chapin and Mary Chapin Carpenter, moviemaker Walt Disney, actors Humphrey Bogart, John Wayne, Anthony Perkins, Jodie Foster, Clint Eastwood, Spencer Tracy, Burt Reynolds, Anthony Perkins, Richard Chamberlain and former British prime minister Boris Johnson. They owe it all to Paignton.

Next to the church are the scant remains of a medieval palace, built as a holiday retreat for the Bishops of Exeter. Some high walls survive along with a corner tower known as the Miles Coverdale Tower, allegedly because Coverdale, who was briefly Bishop of Exeter from 1551–53, wrote his translation of the Bible there. Alas, the dates don't match: Coverdale produced his translation, the first printed translation of the full Bible into English, in 1535, although it is entirely possible that he did stay at Paignton during his brief tenure as Bishop.

Paignton remained a small village until the railway arrived in 1859, bringing holidaymakers with it, and today Paignton is a jolly seaside town with plenty of Victorian villas, novelty rock shops, three beaches of rich red sand, a bracing promenade and a Victorian pier of 1879.

The town's most exuberant and unlikely attraction is OLDWAY MANSION, built in 1871 on the site of an older house by ISAAC SINGER, inventor of the Singer Sewing Machine, who arrived in Paignton having been forced to leave first New York and then Paris, because of a series of scandals. The Statue of Liberty in New York is thought to be modelled on one of Singer's wives, a half-English, half-French actress called Isabella, who in her time was considered the most beautiful woman in Europe. Singer lavished much of his fortune on Oldway but he and Isabella were only able to enjoy their Devon home for a brief time before he died in 1875, leaving the place to his third son Paris.

Between 1905 and 1907 Paris had the house rebuilt in the style of the Palace of Versailles and filled it with beautiful things, including a grand marble staircase, Jacques-Louis David's painting of the Crowning of Josephine by Napoleon, a gallery based on the Hall of Mirrors at Versailles and, best of all, his mistress, the dancer Isadora Duncan. Sadly, the Singers seem to have been one of those families who attract bad luck: Paris and Isadora's child drowned in the Seine and then Isadora herself died while driving her Bugatti along the French Riviera when her trademark long, flowing scarf became entangled in one of the back wheels and she was throttled. The 1968 biopic *Isadora*, starring Vanessa Redgrave as Isadora Duncan, was partially filmed at Oldway.

Used for a while as council offices, Oldway Mansion has been closed since 2013, deemed too

expensive to keep up, but is today being restored. The gardens and grounds are open to the public.

Torquay

The loveliest sea village in England.

Alfred, Lord Tennyson

Originally the quay for Torre Abbey, TORQUAY really got into its stride in the early 19th century when ships of the Royal Navy were anchored in Tor Bay in readiness for action against Napoleon, and the officers would come ashore for supplies and to spend time with their families who were put up in the local hostelries. The town gained a reputation as a good place to stay for wealthy people unable to travel to the Continent because of the war and then expanded rapidly in the Victorian era with the arrival of the railway. Elegant white-painted Victorian terraces and hotels climb the hillside, giving the town a distinctly Mediterranean air.

Torre Abbey
TORRE ABBEY, west of the town, is the best-preserved medieval monastery in the south west and was founded in 1196 as a Premonstratensian monastery. By the time of the Dissolution of the Monasteries it had become the wealthiest such monastery in England. The church and many of the main buildings were demolished but a splendid 14th-century gatehouse remains, and the south and west ranges were converted into a house which was later remodelled in Georgian

Torre Abbey

style. The house was the home of the Cary family from 1662 until 1930 when it was sold to the council and is now used as an art gallery and museum. Nearby stands a 700-year-old tithe barn, known as the Spanish Barn ever since it was used to hold 400 prisoners of war from the Spanish Armada.

Today Torre Abbey is home to the International Agatha Christie Festival, held on 15 September each year to mark the birthday of the celebrated author, who was born in nearby Torquay in 1890. In the medieval gardens you can explore the Agatha Christie Potent Plants Garden, inspired by Agatha's novels and featuring some of the plants that provide the sources of such poisons as cyanide, morphine and ricin, used by Agatha Christie to kill off more than half of her characters' victims.

Kent's Cavern
KENTS CAVERN is a cave system that runs under the cliffs to the east of Torquay. A fragment of jawbone was discovered in the cavern in 1927 which was later dated to over 40,000 years old, making it THE EARLIEST HUMAN FOSSIL EVER FOUND IN NORTH-WEST EUROPE, although these findings are controversial. A Scheduled Ancient Monument since 1957, the cavern, which was once used as a workshop for making beach huts, is now open to the public as a tourist attraction and was the model for Hampsley Cavern in Agatha Christie's novel *The Man in the Brown Suit*.

Born in Torquay
SIR RICHARD BURTON (1821–90) Explorer best known for his exploits in Africa where he was the first European to discover Lake Tanganyika, the second largest and second deepest freshwater lake in the world. He was also an officer of the East India Company and is responsible for introducing the word 'pyjama'

into the English language, which is of Persian and Urdu origin meaning 'a loose garment'.

DAME AGATHA CHRISTIE (1890–1976)
The 'Queen of Crime' was born Agatha Miller, to a wealthy family who lived in a late Victorian villa called Ashfield (alas since demolished) in Barton Road, Torquay. Agatha began writing as a girl while she was confined inside with a cold, at the suggestion of her mother. In 1914 she married a Royal Flying Corps officer, Archibald Christie, and they honeymooned in Torquay's Grand Hotel. During World War One she worked in Torquay hospital where she picked up a useful knowledge of poisons. Her first literary success came in 1920, with the publication of *The Mysterious Affair at Styles*, which introduced the Belgian detective Hercule Poirot. Miss Marple appeared in 1930 in *The Murder at the Vicarage*.

Towards the end of 1926, Agatha discovered that her husband had been having an affair with a young woman called Nancy Neele and in a mystery worthy of one her own novels Agatha disappeared from the Silent Pool car park in Surrey, where her car was discovered with the lights still on. Archibald was suspected of murdering her and the newspapers offered a reward to anyone who could find her. She eventually surfaced ten days later at the Old Swan Hotel in Harrogate where she had booked in as Teresa Neele. Agatha divorced Archibald two years later and in 1930 married archaeologist MAX MALLOWAN, commenting at the time that *'an archaeologist is the best husband a woman can have. The older she gets the more interested he is in her'*. She was made a Dame in 1971.

Agatha Christie is THE MOST SUCCESSFUL NOVELIST, BEST-SELLING FICTION WRITER AND MOST-TRANSLATED INDIVIDUAL AUTHOR OF ALL TIME, and has been outsold only by Shakespeare and the Bible. Her novel *And Then There Were None* has been voted the World's Favourite Christie and has sold over 100 million copies. Her stage play THE MOUSETRAP HAS BECOME THE LONGEST-RUNNING PLAY IN THE WORLD, having premiered at the Theatre Royal in Nottingham in October 1952, and subsequently opening in London in November of that same year.

Agatha Christie used many Devon locations in her novels and some of these, such as Burgh

Island, Elberry Cove and Kents Cavern can be found elsewhere in this book.

In Torquay itself there is now a walk around the town called the AGATHA CHRISTIE MILE which takes in such delights as the Imperial Hotel, which appears in three books, *Peril at End House, The Body in the Library* and *Sleeping Murder* and was visited by both Poirot and Miss Marple – as well as Queen Victoria and Prince Albert, Edward VII and his mistress Lily Langtry and the Beatles. Then there is TORQUAY MUSEUM, which houses THE ONLY DEDICATED AGATHA CHRISTIE GALLERY IN THE WORLD, and the Grand Hotel where Agatha honeymooned with her first husband.

PETER COOK (1937–95)
Actor, playwright and comedian Peter Cook initiated the 1960s satire boom with his comedy stage revue *Beyond the Fringe* which also starred Dudley Moore, with whom Cook established a successful long-running comedy partnership. Together they created an award-winning TV series *Not Only ... But Also* and starred in two films, *The Wrong Box* (1966) and *Bedazzled* (1967). Often called the 'father of modern satire', Peter Cook was voted the greatest comedian of all time in 2005 by over 300 comedians, comedy writers, producers and directors both in the UK and America.

Compton Castle

Set in a deep valley a few miles west of Torquay, COMPTON CASTLE is named after the de Compton family who owned the estate in the 13th century. The Comptons built themselves a manor house centred on a great hall which became the property of the Gilberts when SIR GEOFFREY GILBERT, from another powerful Devon family and MP for Totnes, married heiress Joan de Compton in 1329.

Their descendant John Gilbert fortified the manor house into the small castle we see today, with two portcullises and a massive gateway from which stones and boiling oil could be dropped on attackers. The effect is spectacular but the fortifications were probably more for show than strength, and as the castle has since remained almost unaltered, Compton Castle is without doubt one of the best examples of a Tudor fortified house surviving in England.

Eventually Compton came into the hands of the explorer

Humphrey Gilbert (see below) who, along with others of his family, embarked upon a series of expensive ventures to colonise the New World. This left little time or money for the upkeep of Compton, which was therefore neglected and eventually became derelict. It was sold in 1785, leading to further decline, and then bought back by a Gilbert descendant in 1931, who began to restore the castle, in particular the grand banqueting hall which had lost its roof. The unaltered Great Kitchen inside provides an authentic glimpse of domestic life in medieval England.

Compton Castle is another one of those places where Sir Walter Raleigh is said to have smoked the first pipe of tobacco in England, a claim also made by Greenway and Raleigh's home in Dorset, Sherborne Castle.

SIR HUMPHREY GILBERT
(1539–83)

Humphrey Gilbert was born in the Gilbert family's Tudor manor house of Greenway on the River Dart in 1539. After his father Otho died, Gilbert's mother Catherine Champernowne went on to marry Walter Raleigh of East Budleigh and gave birth to five sons, the youngest of whom grew up to be Sir Walter Raleigh of Elizabethan fame. Thus Sir Humphrey Gilbert and Sir Walter Raleigh were half-brothers and cousins to Sir Richard Grenville, all of them members of a group of buccaneering sailors and explorers who became known as the West Country Men. This group also included Sir John Hawkins and Sir Francis Drake.

Sir Humphrey had long wanted to claim land in the New World for England and in 1583 he sailed from Dartmouth under a charter from Queen Elizabeth to establish a colony on the American continent. His fleet of five ships arrived at the port of St John's on 5 August 1583 and, after some resistance from the port admiral, took possession of this New Found Land (Newfoundland) in the name of His Sovereign Queen Elizabeth and thereby, as it says on a plaque placed close to where he landed in St John's, '*founded Britain's Overseas Empire*'.

> A few days later Gilbert took his fleet to explore the coastline further and after a series of misfortunes, his heavily overloaded ship the *Squirrel* sank in a storm, taking Gilbert and the entire crew with it. As the ship went down Gilbert was heard to cry out *'heaven is as near by water as by land!'* In the hall at Compton Castle there is a model of Gilbert's ship, which is named for the squirrel on the Gilbert family crest.

Teignmouth

Teignmouth is a Saxon fishing village that grew into a small port and holiday town in the early 19th century, and there are many Regency buildings along the waterfront and in the streets behind. The quay was built in 1830 to handle Dartmoor granite, which was shipped from there to build the old London Bridge that now spans the Colorado River at Lake Havasu in Arizona.

A plaque on 20 NORTHUMBERLAND PLACE, in a narrow street of Regency houses just in from the river, informs us that the poet JOHN KEATS lived there in 1818. He was there with his two younger brothers George and Tom, who was dying of tuberculosis, and it was thought the Devon air might help. It is believed that Keats finished *Endymion* while living in Teignmouth – perhaps the surrounding idyllic Devon countryside inspired the first line, '*A thing of beauty is a joy forever.*'

Teignmouth to Exeter Railway

The rail journey from Teignmouth to Exeter is one of the most scenic in Britain, running right alongside the sea. The line was built by ISAMBARD KINGDOM BRUNEL between 1846 and 1859 and involves five tunnels and a series of cuttings. Two of the tunnels run beneath a pair of sea stacks called the Parson and Clerk, which are said to be the Bishop of Exeter and a local priest set in stone by the Devil. The line is often battered by storms and in 2014 was closed for two months when part of the line at Dawlish was washed away.

Brunel had originally intended for the trains on this stretch of line to be propelled by atmospheric power. A pipe was laid along the centre of the track and the air pumped out to create a partial vacuum in front of the train, which was then drawn along by the atmospheric pressure behind the train's piston. However, it transpired that the leather valves running along the top of the pipe were constantly getting soaked with sea spray and quickly degraded, allowing air to leak in and compromise the vacuum. The project swiftly foundered, and the line was eventually converted to running conventional steam trains. This turned out to be Brunel's only major engineering failure.

Between the railway and the bow-fronted cottages of the main street in the village of STARCROSS on the Exe estuary stands a tall tower made from red Devon sandstone. This is the best preserved of the engine houses that stood outside every station along the route and contained the boilers that powered the pumps to create the vacuum that moved the trains.

Powderham Castle

POWDERHAM CASTLE is a fortified manor house that sits on a terrace on the west bank of the River Exe, south of Exeter. The house was begun at the end of the 14th century by a younger son of Hugh Courtenay, Earl of Devon, and was added to in the 19th century to make it appear more castle-like. The Courtenays came over from north-central France in the 12th century and settled first at Okehampton and then Tiverton. They took over as Earls of Devon from the de Redvers family, the first of the Norman earls, but subsequently lost and regained the title many times depending upon who was on the throne – hence the many Courtenays titled 1st Earl of Devon.

When William Courtenay, one of these numerous 1st Earls of Devon, married a daughter of Edward IV, the Courtenays came a little too close to the throne for the Tudors' liking and lost their titles and lands, rendering the earldom dormant. Since there was no Earl of Devon, James I sold the title to William Cavendish, a nobleman and courtier who lived at Chatsworth in Derbyshire. He had no connection to Devon at all and chose to style himself the Earl of Devonshire. The Cavendishes became Dukes of Devonshire in 1694 and have held the title ever since.

The Courtenays of Powderham, meanwhile, stayed out of it all, living quietly as country gentlemen. In 1831 it was decided that they had been the rightful heirs to the dormant earldom all along and William Courtenay of Powderham became the 9th Earl of Devon. He died childless but was succeeded by his cousin William the 10th Earl, from whom the present Earl is descended. Powderham has been the seat of the Earls of Devon ever since.

WELL, I NEVER KNEW THIS ABOUT

SOUTH DEVON

Lying in the 14th-century church at Slapton are SIR RICHARD HAWKINS and his wife LADY JUDITH, Lord and Lady of the Manor of Poole, whose house lay a quarter of mile up the road. When Richard's wife Lady Judith walked to church from Poole House, two pages would go before her unrolling a red carpet onto the ground to save her shoes from the mud. Sir Richard was the son of the Elizabethan explorer and privateer Sir John Hawkins, THE FIRST ENGLISH NAVAL CAPTAIN TO BECOME INVOLVED IN THE SLAVE TRADE. Richard Hawkins, in sharp contradistinction, was THE FIRST NAVAL CAPTAIN TO GIVE HIS MEN LEMON OR LIME JUICE TO PREVENT SCURVY.

In 2006 Totnes, already known for its large New Age community and bohemian lifestyle, became THE WORLD'S FIRST TRANSITION TOWN, with the aim of protecting itself against climate change, reliance on fossil fuels and economic instability by setting up community projects around food production and energy use. Totnes has since become the inspiration for a network of similar Transition Towns all over the world.

Two miles east of Totnes, just outside the village of LONGCOMBE, stands PARLIAMENT COTTAGE, a gorgeous 17th-century cottage with a thatched roof that could rival the Cott Inn at Dartington for length. In the front garden there stands a stone inscribed with the words '*William Prince of Orange is said to have held his first Parliament here in November*

1688', hence the name of the dwelling.

Hiding to the south of Paignton's three popular red sand beaches, below the village of Churston, is little known ELBERRY COVE, a small, concealed beach of white sand and shingle that can only be reached on foot, via a 15-minute walk from Broadsands beach. At one end are the ruins of Lord Churston's bathhouse from the ground floor of which his Lordship and guests could swim out to sea at high tide, before coming back to warm up in a heated seawater pool.

Elberry Cove features in Agatha Christie's novel *The ABC Murders* as the setting for the murder of Sir Carmichael Clarke. Sheltered from the public gaze by woods and blessed with crystal clear waters, Elberry Cove is one of Devon's best-kept secrets.

The lighthouse on Berry Head, the headland at the southern end of Tor Bay above Brixham, is THE SHORTEST LIGHTHOUSE IN BRITAIN, being just 16 feet (5 metres) tall. It is also, thanks to the height of the cliffs on which it stands, THE HIGHEST LIGHTHOUSE IN BRITAIN, being 200 feet (60 metres) above sea level.

PLYMOUTH

Turris Fortissima est Nomen Jehova
'The strongest tower is the name of Jehovah'

Plymouth's motto, referring to the city's successful resistance
to the Royalist siege during the Civil War

The Mayflower Steps

For hundreds of years, Devon men and women have sailed from Plymouth to explore all four corners of the globe and have conferred the name of Plymouth on more than 50 places, mostly in North America and the Caribbean. Perhaps the most significant of these is Plymouth, Massachusetts, 'America's Hometown', founded in 1620 by the Mayflower pilgrims who named their new settlement after the port from where they had left England for the last time. The rock on which they are said to have made their first landfall in the New World is known as Plymouth Rock.

The original Plymouth sits on its own rock 150 feet (46 metres) above the sea, enfolded in the arms of two rivers running down from Dartmoor, the Tamar in the west and the Plym to the east. The city is protected from the sea and the enemy by the vast Plymouth Sound which forms a safe, easily defended harbour.

By the end of the 13th century the River Plym had begun to silt up, leaving the former seaport of Plympton upriver high and dry. Trade moved down to the mouth of the river at Sutton, mentioned in the Domesday Book as Sudtone, the 'town south of Plympton', around which Plymouth developed.

In 1439 Old Plymouth became THE FIRST TOWN IN ENGLAND TO BE INCORPORATED BY PARLIAMENT rather than by the monarch. In 1928 the town became a city, incorporating the previously separate towns of Stonehouse and Devonport, and today it is the largest city in Devon.

Plymouth Sound

Three miles out, at the entrance to the Sound, is the Plymouth breakwater, nearly one mile long and made from some 4 million tons of stone. Begun in 1812 by John Rennie and completed in 1841 by his son Sir John Rennie, it was ONE OF THE FIRST BREAKWATERS TO BE BUILT ANYWHERE IN THE WORLD and, at the time, was THE LARGEST FREE-STANDING BREAKWATER EVER ATTEMPTED. Constructed to protect naval vessels entering and leaving Devonport from the treacherous southerly gales, there is a lighthouse at the western end and a beacon at the eastern end, along with a special cage designed to provide a place of safety for shipwrecked sailors. To celebrate the lighthouse becoming operational in 1844, a horse-drawn carriage full of passengers was driven from east to west along the top of the breakwater to the accompaniment of a military band. Just inside the breakwater is the Breakwater Fort, an oval sea fort built in 1865 to help defend Plymouth Sound.

The volcanic island closer inshore was originally known as St Michael's after a chapel that stood there in 1135. During the 16th century the people of Plymouth began to refer to it as Drake's Island after their town's favourite hero, and the name stuck. At the same time, the island was fortified against the French and Spanish and a barracks built, which later served as a prison. In the 18th and 19th centuries the fortifications were strengthened to defend the deep channel into Devonport. It is now privately owned and run as a museum and heritage centre offering guided tours.

Plymouth Hoe

The Promenade and wide lawns of Plymouth Hoe ('hoe' meaning 'high ridge') were laid out in the 1880s on top of limestone cliffs that rise 150 feet (46 metres) above the waters of Plymouth Sound. The landward side of the Hoe is dominated by the PLYMOUTH NAVAL MEMORIAL, commemorating the 23,000 naval personnel who were lost or buried at sea. It was designed in 1924 by Sir Robert Lorimer and is one of three naval memorials in the country, the others being at Portsmouth and Chatham. After World War Two the memorial was extended by Sir Edward Maufe.

The views along the coast and out to sea from the Hoe are stupendous. On a clear day it is possible to see the Eddystone

Smeaton's Tower

Lighthouse, perched on the Eddystone Rocks 14 miles out to sea.

Smeaton's Tower

The present EDDYSTONE LIGHTHOUSE is the fourth to be built on the rocks of the same name, and the best view of it is to be had from the lantern of its predecessor, the third lighthouse. Known as SMEATON'S TOWER, the upper portion of this former lighthouse was dismantled and rebuilt on the Hoe in 1884.

Originally built in 1759 by engineer JOHN SMEATON, Smeaton's Tower was of pioneering design and its shape was modelled on the trunk of an oak tree, tapering upwards from a broad base. Smeaton was the first modern engineer to employ a type of lime mortar or concrete once used by the Romans which can set underwater, and this proved so durable that the lighthouse continued in operation for over 120 years until it was taken down, not because the structure failed but because the rock beneath it began to erode. The base of the tower proved impossible to break and is still there next to the current lighthouse.

Smeaton's Tower has become a much-loved landmark on the Hoe and the view from the lantern

room, reached by a climb of 93 steps, is sublime.

Bowls

It could be argued that Plymouth Hoe is the birthplace of Britain as a world power, for it was from the Hoe that Sir Francis Drake departed in 1588 to defeat the Spanish Armada and make England mistress of the seas. The story goes that Drake was playing bowls on the Hoe when he was informed of the approach of the Armada. Well aware that the state of the wind and tide meant the English fleet could not set sail for a few hours, Drake is alleged to have said, *'Time enough to play* the game and thrash the Spaniards afterwards.' You can still play bowls on the very Hoe where this momentous event happened, and nearby on the Promenade there is a statue of Drake, a former mayor of Plymouth, by Sir Joseph Boehm, which was unveiled in 1884 by Lady Fuller Drake, a descendant of Drake's brother Thomas.

The Citadel

At the eastern end of the Hoe is the vast complex of the ROYAL CITADEL. This was built in 1665 on the orders of Charles II to protect Plymouth from the Dutch during the Anglo-Dutch Wars, and incorporates a previous fortress built by Sir Francis Drake in 1590. The guns of the Royal Citadel face inland as well as out to sea, a message from the King to the people of Plymouth who had supported Parliament during the Civil War. For over 100 years the Citadel was THE BIGGEST AND MOST IMPORTANT OF ENGLAND'S COASTAL DEFENCES and is still in use by the military today as home to 29 Commando Regiment. One of few star-shaped forts in the country that is still operational, and one of only ten places in Britain that is allowed to fire a 21-gun salute, the Citadel is only accessible to the public via guided tours.

The Barbican

The Royal Citadel overlooks SUTTON POOL, Plymouth's original harbour, named after the little fishing village of Sutton from which Plymouth developed. The area around the harbour is called the Barbican and forms the historic heart of Plymouth. One of the few areas of the city to survive the Plymouth Blitz in World War Two, the Barbican can boast a fine collection of more than 200 listed buildings, many of them Tudor or Jacobean, and also has THE HIGHEST CONCENTRATION OF COBBLED STREETS IN BRITAIN.

Sutton Pool has been the scene of many pivotal moments in England's history. Here, in 1445, came Margaret of Anjou to meet her future husband Henry VI, and here, in 1501, came Catherine of Aragon, on her way to marry Prince Arthur, eldest son of Henry VII. King Philip of Spain stopped off here in 1554 on his way to Southampton and then Winchester to marry Queen Mary, little knowing that just over 30 years later a man playing bowls on the Hoe above would be instrumental in the defeat of his mighty Armada.

Martin Frobisher sailed from here in 1578 to search for the

Northwest Passage, while the Devon men who helped open up the New World also sailed from Sutton Pool, Humphrey Gilbert for Newfoundland in 1583, Richard Grenville for Virginia in 1585, Walter Raleigh for Guiana in 1594.

Mayflower Steps

Standing at the entrance to the inner harbour, the MAYFLOWER STEPS commemorate the departure of the *Mayflower* from Plymouth on 6 September 1620, carrying 102 English Puritan pilgrims, sailors and craftsmen to the New World, where they founded a colony that 400 years later has grown into the most powerful country in the world. Plymouth was the last place in the country of their birth that these remarkable men and women ever set foot, and they named their first landfall in America after it, Plymouth Rock, and their first settlement, Plymouth, now known as 'America's Hometown'. The actual site from where the *Mayflower* cast off is thought to be where the Victorian Admiral MacBride pub now stands.

The ELIZABETHAN HOUSE at 32 New Street, The Barbican, is a rare example of a house from the late 1500s, while overlooking the inner harbour is Island House where a number of the *Mayflower* pilgrims were entertained before they left – this could be the last

house in England they ever knew. Tucked away down narrow Southside is JACKA BAKERY, THE OLDEST WORKING COMMERCIAL BAKERY IN BRITAIN, which has been making bread since the time of the Armada and baked the ship's biscuits for the *Mayflower*.

Plymouth Gin

PLYMOUTH GIN, the official gin of the Royal Navy, has been made at Black Friar's Distillery, THE OLDEST WORKING GIN DISTILLERY IN ENGLAND, since 1793. Occupying the buildings of the old Black Friars Monastery on Southside that some of the *Mayflower* pilgrims stayed at, the distillery recalls its long history in the ship on the label of each bottle of Plymouth Gin, depicting the *Mayflower*. Plymouth Gin is 57 per cent ABV, what they call Navy Strength: a higher alcohol content than other gins because it had to be stored below decks next to the gunpowder, which ordinary gin, at 41.2 per cent, would damage if it leaked, meaning that the gunpowder wouldn't light. Navy Strength, on the other hand, being flammable, would actually help to light the gunpowder!

St Andrew's Church

Not far away in the city centre, standing next to the grand Victorian Gothic Guildhall of 1875, is St Andrew's church, THE LARGEST PARISH CHURCH IN DEVON. Dating largely from the 15th century, it sits on the site of the original Saxon church of Sutton and is much restored after being heavily bombed in World War Two. CATHERINE OF ARAGON came to St Andrew's to give thanks for her safe journey to England from Spain, Sir Francis Drake worshipped in the church, and he and the other victorious commanders of the English fleet came here to give thanks for their victory over the Spanish Armada in 1588. Lying beneath a simple stone in front of the chancel steps is the heart of ADMIRAL ROBERT BLAKE (1598–1657), commander of Oliver Cromwell's navy during the Commonwealth and known as '*Father of the Royal Navy*' for his success in consolidating the Royal Navy's supremacy on the seas. Next to him is the heart of the explorer MARTIN FROBISHER, who put many new names on the map of the world and was one of Drake's companions in the defeat of the Armada. CAPTAIN BLIGH OF the HMS *Bounty* was baptised here in 1754.

The Door of Unity

Beside St Andrew's is Plymouth's oldest building, Prysten House, a courtyard house built in 1498 for merchant Thomas Yogge and now used as a museum. Built into the north wall of the house is a tombstone with the words *'Here lie the brave'* inscribed on it. This is a tribute to two American naval officers who were killed in 1813 during a battle between the American brig *Argus* and the English ship *Pelican* in the British–American War of 1812. Their bodies were brought to Plymouth for burial in St Andrew's churchyard and in 1930, in a special ceremony organised by the National Society United States Daughters of 1812, their headstone was placed next to the door from Prysten House into the churchyard and the door was dedicated the 'Door of Unity' as a show of friendship between the peoples of America and Plymouth, from where so many of the first European Americans came.

Devonport

The east bank of the Hamoaze, the stretch of the River Tamar south of the Royal Albert Bridge, is lined with the docks of Devonport Naval Base, established in the late 17th century as a royal dockyard called Plymouth Dock and now the largest naval base in western Europe. In 1768 Captain Cook set out from Plymouth Dock on his voyage to Australia.

By the early 19th century Plymouth Dock had become the biggest town in Devon and Cornwall, and in 1823 was renamed Devonport to distinguish it from neighbouring Plymouth. In celebration, architect John Foulston designed and built the splendid Devonport Guildhall and next to it the equally splendid Devonport Column, 124 feet high with a viewing platform at the top reached by a climb of 137 steps. In 1849 the column was used for one of the world's first experimental demonstrations of electric light when the Plymouth-born electrical engineer John Nash Hearder set up a light that burned for three hours. The light shone so brightly that, with the help of a reflector, his assistant was able to read a book while standing on the ramparts of Trematon

Castle, nearly four miles away near Saltash in Cornwall. Completing what is the finest surviving collection of Regency architecture in Plymouth is the extraordinary ODD FELLOWS HALL, ONE OF ONLY TWO 'EGYPTIAN' HOUSES IN BRITAIN, the other being in Penzance.

Born in Devonport

ROBERT FALCON SCOTT (1868–1912), Antarctic explorer, remembered with a monument on Mount Wise, a viewpoint just east of the Devonport docks.

LESLIE HORE-BELISHA (1893–1957), politician and Minister of Transport who introduced the driving test, the 30mph speed limit and the Belisha Beacon, indicating a pedestrian crossing.

GUY BURGESS (1911–63), spy and Soviet double agent and member of the Cambridge Five. He defected to the Soviet Union in 1951.

Stonehouse

Stonehouse is home to THE OLDEST BARRACKS IN BRITAIN, THE ROYAL MARINE BARRACKS, a superb complex of Georgian buildings built in the mid-18th century and known as the spiritual home of the Royal Marines. In 1831 the racquets court of the barracks was converted into the Globe Theatre, which survives as a rare example of a Regency theatre. Today, the barracks are known as RM Stonehouse and currently serve

Devonport Guildhall and Column

as headquarters of 3 Commando Brigade.

Stonehouse is also the site of Plymouth's cathedral, THE ROMAN CATHOLIC CATHEDRAL CHURCH OF ST MARY AND ST BONIFACE, seat of the Bishop of Plymouth. It was designed and built in the 1850s by JOSEPH HANSOM, creator of the Hansom cab, and his brother Charles.

Royal Albert Bridge

The River Tamar forms the border between Devon and Cornwall for all but four miles, as it has done since the 10th century when it was declared to be the border by the Saxon king Athelstan. The most spectacular crossing of the Tamar is the distinctive ROYAL ALBERT BRIDGE, which carries the Cornish Main Line in and out of Cornwall. It is one of the world's great railway bridges and an iconic image of the transition from England into Cornwall.

The bridge was designed and built by ISAMBARD KINGDOM BRUNEL and was the third major wrought iron bridge ever to be built. Its unique design, a mix of arch and suspension, is based on the two previous wrought iron bridges, the High Level Bridge across the River Tyne in Newcastle and the Britannia Bridge across the Menai Straits to Anglesey, both by Robert Stephenson. The Royal Albert Bridge is a little over 2,000 feet long and 172 feet high, with the deck being 100 feet above the river. It was opened by Prince Albert himself in 1859, though Brunel was too ill to attend the opening and died later that year; his name was inscribed in huge letters on the portals at each end of the bridge as a memorial. Running along the north side of the railway bridge and taking the A38 road across the river is the Tamar Suspension Bridge which

opened in 1962. South of the two bridges, the Tamar River is joined by the St Germans River and the estuary formed by confluence is known as the HAMOAZE.

Plymouth: First and Last

Plymouth has been the first and last port of call for great figures from history down the ages, from kings and queens, naval heroes, explorers and empire builders to pilgrims, pirates, adventurers and round-the-world sailors.

In the 14th century, along with Dover, Plymouth became one of two licensed English ports from which pilgrims could travel to Spain without obtaining special permission from the king.

In 1355 EDWARD THE BLACK PRINCE assembled the English fleet in Plymouth Sound before departing for the Battle of Poitiers.

In 1445 MARGARET OF ANJOU landed at Plymouth to meet her future husband, Henry VI.

In 1501 CATHERINE OF ARAGON landed at Plymouth on her way to marry Prince Arthur, eldest son of Henry VII.

KING PHILIP OF SPAIN landed at Plymouth on his way to Southampton and then Winchester to marry Queen Mary in 1554.

SIR FRANCIS DRAKE left from Plymouth in the *Pelican* at the start of his circumnavigation of the world in 1577, and in 1588 he sailed from Plymouth to confront the Spanish Armada.

In 1620 the *MAYFLOWER* set sail for the New World from Plymouth carrying 101 pilgrims, sailors and craftsmen seeking a new life free from religious persecution.

CAPTAIN JAMES COOK set sail from Plymouth on each of his three famous voyages of discovery that mapped and explored the Pacific Ocean in 1768, 1772 and 1776. Plymouth was the last place in England he ever saw, as he was killed by natives on the Sandwich Islands (now Hawaii) during the third voyage and was buried at sea.

CHARLES DARWIN'S VOYAGE ON HMS *BEAGLE* set sail from Plymouth in December 1831. Discoveries made on the voyage inspired Darwin's Theory of Evolution.

The TOLPUDDLE MARTYRS sailed into to Plymouth on their return from Australia in 1837–9.

ERNEST SHACKLETON twice sailed from Plymouth to the Antarctic, in 1914 on the *Endurance*, which became trapped in ice and sank, and in 1921 on the *Quest*, where he died on board while the ship was moored off South Georgia.

Plymouth has been the finish of the iconic Fastnet Race since it started in 1925.

Plymouth was the starting point for ELLEN MACARTHUR's record-breaking solo circumnavigation of the globe in 2005.

In September 2018 sixty-year-old JOANNA (ASIA) PAJOWSKA's single-handed non-stop circumnavigation of the globe began in Plymouth, and ended there in 2019.

GRETA THUNBERG set sail from Plymouth on 14 August 2019 on her 15-day trip across the Atlantic on board the zero-carbon sailboat *Malizia II*.

Plymouth was the starting point for SIR FRANCIS CHICHESTER's epic journey to become the first person to sail single-handed around the globe in August 1966. He succeeded and arrived back in Plymouth 226 days later. He was later knighted at the Old Royal Naval College in Greenwich by Queen Elizabeth II using the same sword that Queen Elizabeth I used to knight Sir Francis Drake after he became the first Englishman to sail around the world in 1577–80.

Born in Plymouth

Sailors

SIR JOHN HAWKINS (1532–95) Both hero and villain, Hawkins was a controversial naval commander and is reckoned to be the first English merchant to profit from the Triangular Slave Trade between Africa and the Spanish West Indies. As Treasurer of the Navy he redesigned the English fighting ships, making them better armed, faster and more manoeuvrable, enabling the English navy to defeat the larger and more powerful ships of the Spanish Armada, a battle in which he fought as Vice Admiral. He died off Puerto Rico while sailing to capture Spanish treasure ships in the Caribbean.

WILLIAM BLIGH (1754–1817) William Bligh joined the Royal Navy at the age of seven and in 1776 accompanied Captain Cook on his third voyage to the Pacific Ocean as sailing master of Cook's ship *Resolution*. After Cook was killed by Hawaiian islanders, his ailing second in command Charles Clerke died of tuberculosis and the young Bligh was left to navigate the expedition back to England. In 1787 he sailed back to the Pacific as Captain of the *Bounty* in search of breadfruit on the island of Tahiti. In 1789, after leaving Tahiti, a mutiny broke out on board led by Master's Mate Fletcher Christian. Bligh and his officers were set adrift in the ship's launch and the *Bounty* sailed for Pitcairn Island where the mutineers settled. Bligh managed to navigate the launch west across the Pacific for over 4,000 miles to land safely on Timor in the Dutch East Indies. He was later appointed Governor of New South Wales and died in London where he is buried in the churchyard of St Mary-at-Lambeth at the gates of Lambeth Palace. There have been three films about the Mutiny on the *Bounty* with Bligh portrayed by Charles Laughton (1935), Trevor Howard (1962) and Anthony Hopkins (1984).

Adventurers and Explorers

ROBERT FALCON SCOTT (1868–1912) Born in Devonport. Made the first balloon flight over Antarctica and in 1911 set off on the Terra Nova Expedition, an overland race to become the first person to reach the South Pole. He arrived at the Pole on 18 January 1912 only to find the Norwegian flag already planted there by Roald Amundsen, who had beaten him by over a month. Scott and his four companions perished on the return journey, leaving behind a diary in which the last entry read, '*Had we lived I should have had a tale to tell of the hardihood, endurance and courage of my companions which would have stirred the heart of every Englishman.*' It was on this expedition the Captain Lawrence Oates, who knew he was dying from hypothermia and didn't want to compromise his companions' chances of survival, left the tent uttering the immortal words, '*I am just going outside and may be some time.*'

LEWIS PUGH (b. 1969) Endurance swimmer and UN Patron of the Oceans, Lewis Pugh was the first person to undertake a long-distance swim in every ocean of the world. He pioneered the first swim across the North Pole, swam under the Antarctic ice sheet and was the first person to swim the length of the English Channel, setting off from Land's End on 12 July 2018 and finishing at Dover on 29 August 2018. The swim was 348 miles in length and took 49 days.

Artist and Scientists

JOSEPH GLANVILL (1636–80) Philosopher and writer who was one of the first to advance natural philosophy, the study of nature and the physical universe that paved the way for modern science. In 1661 he even predicted modern communications: '*To converse at the distance of the Indes by means of sympathetic conveyances may be as natural to future times as to us is a literary correspondence*'.

JAMES NORTHCOTE (1746–1831) Prolific and much-admired portrait painter who began his career as a pupil of fellow Plymouth-born artist Sir Joshua Reynolds. Known especially for his paintings of historic scenes such as the Princes in the Tower. There is a memorial to him by Sir Francis Chantrey in Exeter Cathedral.

SAMUEL PROUT (1783–1852) Painter known for his architectural watercolours who became 'Painter in Water-Colours in Ordinary' to George IV and then Queen Victoria. His pupil John Ruskin said of him, '*Sometimes I tire of Turner, but never of Prout*'.

BENJAMIN HAYDON (1786–1846) Artist and tutor to fellow Plymouth-born artist Sir Charles Lock Eastlake (see page 137), Haydon was famous for huge, grand historical paintings. The two most celebrated of these are *The Reform Banquet*, depicting a celebratory dinner held at the Guildhall in July 1832 for supporters of the Great Reform Act, including Prime Minister Earl Grey, which contained 597 individual portraits, and *The Anti-Slavery Society Convention*, 1840, showing Thomas Clarkson addressing the delegates – Haydon was a well-known anti-slaver. He was also a great champion for the displaying of art in public buildings, the public funding of art education and free public museums. Part of the Romantic movement in art and literature, one of Haydon's most famous paintings was of his fellow Romantic William Wordsworth lost in thought on Helvellyn in the Lake District. Both Wordsworth and Keats wrote sonnets in praise of Haydon. Overcome by constant financial difficulties, he took his own life in his studio in London. He is portrayed by Martin Savage in the 2014 film *Mr. Turner*.

WILLIAM ELFORD LEACH (1791–1836) Zoologist and marine biologist who developed modern zoology and paved the way for Charles Darwin and Alfred Russel Wallace.

SIR CHARLES LOCK EASTLAKE (1793–1865) Painter who became President of the Royal Academy, the first Director of the National Gallery and first President of the Royal Photographic Society. As Secretary to the Fine Arts Commission, he was responsible for finding artists to decorate the new Houses of Parliament. As President of the Royal Academy, he opened up the Academy to engravers and female students and encouraged foreign students to exhibit at the Summer Exhibition. He travelled Europe purchasing paintings for the National Gallery, of which he became the first director and during his tenure revolutionised the curation and display of the pictures in historical sequence, an arrangement the National Gallery and others around the world still follow to this day. His most famous work is *Napoleon on the Bellerophon*, painted in 1815 while Napoleon was being held on the *Bellerophon* in Plymouth Sound after his defeat at the Battle of Waterloo. He is portrayed by James Fox in the 2014 film *Effie Gray*.

CHARLES LOCKE EASTLAKE (1836–1906) Nephew of the painter Sir Charles Lock Eastlake, the younger Eastlake became an architect and furniture designer. His architectural and design style was a mix of Queen Anne, Arts and Crafts and Gothic Revival and gave rise to the Eastlake Movement in North America. Perhaps the most famous examples of the Eastlake Movement are the distinctive Victorian houses of Carroll Avenue in Los Angeles, one of which (1330) appeared in Michael Jackson's *Thriller* video, while 1329 is the famous

'Charmed House' from the TV series *Charmed*.

HENRY AUSTIN DOBSON (1840–1921) Biographer and poet who wrote the first 'ballade', a form of medieval French poetry, in English. His biographies of Henry Fielding, Thomas Bewick, Richard Steele, Oliver Goldsmith, Horace Walpole and William Hogarth are considered the best of all such biographies. Amongst his most famous lines are:

Time goes, you say? Ah no!
Alas, Time stays, we go ...

From 'The Paradox of Time'

Old books, old wine, old Nankin blue; – All things, in short, to which belong. The charm, the grace that Time makes strong, – All these I prize, but (entre nous) Old friends are best.

From 'To Richard Watson Gilder'

SIR JOHN COLLINGS SQUIRE (1884–1958) Author and poet who, as editor of the progressive literary magazine *London Mercury*, gathered a coterie of writers around him known as the Squirearchy. His most famous quote is '*I am not so think as you drunk I am*' which comes from his *Ballade of Soporific Absorption*, lampooning his own reputation as a heavy drinker.

SIR DESMOND MACCARTHY (1877–1952) Author, drama critic, *Sunday Times* literary critic and member of the Bloomsbury Group.

LEONARD STRONG (1896–1958) Prolific writer of novels, short stories, plays and history.

DONALD SINDEN (1923–2014) Much-loved and award-winning film, television and theatre actor known for his rich, plummy voice and remembered for such films as *The Cruel Sea* (1953), *Doctor in the House* (1954) and *Doctor at Large* (1957), for the TV sitcoms *Two's Company* with Elaine Stritch and *Never the Twain*, and in the theatre for his appearances in the Ray Cooney farces. He was the last person living to have known 'Bosie', Oscar Wilde's lover Lord Alfred Douglas.

Ron Goodwin (1925–2003) Composer known for his film scores which include *633 Squadron* (1964), *Those Magnificent Men in their Flying Machines* (1965), *Where Eagles Dare* (1968) and *The Battle of Britain* (1969). Goodwin's eponymous main theme from the 1966 film *The Trap* is used by the BBC as the London Marathon TV coverage theme tune, while a variation of his score for the 1969 film *Monte Carlo or Bust!* is used as the intro music for BBC Radio Four's panel show *I'm Sorry I Haven't a Clue*. The road in Plymouth where Goodwin lived for a time with his family is named Goodwin Crescent in his memory.

George Passmore (b. 1942) One half of the famous collaborative artist duo Gilbert and George. Together they won the highly prestigious Turner Prize in 1986.

Wayne Sleep (b.1948) Dancer and choreographer who danced with Princess Diana of Wales at the annual Christmas party of the Friends of Covent Garden at the Royal Opera House in 1985. The episode was recreated in the TV series *The Crown* in which Sleep was portrayed by Jay Webb. He is the world record holder for the entrechat-douze, a dance step in which the dancer jumps into the air and rapidly crosses and recrosses his legs 12 times before landing.

Others

Robert Stephen Hawker (1803–1875) Parson who invented the Harvest Festival. He was the grandson of Robert Hawker, vicar of Charles Church and was born in the Charles Church Clergy House.

Stuart Rendel, 1st Baron Rendell (1834–1913) Liberal politician and industrialist with engineering company Armstrong Mitchell. He was one of the pallbearers at Prime Minister William Gladstone's state funeral in Westminster Abbey along with future kings Edward VII and George V.

Michael Foot (1913–2010) Eccentric left-wing intellectual who became editor of the *Evening Standard* before he was 30. Leader of the Labour Party from 1980–1983.

Herchel Smith (1925–2001) Chemist whose research led to the development of the contraceptive pill.

Trevor Francis (1954–2023) In 1979 he was transferred from

Birmingham City to Nottingham Forest for £1 million, becoming THE FIRST £1 MILLION PLAYER IN ENGLISH FOOTBALL.

KATE NESBIT (b.1988) THE FIRST FEMALE MEMBER OF THE ROYAL NAVY, and the second woman in the British Armed Forces to receive the Military Cross, awarded for administering emergency medical treatment and saving the life of a fellow soldier during a Taliban ambush while on operational tour in Afghanistan in 2009.

Plympton

Plympton was a Borough Town

When Plymouth was a fuzzy down

So runs the boast of Plympton, a significant place long before Plymouth: the site of an important priory, a borough from the 12th century, a stannary town where tin from the local mines was regulated and traded, and a busy seaport. The town sent two representatives to Edward I's Model Parliament in 1295 and, as a Rotten Borough with a tiny electorate, continued to send two local landowners to Parliament as MPs for the next 537 years until the Great Reform Act of 1832 – in fact Plympton folk were surprisingly influential in the 17th-century world of politics and, indeed, in the world of 18th-century art.

Now a north-western suburb of Plymouth, Plympton is made up largely of two distinct communities, Plympton St Mary and Plympton St Maurice.

Plympton St Mary

St Mary is the older of the two and stands on the site of a Saxon monastery dating from around AD 900. In 1121 Warelwast, Bishop of Exeter and a nephew of William the Conqueror, disbanded the community of canons that occupied the monastery and in its place founded the Augustinian Priory of St Peter and St Paul, which grew into THE RICHEST RELIGIOUS HOUSE IN THE WHOLE OF DEVON and THE FOURTH RICHEST AUGUSTINIAN PRIORY IN ENGLAND.

There's not much left of the Priory except for the remains of the gatehouse incorporated into what's known as Tower House, a few small sections of stone wall south of the churchyard, and the stately CHURCH OF ST MARY. The church was built in 1311 to serve as the Priory chapel in place of an earlier chapel, extended in the 15th century, and then became the parish church after the Priory was dissolved by Henry VIII.

Lying under a canopy in the north aisle of the church is the armoured figure of RICHARD STRODE OF NEWNHAM (a small village half a mile to the north), who died in 1464. In the niches of this beautiful tomb are 11 mourners each holding rosaries and other items, including a tiny prayer book and the figure of a child (the Baby Jesus?) less than an inch high and said to be THE SMALLEST FIGURE OF A CHILD ON ANY TOMB IN AN ENGLISH CHURCH. Nearby, on the wall of the north aisle, is a monument to Richard's descendant SIR WILLIAM STRODE, seen kneeling between his two wives with his seven daughters and three sons depicted in a panel below.

The Strode family of Plympton would go on to make their mark in politics. Richard Strode of Newnham's younger son, another Richard, instigated the STRODE ACT which was responsible for the introduction of Parliamentary Privilege. The second son of Sir William Strode, another William, strode into history as one of the five Members of Parliament who just managed to escape before Charles I came to the Commons to arrest them, causing the King to exclaim *'I see my birds have flown'*. The incident saw the monarch banned from entering the Commons for evermore,

Plympton Grammar School

an episode still remembered at the Opening of Parliament when the monarch's representative Black Rod has the door of the Commons slammed in his or her face.

Plympton St Maurice
I love every stone in Plympton.

Sir Joshua Reynolds

Here, gloriously and unexpectedly, is one of Devon's hidden delights.

Plympton St Maurice lies about half a mile to the southeast of St Mary and gathers about the high grassy mound of Plymouth's Norman motte and bailey castle, built around 1100 on the site of a Saxon fort by RICHARD DE REDVERS, a friend of William the Conqueror. De Redvers's son Baldwin was a supporter of the Empress Matilda during the war between Matilda and Stephen known as the Anarchy, and King Stephen had the castle razed to the ground. Baldwin, created the first ever 1st Earl of Devon by Matilda, rebuilt the castle in stone and it is the remains of Baldwin's castle that we see there today. A Royalist stronghold in the Civil War, the castle was finally destroyed by Cromwell's men in 1647. The bailey area is now used for village fetes and other entertainments while there are stupendous views over Plymouth, Dartmoor and the surrounding countryside from the top of the motte.

The motte is the best place to see over the high wall that hides the rather handsome PLYMPTON HOUSE, begun around 1690 by SIR GEORGE TREBY, the local MP and Lord Chief Justice, and completed by his son, also named George, in 1715. One of the loveliest houses in Devon, Plympton House is designed in traditional William and Mary style, possibly by Treby's friend SIR CHRISTOPHER WREN, who was briefly an MP for Plympton from 1685–87 along with Richard Strode of Newnham. Having served as Dr Duck's Asylum for almost a century between 1835 and 1933 and then as a care home, Plympton House is once more a private home while the outbuildings have been converted into residential properties.

Just down from the house is the splendid former home of PLYMPTON GRAMMAR SCHOOL, the schoolroom set above a picturesque many-arched cloister and supported on granite columns. Dated 1664, the building is considered by some to be THE FINEST JACOBEAN BUILDING WEST OF BRISTOL. The school was founded in 1658 with a bequest from local landowner and Treasurer to James I, ELIZE HELE, whose only son died at the age of 12 prompting Hele to leave his fortune to 'pious purposes'. In front of the schoolroom stood the Old School House, demolished in 1871, where the artist SIR JOSHUA REYNOLDS, seventh son of the headmaster Samuel Reynolds, was born in 1723. As well as Sir Joshua Reynolds himself, the school was attended by a number of influential local artists including James Northcote, Benjamin Haydon and Charles Lock Eastlake, prompting many people to call Plympton Grammar School a 'cradle of English art'.

Another famous pupil was the 'Sporting Parson' Jack Russell.

The infant Joshua Reynolds was christened in the heavily restored 15th-century Church of St Maurice across the road, which had formerly been the castle chapel.

FORE STREET, which curls around the southern base of the castle mound, is one of the loveliest I have walked down in all my travels around England. The narrow street is lined with smart doorways and Georgian frontages, many of them hiding older buildings behind with some dating as far back as 1275, all

Plympton Guildhall

jostling side by side with 16th- and 17th-century houses, a few with their upper storeys extending out over the pavement and resting on stone pillars.

Amongst the finest are the early 18th-century Rectory at No. 9, the steep-roofed Tudor Lodge, formally a brewery and resting on 14th-century foundations and, at the other end of the street, the late-eighth-century Plympton St Maurice House with its tiny service cottage attached and looking all of a piece. The gardens on the south side of Fore Street retain the form of medieval burgages, long, narrow plots of land of the same width as the street frontage of the house (see below).

> Burgages were long, thin strips of land extending back from the street that measured the same width as the street frontage of the house. The buildings facing the street were usually used for business purposes such as shops, workshops or taverns and the narrow frontages maximised the number of properties that could be accommodated – all good for business. Taxes and rents were levied according to the width of the frontage, so the wider the frontage, the higher the tax or rent.

Many of the Fore Street gardens were planted with apple trees and Plympton is THE FIRST PLACE IN DEVON RECORDED AS PRODUCING THE CIDER FOR WHICH DEVON HAS BECOME FAMOUS. Plympton, according to the accounts of the Earl of Devon in 1295, had '*a small quantity of cider remaining from the previous season*'.

The most distinctive building in the street is the PLYMPTON GUILDHALL, a classical building whose upper floor rests on an arcade of granite pillars. There has been a guildhall here since the 13th century although the present building is late 17th century and was given to the town by the Trebys of Plympton House. Sir Joshua Reynolds held court here as Mayor of Plympton in 1773, four years after receiving a knighthood from George III. The story goes that on meeting the monarch some time later in Hyde Park, Reynolds thoughtlessly told the King that being elected Mayor was '*the greatest honour I have ever received*' before quickly adding, '*save for being honoured with a knighthood by my gracious sovereign, of course*'.

Born in Plympton

DAVID OWEN (b.1938) Foreign Secretary in James Callaghan's Labour government and one of the 'Gang of Four' who founded the Social Democratic Party (SDP) in 1981. From 1992 to 1995 he was EU co-chairman of the Conference for the Former Yugoslavia. Styled Baron Owen of Plymouth in the County of Devon.

SIR JOSHUA REYNOLDS (1723–92) Joshua Reynolds, lauded as the greatest portrait painter of the 18th century, was born in the Old School House of Plympton Grammar School, where his father Samuel Reynolds was headmaster and where Joshua was educated. His early enthusiasm and aptitude for art was encouraged by his older sister Mary and after leaving Plympton he was apprenticed to the fashionable London portrait painter Thomas Hudson, a fellow Devonian.

After travelling through Europe studying the Old Masters, Reynolds established himself in London as a portrait painter and rapidly acquired an aristocratic clientele such as the Dukes of Devonshire, Grafton and Cumberland, the latter being the third son of George II. In 1760 he moved into the house where he lived for the rest of his life, on the west side of Leicester Fields, now Leicester Square.

Due to success as a portrait painter, Reynolds mixed with all the wealthy and artistic figures of his day and in 1764 he and Dr Samuel Johnson founded The Club, a dining club that met every Monday evening at the Turks Head in Gerrard Street, Soho, a venue that has long since disappeared and is now marked only by a plaque. Fellow members included the actor David Garrick and writer Oliver Goldsmith.

In 1768 Reynolds was appointed the first President of the Royal Academy, a position he held until his death, and in 1769, he was knighted by King George III, only the second English artist to be so honoured after Sir James Thornhill.

In 1772 Reynolds commissioned the architect Sir William Chambers to build him a house on Richmond Hill in South London, as a place where he could get away from the bustle of the capital. Wick House had a bow window on the first floor from which Reynolds could admire the prospect of the Thames; although best known as a portrait painter he enjoyed landscape painting too and one of his best known works was his 1788 landscape *The Thames from Richmond Hill*, now THE ONLY ENGLISH LANDSCAPE VIEW WHICH IS PROTECTED BY AN ACT OF PARLIAMENT.

Reynolds was held in great esteem by those who knew him. The artist James Northcote, a fellow pupil at Plympton Grammar School, said of him, *'I know him thoroughly, and all his faults, I am sure, and yet almost worship him'*. The philosopher Edmund Burke, who was with Reynolds on the night he died, began his eulogy with the lines, *'Sir Joshua Reynolds was on very many accounts one of the most memorable men of his Time. He was the first Englishman who added the praise of the elegant Arts to the other Glories of his Country'*.

Works by Sir Joshua Reynolds are now worth millions. His *Portrait of Lady Worsley* sold for £25 million in 2025, while in 2023 his *Portrait of Omai* sold for £50 million.

Sir Joshua Reynolds is buried in St Paul's Cathedral.

WELL, I NEVER KNEW THIS ABOUT

PLYMOUTH

JOHN HOWLAND fell overboard from the *Mayflower* on its fateful journey to America during a storm and was almost lost at sea but managed to grab a rope, giving the crew enough time to rescue him with a boat hook. Had he been lost we would never have known his descendants, who include Franklin D. Roosevelt, George H.W. Bush, George W. Bush, the essayist and poet Ralph Waldo Emerson and the actor Humphrey Bogart.

In 1774 THE WORLD'S FIRST RECORDED SUBMARINE FATALITY occurred in Plymouth Sound, just north of Drake's Island, when a carpenter called John Day descended from the sloop *Maria* in a wooden diving chamber he had built himself. Weighted down with some 50 tons of ballast, the chamber sank out of sight and failed to resurface. It has never been found.

Plymouth Synagogue, built in 1762, is THE OLDEST ASHKENAZI SYNAGOGUE STILL IN REGULAR USE IN THE ENGLISH-SPEAKING WORLD.

The Port of Plymouth Sailing Regatta is one of the oldest regattas in the world. It started in 1823.

Local legend has it that when the Tolpuddle Martyrs returned from Australia between 1837 and 1839, they stayed in the Dolphin Hotel on the Barbican.

STANLEY GIBBONS founded his famous stamp collecting business in Plymouth in 1840, the same year that the penny black stamp was launched.

Sherlock Holmes author Sir Arthur Conan Doyle assisted at a medical practice in Durnford Street in Plymouth in 1882. Holmes is rumoured to have been based on his colleague there, Dr Budd, although Conan Doyle's tutor at Edinburgh University is a more likely claimant.

It is somewhat fitting that Plymouth, from where Humphrey Gilbert sailed in 1583 to take possession of Newfoundland, should, over 300 years later, be the end point for THE FIRST EVER TRANSATLANTIC FLIGHT, from Newfoundland to England. On 31 May 1919 a Curtiss NC-4 seaplane crewed by US Navy aviators landed in Plymouth Sound having crossed the Atlantic, stopping at the Azores for refuelling. Two weeks later Alcock and Brown completed the first ever non-stop transatlantic flight, from Newfoundland to Ireland.

In 1919, Plymouth's NANCY ASTOR became THE FIRST FEMALE MP TO TAKE A SEAT IN THE HOUSE OF COMMONS. She was introduced to Parliament on 1 December 1919.

Plymouth's Art Deco LIDO opened in 1935 and is regularly featured in national press as one of the finest places in the UK to swim.

Plymouth has THE HIGHEST NUMBER OF POST-WAR LISTED BUILDINGS IN THE UK OUTSIDE LONDON.

SALTRAM HOUSE, the home of the Parker family since 1712, is set in its own extensive grounds on the eastern outskirts of Plymouth. Originally a Tudor mansion, it was remodelled in 1743 in Palladian style by John Parker and his wife Lady Catherine, who largely funded the works. Robert Adam was later commissioned to refurbish the interior and Saltram's Saloon is rated amongst some of his finest work. The house generally is regarded as one of the finest early Georgian houses in England. Saltram and its collection of ten Joshua Reynolds paintings was handed over to the National Trust in lieu of death duties in 1957.

Across the harbour entrance from the Mayflower Steps by Sutton Pool in Plymouth is the National Marine Aquarium, THE LARGEST AQUARIUM IN BRITAIN, with THE DEEPEST TANK IN EUROPE, the Atlantic Ocean Tank.

In March 2019 the Theatre Royal Plymouth unveiled *MESSENGER*, THE UK'S LARGEST BRONZE SCULPTURE, created by the artist JOSEPH HILLIER. Messenger is 23 feet (7 metres) tall, 30 feet (9 metres) wide and weighs ten tonnes.

NORTH CORNWALL

The golden and unpeopled bays
The shadowy cliffs and sheep-worn ways

Sir John Betjeman

Bude Castle

Morwenstow

EVERYTHING PETERS OUT at the church at MORWENSTOW. The road peters out into a cliff path. Cornwall peters out into Devon, this being Cornwall's most northerly parish, and England peters out altogether, as there is no more land to the west between here and America, just ocean. This is the wild West Country: bare fields, tall, broken cliffs, Atlantic rollers, seagulls.

St Morwenna's Church

The robust, grey-turreted, 15th-century tower of St Morwenna's church peeps out from a fold above a steep combe that runs down to the sea. There was a Celtic church here marking the grave of St Morwenna, who was one of the many children of the 5th-century Celtic king Brychan and who evangelised throughout Cornwall. Surviving from that Celtic church, and now standing at the west end of the present building, is a gorgeously primitive tub font with carved cable moulding tied around the middle like a belt. You enter the church through a rugged Norman doorway sheltered by a rugged Norman porch, both having rugged Norman arches carved with numerous zig-zags, flowers, pine cones and beasts including a mermaid, dragon, dolphin and whale. Inside and out, St Morwenna's is renowned

for some of the most superlative Norman sculpture to be found in any English church.

Three bays of the north arcade are Norman, consisting of some of Cornwall's best Norman arches, each adorned with many heads, including those of a monk, an antelope and a hippopotamus. One of the capitals of the Perpendicular south arcade is inscribed with the words, '*This is the House of the Lord*', carved upside down so that it can be read by the angels in Heaven. There are over 100 medieval bench ends and over a mile of wonderfully carved wooden roofing.

On the north wall of the chancel are traces of a 15th-century wall painting, thought to be of the church's patron saint and founder Morwenna.

A Poet Parson

In the south aisle is the Hawker Memorial Window, dedicated in 1904 and showing Morwenstow's famous parson with his dog. ROBERT STEPHEN HAWKER was vicar of Morwenstow from 1834 until his death in 1875. When he arrived, the church and parish had been long neglected: remote and inaccessible, they were battered by Atlantic storms and populated mainly by smugglers and wreckers, who enjoyed rich pickings from the many ships that were cast on the rocks of this merciless coastline. Hawker put a stop to the wreckers and made sure that seamen washed up on the shore were given a Christian burial in St Morwenna's churchyard. The figurehead of the *Caledonia*, wrecked on the coast in 1842 in the first major disaster of Hawker's tenancy, hangs on a wall inside the church as a memorial.

Hawker is remembered for his eccentricities as well as his compassion. He talked to the birds, wore fishermen's boots under his cassock, sometimes dressed up as a mermaid with seaweed for hair, took his pigs for long walks and brought his nine cats into church, despite excommunicating one of them for catching mice on a Sunday.

He built the nearby vicarage and modelled the chimneys on the tower at Magdalen, his Oxford college, and the towers of the churches where he had served were modelled after Tamerton, where he was curate, Welcombe, next door in Devon, and Morwenstow.

One of Hawker's many accomplishments was THE INVENTION OF THE HARVEST FESTIVAL in the modern Christian tradition. In 1843, on 1 October, he invited his parishioners to a special service of

Thanksgiving for the harvest and encouraged them to decorate the church with their home-grown produce, while he also served Communion bread made from the first cut of corn. The idea was copied at other churches in Devon and Cornwall and then spread rapidly throughout England.

Not far away from the church on the coast halfway down the HENNA CLIFF – which at 472 feet (144 metres) is THE SECOND TALLEST SHEER CLIFF IN ENGLAND after Beachy Head – is MORWENNA'S WELL, a little stone dwelling where Morwenna lived in perfect isolation 1,500 years ago. Until recently it was possible to reach it down a steep path with the help of a rope, but the way is now overgrown with brambles and almost inaccessible, except for those with a bit of local knowledge.

THE BUSH INN at Morwenstow dates from the 13th century, making it already one of the oldest pubs in Cornwall, but there has been some sort of tavern on the site since as far back as AD 950. Naturally, it is haunted ...

HAWKER'S HUT

Robert Hawker was also something of a poet and he built himself a small hut made out of driftwood on the edge of the cliffs, where he could sit and write and meditate, 'communing with St Morwenna' (usually while smoking opium). Here he composed the unofficial Cornish anthem 'Trelawny', or 'The Song of the Western Men', which includes these famous lines:

And shall Trelawny die?
Here's twenty thousand Cornish men
Will know the reason why!

Hawker even entertained fellow poets such as ALFRED, LORD TENNYSON and CHARLES KINGSLEY in his hut, which can still be reached via a path over the stile opposite the church porch. It is now looked after by and is THE SMALLEST PROPERTY OWNED BY THE NATIONAL TRUST.

Hawker's Hut

Bude

BUDE was once a busy port but today is a largely Victorian resort based around the golden sands of Summerleaze Beach, which as with so many of the beaches in North Cornwall, is pounded by white-tipped Atlantic rollers, formerly the bane of sailors but popular nowadays with surfers.

Overlooking the beach, atop its own sand dune, is BUDE CASTLE, constructed in 1830 and THE FIRST PERMANENT STRUCTURE IN THE WORLD TO BE BUILT ON SHIFTING SANDS. It was the work of the Cornish scientist and inventor SIR GOLDSWORTHY GURNEY (1793–1875), who overcame the unstable nature of the ground by laying a concrete platform directly on to the sand as a base for the foundations. The technique is still widely used in the modern construction industry, an example being what were once the world's tallest buildings, the Petronas Towers in Kuala Lumpur, Malaysia, which were built on soft, wet limestone using Gurney's method. His story is told in Bude Castle's Heritage Centre and in this book on page 154.

Bude Canal

Below the castle a sea lock, one of the last working locks of its kind in Britain, guards the entrance to the Bude Canal, THE MOST WESTERLY OF BRITAIN'S MAJOR CANALS. It was built in 1823 to transport

lime-rich Bude sand, used in fertiliser, to Launceston, 35 miles away. The first part of the canal rose over 400 feet in six miles using inclined ramps, up which wheeled tub boats were hauled on metal rails. The tubs were hooked on to a long chain driven by a waterwheel. The Bude Canal is THE LONGEST TUB BOAT CANAL EVER BUILT. The sea lock still works and the two-mile stretch of the canal to the bottom of the first incline can be followed along the towpath.

Sir Goldsworthy Gurney

Born at Treator near Padstow in 1793, GOLDSWORTHY GURNEY was a distant cousin of the Norfolk Gurneys, who founded what later became Barclays Bank, and so was wealthy enough to devote himself to science and invention. A meeting with fellow Cornishman, steam pioneer Richard Trevithick (see page 170), fired his enthusiasm and his first invention was the blast-pipe, a high-pressure steam jet (later adapted by George Stephenson for his *Rocket*) which he used to power a road-going steam engine with a passenger carriage in tow called a Gurney drag. In 1829 this travelled from London to Bath at an average speed of 15mph in THE FIRST LONG JOURNEY BY A SELF-PROPELLED VEHICLE AT A SUSTAINED SPEED ANYWHERE IN THE WORLD. Gurney established a daily service between Cheltenham and Gloucester, THE

WORLD'S FIRST REGULAR STEAM-PROPELLED COACH SERVICE, but was bankrupted when rival horse-drawn carriage owners forced the government to impose a ruinous tax on his enterprise.

Gurney returned to Cornwall and set about building himself a family home on the dunes of Bude beach, for which he devised a concrete raft to provide firm foundations. The result, Bude Castle, still stands today.

Gurney lit his new house with a revolutionary lighting system created by forcing a mixture of oxygen and hydrogen through a blowpipe to produce a hot flame and then adding lime to make the light burn especially bright: LIMELIGHT. Using just one limelight and a series of mirrors and lenses, he was able to light the whole house and he developed just such a set-up to light the Houses of Parliament in place of the thousands of candles required previously. His limelight was also used in a revolving frame to improve the intensity and visibility of lighthouses, saving thousands of lives, and in the theatre – the origin of the phrase to be *'in the limelight'*.

Amongst his other inventions were the steam cleaner, ventilation systems for mines and sewers, and the Gurney stove for heating large buildings, still in use in Tewkesbury Abbey and Chester, Ely and Durham cathedrals.

St Swithin's Church, Launcells

Launcells

Sir Goldsworthy Gurney is buried five miles away from Bude in the churchyard of ST SWITHIN at Launcells, a church considered by John Betjeman to be the '*least spoiled church in Cornwall*'. It is tucked away in a dell down its own sunken lane, just the tips of the high, turreted tower waving above the hedgerows. The Victorian restorers missed it and hence what we see today is the unblemished artistry of Cornish 14th- and 15th-century builders.

The ancient door swings open to reveal a church that is nearly as wide as it is long, with a nave and two aisles, each with their own lovely waggon roofs, the aisles boasting elaborately carved ribs and bosses, the nave roof plain. The arcades are different from one another, the north one of granite, the south made with Cornish stone from the quarries of Polyphant, near Launceston.

The floor of the chancel is set with 15th-century glazed tiles from Barnstaple showing lions, griffins, pelicans and flowers. Next door, at the east end of the south aisle, is the grand Jacobean monument of Sir John Chamond (d.1624), who is shown in effigy lying sideways, with his head on his hand and a rather puffy look on his face. There is a Georgian pulpit with a tester and some box pews in the north aisle, while high on the north wall are traces of a painted text, part of a letter written by Charles I in 1643 in which he thanks his loyal Cornish subjects for their support against the Roundheads.

There is also an extremely rare post-Reformation wall painting dated to 1680, but what really takes the breath away is the dazzling carving on the Tudor pews, rich and sumptuous as icing on a chocolate cake. Cornish churches are renowned for their wood carvings, and these are

amongst the best. The first and last pews are decorated along their fronts and backs while the others, some 30 in all, are decorated at each end. The carvings show the Instruments of the Passion such as the Crown of Thorns, the Nails of the Cross and the Thirty Pieces of Silver, and allegories of Biblical stories such as the Ascension (with Christ's feet disappearing into the clouds) and Easter Day, with Christ the gardener represented by a spade. There is not a human figure amongst them – it is great fun to go around the pews attempting to interpret the pictures, although the temples do start to throb after a while.

If you need to take a break then you could do worse that go out into the churchyard and have a look at the grave of Sir Goldsworthy Gurney, Cornwall's forgotten genius (see page 154).

ST SWITHIN'S WELL, in the woods beside the church, is reputed to never run dry and the waters are said to be good for the eyes.

Boscastle

From Padstow Bar to Lundy Light

Is a sailor's grave by day or night.

So say the locals of this perilous stretch of the Cornish/Devon coast. BOSCASTLE is the only haven for 20 miles along the coast, a natural inlet that twists and turns past rocky headlands to an inner harbour protected by walls built by Sir Richard Grenville (see page 53) in 1584. Even so, the harbour can only be entered when the sea is calm – when the river in spate meets the incoming tide, the result is awesome. Either side of low tide the DEVIL'S BELLOWS, a natural blowhole at the harbour entrance, roars like a volcano as it spews out a spectacular horizontal jet of water.

The harbour lies in a deep cleft, and the village streets creep up the steep hillside past sturdy stone cottages and rushing waters. At the bottom is the celebrated MUSEUM OF WITCHCRAFT AND MAGIC, home to THE WORLD'S LARGEST COLLECTION OF ITEMS RELATING TO WITCHCRAFT, MAGIC AND THE OCCULT, which was transferred here from the Isle of Man by CECIL WILLIAMSON in 1960. He chose Cornwall since the county has a reputation as a land of legend and mystery – certainly, when the seas are raging and the wind howling, it is quite easy to imagine broomsticks and wizards and ghouls swooping over the clifftops. Indeed, the nearby 16th-century WELLINGTON HOTEL is not just one of the oldest coaching inns in Cornwall but also one of the most haunted, with reported sightings of a ghostly coachman ...

On a slightly more sombre note, the village sits at the confluence of two rivers, the Valency and the Jordan, and in August 2004 heavy rain caused flash floods that hit the village at high tide, submerging the roads, sweeping cars into the harbour and demolishing the bridge. The resultant rescue operation became the biggest rescue operation ever conducted in Britain in peacetime. The disaster and its aftermath were caught on film as the BBC was at the time recording a documentary following the life of Boscastle's new rector, Rev Christine Musser, for the series *A Seaside Parish*.

Much of Boscastle and the surrounding land is owned by the National Trust, who run a shop and cafe overlooking the harbour.

Tintagel Castle

St Juliot

A couple of miles to the north-east, tucked away down a maze of narrow country lanes, lies ST JULIOT, a simple hamlet that has become a place of pilgrimage for fans of the author THOMAS HARDY, then an aspiring architect, who came here in 1870 to carry out restoration work on the church. He stayed at the Rectory and there fell in love with the rector's sister-in-law EMMA GIFFORD. They later married and Hardy's novel *A Pair of Blue Eyes* tells the tale of their romance. When Emma died in 1912, Hardy returned to St Juliot to place a memorial to her in the church and to write a series of poems honouring her memory, featuring the surrounding countryside where they had wandered together during their courtship.

Tintagel

The north Cornish coast is at its most romantic at TINTAGEL, a long straggling village set on the clifftops 300 feet (91 metres) above the sea and linked to a rocky headland by a thin strip of wave-lashed causeway. An ancient place dripping in mist and legend, the village sprang to fame in the 19th century thanks to Tennyson's *Idylls of the King*, which was written while he was staying in Tintagel. The poem cycle publicised Tintagel's links to King Arthur, first put forward in Geoffrey of Monmouth's imaginative *The History of the Kings of Britain*, written in the 12th century.

Tintagel means 'fortified neck of land' and while there is no proof that Tintagel was the birthplace of King Arthur, the dramatic scenery and atmospheric ruins cannot help but suggest that it could have been. A footpath leads from the village to the ruins of Tintagel Castle which was built in the 13th century for RICHARD, EARL OF CORNWALL, brother of Henry III, who was drawn to Tintagel by its Arthurian connections as chronicled by Geoffrey of Monmouth. The castle is split asunder by a deep crevice that separates the mainland from the island where the bulk of the castle lies. The original land bridge across the gap was washed away in the 15th century and for a long time visitors had to descend a steep staircase to a short bridge across the gap and then climb more steps up through the castle ruins to reach the top of the island, where there are the scant remains of a 6th-century Celtic monastery. A new bridge opened in 2019 and runs at the same height as the original crossing, thus avoiding the steps.

You can still follow the old steps down to the pebbly beach, known as the Haven, and explore MERLIN'S CAVE, where Arthur first met Merlin the Wizard.

North across the Haven from the island is the headland of BARRAS NOSE, which came to the National Trust in 1897 as THE NATIONAL TRUST'S FIRST ENGLISH COASTAL ACQUISITION. Looming just back from the headland is a huge, castle-like Victorian hotel now called the Camelot Castle, which was built in the late 19th century by the London and South Western Railway to accommodate passengers visiting Tintagel in search of King Arthur.

The highlight of the village itself is the OLD POST OFFICE, a gloriously crumpled and weather-beaten 14th-century yeoman's farmhouse which became a post office in the 19th century and is now owned by the National Trust.

St Materiana

Situated in splendid isolation on the cliffs to the south of Tintagel is the early Norman church of ST MATERIANA, occupying the site of an earlier 6th-century chapel. A stone inscribed with the name of the 4th-century Roman Emperor LICINIUS that was found nearby stands in the south transept, while out in the vast churchyard is the tomb of JOHN DOUGLAS COOK (d.1868), founding editor of the London weekly newspaper the *Saturday Review*.

Old Post Office

THE STORY OF KING ARTHUR AT TINTAGEL, AS TOLD BY GEOFFREY OF MONMOUTH

Uther Pendragon, a king of ancient Britain, lusts after Ygerna, wife of Gorlois of Cornwall. Gorlois sends Ygerna to the impregnable fortress at Tintagel for safety, and for a while this ruse thwarts the King, who then turns to his wizard, Merlin, for advice. Using a magic potion, Merlin alters Uther so that he looks just like Gorlois and in this guise Uther is granted access to the castle and Ygerna's bed. *That night she conceived Arthur, the most famous of men, who subsequently won great renown for his outstanding bravery.*

There is no doubt that the legend of King Arthur is based on a real Christian Celtic leader who emerged from the west in the 5th century to lead the British resistance against the invading pagan Saxons, just as Britain was being abandoned by the Romans, and who had some success in halting their advance with a famous victory at Mount Badon, thought to be somewhere near Bath. Arthur has since become a symbol of hope and courage for the English in times of adversity; in medieval days the warrior king became associated with the code of chivalry, brought over from France by the Plantagenet kings ('chivalry' being derived from the French word *'chevalier'* meaning 'knight', which in turn comes from *'cheval'*, the French for 'horse'). King Arthur and the Knights of the Round Table fused the soldier with the *chevalier* to create the definitive hero, claimed by the English and Welsh alike.

Tintagel also features in another medieval legend, that of Tristan and Isolde. Tristan, a Cornish knight, falls in love with the Irish princess Isolde, who is destined to be married to his uncle, King Mark of Cornwall, which inevitably leads to unfortunate consequences ending with the death of the lovers. Much of the action takes place at King Mark's royal fortress, none other than Tintagel.

Polzeath

A stone plaque set on the cliffs above POLZEATH, between Pentire Point and Rumps Point north of Padstow, commemorates the spot where some of the most moving lines of all time were inspired and composed.

They shall grow not old, as we that are left grow old:
Age shall not weary them, nor the years condemn.
At the going down of the sun and in the morning
We will remember them.

The words are from the poem 'For the Fallen', written in 1914 by LAURENCE BINYON (1869–1943), a poet and playwright who worked at the British Museum as an expert in Oriental art and literature and later volunteered to go to the Front to work for the Red Cross. They were written in honour of the soldiers of the British Expeditionary Force who died in the Battle of Mons and the Battle of Marne at the beginning of World War One, and have since been adopted as a tribute to all casualties of war from every nation, becoming an integral part of the Remembrance Day Services

St Enedoc Church

St Enodoc Church

*So grows the tinny tenor
  faint or loud.*

*All all things draw
toward St Enodoc.*

Sir John Betjemen

Plugged in the middle of a bunker on St Enodoc Golf Course at Tretherick, north of Padstow, sits the 12th-century CHURCH OF ST ENODOC, its stubby and twisted stone spire peeking arthritically above the dunes that protect it from the sea. Not too long ago the church was full of sand and the vicar and congregation had to be lowered in through the roof to attend services. St Enodoc, known affectionately as 'Sinking Neddy', is an eternal part of the landscape and the spectacle from the top of the dunes of church and greensward, sand and sea, is one of those timeless views of England that warm the heart.

It seems only fitting that the man who did more than most to celebrate and save the country churches of England should be buried here in one of the loveliest churchyards of them all. SIR JOHN BETJEMEN spent many happy holidays in Tretherick as a boy and returned in later life to buy a home here, where he died in 1984 aged 77. He was buried in the churchyard of his favourite church, St Enodoc, in a grave by the path near the lychgate. His mother lies nearby and there is a memorial to his father inside the church.

Also in the churchyard, in the corner furthest from the entrance gate, is a memorial tablet to FLEUR LOMBARD (1974–96), the first female firefighter to die in action in Britain. Placed on the seat in the south porch is a slate memorial to JOHN MABLY and his daughter ALICE who died within days of each other in 1687. Theirs is the last slab incised with effigies found in England.

Padstow

Once the most thriving port on Cornwall's north coast, PADSTOW's importance declined as the entrance to the RIVER CAMEL became blocked by the DOOM BAR, a large shifting sandbank that made the channel too shallow for larger boats and caused many shipwrecks. The Doom Bar has become famous worldwide as the name of the flagship ale of local brewers Sharp's, founded across the Camel at Rock in 1994. It is now sold across the world. In 2008 Doom Bar became THE FIRST EVER OFFICIAL BEER SPONSOR OF THE BOAT RACE – and is the favourite drink of J.K. Rowling's private detective, Cornishman Cormoran Strike, because it tastes of 'home, peace and long-gone security'.

In the 19th century, having declined as a port, Padstow was described as an *'antiquated, unsavoury fishing town'*. Today, although it retains the allure of a traditional fishing village, with its narrow streets and old weathered houses tumbling down to the harbour, Padstow is more of a 'fish and chip' town, prospering as a tourist destination. Many such tourists are attracted by the restaurants and cafes of TV chef RICK STEIN, to such degree that Padstow is often referred to as 'Padstein'.

The village is overlooked by PRIDEAUX PLACE, a fine Elizabethan house, with Strawberry Hill Gothic additions, that has been owned by the Prideaux family since it was built in 1592. The Great Chamber has what is considered one of the finest Elizabethan plastered ceilings in England while in the Armoury is ENGLAND'S OLDEST CAST-IRON CANNON, dating from the middle

of the 16th century. The deer park is home to one of the oldest herds of deer in England and legend has it that if the deer die out then so do the Prideaux family, so they are well looked after.

Prideaux Place appears frequently in the *Poldark* books of Winston Graham, who was a great friend of the Prideaux family and wrote much of his twelfth and last *Poldark* novel, *Bella Poldark*, while staying at Prideaux Place. A serious fire broke out in the house while he was there but fortunately Graham's handwritten manuscript was rescued from the flames.

Newquay

The 'new' quay that Cornwall's biggest resort sprang from dates from the 17th century, while the town that built up around it became rich on pilchards. A symbol of those days is the quaint, crooked, white-painted building that looks like a mini fort perched on the cliffs above the harbour. This is the unique Huer's Hut from which a 'huer' would scan the bay for the telltale signs of shoals of pilchards and upon spotting them would alert fishermen by crying 'heva, heva!' Once the fishing boats were launched the huer would direct the boats to the

location of the shoals, employing semaphore signals using furze bushes covered with some kind of cloth, visible from the sea.

The Huer's Hut stands on the site of a hermitage dating from the 14th century. The hermit was responsible for keeping alight a beacon for guiding shipping in the bay.

During the 19th century, as the pilchards moved away, so the tourists moved in, attracted by the town's nine sandy beaches and transported to Newquay by the railway which arrived in the 1870s. High on Towan Head, overlooking Fistral Beach, is one of the hotels built to cater for those tourists: the grand, monumental Victorian hotel the Headland, built in 1900 and similar in Gothic institutional appearance to the Camelot Castle at Tintagel. This was the location for the film of Roald Dahl's *The Witches* and featured in Rosamunde Pilcher's novel *The Shell Seekers*.

For those who want particularly exclusive accommodation there is THE HOUSE IN THE SEA, a hideaway cottage perched on top of Towan Island, an 80-foot-high rock outcrop on Newquay's Tolcarne Beach, which is cut off at high tide and reached only by a gated suspension bridge. It was built originally as a Victorian tearoom but converted to a three-bedroom house in the 1930s and was once owned by SIR OLIVER LODGE (1851–1940), the pioneer of electromagnetic waves and inventor of the spark plug. It is today available for holiday let at up to £6,000 a week.

Newquay today is renowned as THE SURFING CAPITAL OF BRITAIN and Fistral Beach hosts the annual English National Surfing Championships.

St Piran's Oratory

The walls of ST PIRAN'S ORATORY, one of the oldest known Christian churches in Britain, lie buried in the sands of Penhale Beach, north of Perranporth. The chapel was built by St Piran in the 6th century in thanks for his survival after he was exiled from Ireland. Apparently, having for some reason angered an Irish chieftain, he was thrown off a high cliff tied to a millstone, but instead of drowning he floated across the sea to Cornwall and landed at the spot now named Perranporth (Piran's port). His first Cornish convert was a badger, but he soon progressed to Cornish men and women who were impressed not just by his inspirational preaching but also by his prodigious ability to drink, a virtue that purportedly enabled him to live for over 200 years. He became the patron saint of Cornwall and especially of tin miners, and the Cornish flag is taken from St Piran's white cross on a black background.

By the 10th century St Piran's Oratory had been engulfed by sand, and a new church was built a little way further inland. This too was lost to the sand and abandoned in 1804. Both were excavated and in 1910 the chapel was covered by an ugly concrete structure to protect it from the elements and visitors who helped themselves to bits of the stonework as souvenirs. By 1980 everything was buried in sand once more and it wasn't until 2014 that money was raised to dig it out again. Today the oratory can be visited, although only from behind a locked gate. Every year on St Piran's Day, 5 March, hundreds of Cornish folk dressed in white, gold and black process to the chapel in celebration of the patron saint while festivities take place across Cornwall.

St Agnes

ST AGNES BEACON rises like a pyramid to a height of 629 feet above the town of ST AGNES. The view stretches from Newquay to St Ives and encompasses 32 churches. Beacons were lit on the summit in 1588 to warn of the approach of the Spanish Armada and during the Napoleonic Wars a guard was stationed there to look out for French ships. Beacons were lit again in 1977, 2002 and 2012 to celebrate Elizabeth II's Silver, Golden and Diamond Jubilees. The town of St Agnes has been at the centre of Cornwall's tin mining industry for 2,000 years and in the early 19th century the local Polperro mine employed more than 500 people, producing more tin than anywhere else in Britain and possibly the world. From Roman times until the 20th century, Cornwall was THE BIGGEST PRODUCER OF TIN IN EUROPE. Today, however, the BLUE HILLS MINE in St Agnes, which opened on site in 1974, is the last tin production centre in Britain.

The landscape around St Agnes is dotted with evocative ruins of engine houses and chimneys. Tumbled blocks of granite are all that remain of the harbour down in Trevaunance Cove from where the tin was shipped. In St Agnes itself, 18th-century houses of granite and slate line the streets while marching down the valley is a steeply stepped terrace of miners' cottages called STIPPY STAPPY, which features in the *Poldark* novels of Winston Graham – St Agnes becomes St Annes in the stories.

Wheal Coates

The remnants of the WHEAL COATES MINE buildings cling precariously to the cliffs south of St Agnes Head, creating a uniquely Cornish landscape. '*Wheal*' means 'workplace' and prefixes many a Cornish mine name.

Redruth

REDRUTH began life as a small village gathered around St Euny's church in what is now called Church Town. The village lies in a deep wooded valley with shallow lodes of tin and copper running through it; the river flowing through the valley was made red by the process of extracting the ores, hence the name Redruth. The 'red' in the place name actually means 'ford', from the Cornish word '*rhyd*', while the colour red comes from the Cornish word '*ruth*', hence 'Rhydruth' or 'ford-red'.

As the copper and tin mining industry grew, so Redruth expanded to the east and, together with Camborne to the south-west, became the centre of THE RICHEST MINING AREA IN BRITAIN.

Murdoch House

The jewel of Redruth is 17th-century MURDOCH HOUSE in Cross Street, formerly a chapel and prison. Small, grey and unassuming, Murdoch House is probably one of the most significant houses

in the world. Scottish engineer WILLIAM MURDOCH came to live here in 1782, his job to install and maintain the many Boulton and Watt steam engines used in the surrounding mines for pumping out water. He had a brilliant mind and was often years ahead of others in his ideas and in 1784, in the front room of Murdoch House, he stunned the invited guests by unveiling a tiny steam engine on wheels that ran around the room by itself in THE FIRST EVER DEMONSTRATION OF A SELF-PROPELLED STEAM ENGINE. This was THE FIRST SELF-PROPELLED VEHICLE THE WORLD HAD EVER SEEN and it changed everything – 2025 saw the 200th anniversary of the first journey ever made by a steam train carrying fee-paying passengers on a public railway, the Stockton and Darlington Railway, and it all began here in 1784, in MURDOCH HOUSE in Redruth. Later that year Murdoch built a full-size version, THE *FLYER*, which he ran through the streets of Redruth late at night, terrifying the local vicar who thought the hissing fiery apparition the Devil.

Murdoch was unable to interest his employers in his invention and he turned his talents elsewhere, coming up with another innovation he trialled at Murdoch House a few years later. In 1794 he built a closed coal fire in the garden and ran a pipe from it into the house, where he ignited the gas coming through from the burning coals to produce light. Thus, Murdoch House became THE FIRST HOUSE IN THE WORLD TO HAVE GAS LIGHTING.

Murdoch House now houses archives of the Cornish diaspora and is open to the public on Fridays or by appointment. It should be better known and celebrated as one of the most important places that gave birth to the modern world.

Camborne

Like its neighbour Redruth, the mining and market town of Camborne has played its part in the story of steam propulsion, thanks to the Cornish Giant, engineer RICHARD TREVITHICK, a colossus of a man whose party trick was to throw a sledgehammer over an engine shed. Trevithick was born in a cottage in TREGAJORRAN, a small village between Redruth and Camborne, in 1771 and the site of his birthplace is marked by a stone plaque.

Richard Trevithick

Trevithick, the son of a miner and born into the world's most prolific mining community, grew up fascinated by mining and the technological challenges faced by the industry. As a youngster he watched on goggle-eyed as William Murdoch demonstrated his '*Flyer*' through the streets of Redruth. Unlike Murdoch's employers, Boulton and Watt, he could see the potential and went away determined to invent his own steam carriage. This he did and on Christmas Eve 1801 Trevithick's '*PUFFIN' DEVIL*' carried six passengers through the streets of Camborne and up Camborne Hill, the steepest hill in town, a feat beyond any horse-drawn carriage.

THIS WAS THE FIRST TIME ANYONE HAD BEEN CONVEYED ANYWHERE BY STEAM and a plaque at the bottom of the hill marks the starting point of this momentous journey. From there you can follow *Puffin' Devil*'s route up the hill to where another plaque commemorates the conclusion of the ground-breaking achievement. Two years later Trevithick constructed THE WORLD'S FIRST HIGH-PRESSURE STEAM LOCOMOTIVE TO RUN ON RAILS which, in 1804 at Merthyr Tydfil in South Wales, completed THE WORLD'S FIRST EVER STEAM-POWERED RAILWAY JOURNEY.

Camborne is proud of its pioneering son and a statue of Trevithick gazing up the hill stands in front of Camborne Library. The Cornish Giant was a giant in more ways than one, but in the grand old tradition, the man who gave the world the gift of locomotion never made a penny from his invention. The glory went to others who knew how to exploit

Puffin' Devil

it, while Trevithick died broke and is buried in a pauper's grave in Dartford in Kent.

William Bickford (1774–1834)

Another West Countryman whose brilliance made mining safer and saved countless lives in Cornwall and all over the world was WILLIAM BICKFORD. Born in Ashburton in Devon, Bickford joined the leather trade and moved from Devon to Illogan, north of Redruth, to set up a leather business at the centre of Cornwall's mining industry, which required leather for miners' helmets, boots and gloves.

Bickford became appalled at the injuries and loss of life caused by uncontrolled explosions of gunpowder in the mines and determined to find a way to lessen the risk. Most of the injuries were caused by unreliable fuses and after watching a friend making rope by twisting strands of fibre tightly together, Bickford came up with the idea of making a fuse by winding strands of rope around a central core of gunpowder. The rope was then varnished and, when lit, the fuse burned at a steady pace. HE HAD INVENTED THE SAFETY FUSE.

Bickford took out a patent for his new safety fuse in 1831 and set up a factory in TUCKINGMILL just outside Camborne but died before the factory opened. His business partner GEORGE SMITH took the company on and in its first year the Bickford–Smith fuse factory produced 45 miles of fuse and would go on to become the world's leading producer of fuses until the invention of electrical fuses in the early 20th century.

In 1836, Richard Bacon from Connecticut travelled to Tuckingmill to obtain the American patent for the safety fuse and the company he established still exists as ENSIGN-BICKFORD which works on the testing and production of safety products with NASA and the aerospace and defence industries.

In Cornwall, the factory was run by dynamite manufacturer Nobel Industries from 1926 until it closed in 1962. The factory site on Pendarves Road in Tuckingmill is now derelict and undergoing redevelopment although the smart stone office facades and entrance gates to THE WORLD'S FIRST SAFETY FUSE FACTORY are still there and, being listed, will remain so for the future.

CORNWALL'S MINING HERITAGE

Cornwall has been mined for thousands of years, certainly since the Bronze Age (2100–750 BC), when copper and tin were needed for making bronze. In Roman times, the world came to Cornwall for tin, and before then, the Phoenicians.

In 1201 the Stannary Charter gave miners the right to mine for tin anywhere in Cornwall, even on private land. Miners were subject to their own stannary laws and taxes, which continued into the 19th century, and could only be arrested and judged by the Lord Warden of the Stannaries.

The Cornish mines became a testing ground for all sort of technological advances, from gunpowder in the 17th century, which enabled miners to blast through granite that before had been impenetrable, to steam engines in the 18th century, which could pump out water from the mines and allow the miners to dig deeper.

By the middle of the 19th century, two thirds of the world's copper came from Cornwall and at the same time Cornwall produced more than half the world's arsenic, a by-product from the processing of copper and tin, which is used in paint and insecticide. Miners would have to cover their skin with clay and their faces with rags to protect themselves from the poison.

The many Cornish mining sites, along with those in West Devon, make up the Cornwall and West Devon Mining Landscape, Britain's largest industrial UNESCO World Heritage Site, covering almost 50,000 acres.

Notable Mines near Camborne and Redruth

Tresavean Mine. In the early 19th century, the Gwennap mining district five miles southeast of Redruth was known the richest copper mining district in Cornwall, which probably means in the whole world, as at that time Cornwall was supplying two thirds of the world's copper.

On 5 January 1842 THE WORLD'S FIRST MAN ENGINE was installed at the Tresavean Mine in Gwennap. Based on an idea from Germany, it was the work of a Cornish engineer called Michael Loam (1797–1871) and was designed to relieve miners of the back-breaking climb down ladders to the mine face, which could be up to 2,000 feet below the surface. The man engine was an early kind of lift consisting of a series of stepped wooden rods which were moved up and down between platforms fixed to the wall of the mine shaft. The miner would step off a platform onto a moving rod, get off at the next platform and wait for the next rod and so on. The whole caboosh was powered in the early days by a waterwheel and, although slow, it was safer and less exhausting than climbing ladders. The first ever lift accident occurred in 31 September 1843 when a 14-year-old miner missed his step and plunged 100 feet to his death. Steam engines soon replaced waterwheels and made the lifts much faster and eventually cages were provided to keep the men from falling. The last man engine was dismantled at the Levant Mine near St Just in 1919 (see page 184).

South Crofty Mine, midway between Camborne and Redruth, began production in the late 16th century and closed in 1998, THE LAST CORNISH TIN MINE TO CLOSE. The mine is now owned by Cornish Metals who are looking to re-open the mine as it produces exceptionally high-grade tin, much sought after globally.

Dolcoath Mine, east of Camborne, was known as 'the Queen of Cornish Mines', and by the middle of the 19th century was THE RICHEST AND LARGEST MINE IN CORNWALL. It was also THE DEEPEST MINE IN THE WORLD reaching a depth of 3,330 feet (1,000 metres).

THE CORNISH PASTY

The Cornish pasty, meat and vegetables baked together in a pastry casing, evolved as a convenient way of providing the tin miners with a complete meal that was easy to handle while working down in the dark, narrow tunnels. The miners' initials would be raised on the pastry casing so that each one could be recognised by touch, with the initials at one end so that if only half the pasty was eaten the other half could still be recognised. The pasties also had a crimped edge which served as a convenient handle, allowing the miners to eat the pasty without their dirty fingers, possibly laced with arsenic, touching the food.

Originally, the pasty would have contained meat and vegetables in one half and fruit in the other half. The traditional filling now is beef, onion and potato although pretty much any filling is considered acceptable these days – except fish. Cornish fishermen refused to take pasties to sea as they were thought to bring bad luck, a superstition put about by the miners who wanted to keep their pasties for themselves.

Hard-up Cornish miners' wives were known to put almost anything into a pasty, even the Devil himself, and as a result the Devil is fearful of entering Cornwall in case he ends up as a filling in a Cornish pasty.

Cornish miners were in demand around the world for their mining expertise and wherever they went they took their pasty with them, hence the dish is known far and wide – but only a pasty actually made in Cornwall is allowed to call itself a Cornish pasty.

WELL, I NEVER KNEW THIS ABOUT
NORTH CORNWALL

Just outside Bude is EBBINGFORD MANOR, a private home dating back some 850 years and said to have THE SMALLEST PRIVATE CHAPEL IN ENGLAND.

WIDEMOUTH BAY, two miles south of Bude, is rumoured to be where the 'hotline' between 10 Downing Street in London and the White House in Washington, DC comes ashore.

HIGH CLIFF, eight miles south of Bude beyond Crackington Haven, rises sheer from the sea for 735 feet, CORNWALL'S HIGHEST CLIFF and THE HIGHEST SHEER CLIFF IN SOUTHERN ENGLAND.

Four miles south of Tintagel is the village of Delabole, home of DELABOLE QUARRY, almost 500 feet deep and over one and a half miles around, THE LARGEST SLATE QUARRY IN ENGLAND. DELABOLE has been operating continuously since at least the 15th century, possibly since the time of King Stephen in the 12th century, and is still being worked, making it also THE OLDEST WORKING SLATE QUARRY IN ENGLAND.

At 800 feet (240 metres) above sea level Delabole is the third highest village in Cornwall and one of the windiest, and in 1991 became the site of THE UK'S FIRST COMMERCIAL ONSHORE WIND FARM, THE DELABOLE WIND FARM.

PORT ISAAC is one of the few working fishing villages on Cornwall's north coast and has found fame

as the setting for the popular ITV series *Doc Martin*. It is a beautiful, almost unspoilt Cornish village of whitewashed overhanging 18th-century fisherman's cottages bedecked with flowers and streets so narrow that two people can scarcely pass without breathing in. SQUEEZY BELLY ALLEY, impassable to those who have just indulged in a Cornish cream tea is said to be THE NARROWEST THOROUGHFARE IN ENGLAND, with an average width of just 18 inches (46 centimetres).

'*St Endellion! St Endellion! The name is like a ring of bells*,' said Sir John Betjeman, and the name was certainly music to the ears of former prime minister DAVID CAMERON and his wife SAMANTHA, who named their daughter FLORENCE ROSE ENDELLION after this tiny Cornish village near Port Isaac. They were on holiday in nearby Rock when she was born. The large 15th-century Perpendicular church, once the parish church of Port Isaac, is dedicated to St Endelienta, another of the daughters of the 5th-century Welsh king Brychan (see Morwenstow, page 150) and supposedly a god-daughter of King Arthur. Nearby to Endellion are two of Cornwall's oldest farms, both used as film locations and offering self-catering accommodation, ROSCARROCK, built by Nicholas Roscarrock in the 14th century, and the battlemented 17th-century TRESUNGERS, built around a 13th-century core.

In 2012 PRINCE WILLIAM and PRINCE HARRY were spotted surfing off POLZEATH, and since then the village has become a popular spot for celebrities such as Chris Martin from Coldplay, thought to own a property there, and regular sightings of the likes of Gwyneth Paltrow, Stanley Tucci and Hugh Grant. In 2024 Polzeath was named BRITAIN'S POSHEST SEASIDE VILLAGE in a *Daily Telegraph* survey.

ROCK, a small fishing village across the River Camel from Padstow, has THE HIGHEST PERCENTAGE OF SECOND HOMES IN CORNWALL. The village is home to SHARP'S BREWERY, whose flagship ale, Doom Bar, named after a sandbar at the entrance to the Camel estuary, has been named by former prime minister David Cameron as his favourite ale.

The village of ILLOGAN just north of Redruth is the site of the only substantial Roman remains discovered west of Exeter, consisting of the remnants of a small Roman villa along with a stretch of Roman pavement, 25 feet long and 8 feet wide.

CHESTEN MARCHANT, who died in 1676 at Gwithian, a small village on the north edge of St Ives Bay, IS THE LAST PERSON KNOWN TO HAVE SPOKEN ONLY CORNISH AND NO ENGLISH. Apparently, she lived to the age of 164, a good advertisement for the bracing Cornish sea air.

GODREVY POINT sits at the northern end of four miles of golden sands stretching south-west to Hayle and commands spectacular views of St Ives Bay and Godrevy Island. The lighthouse on the island was the inspiration for Virginia Woolf's novel *To the Lighthouse*. It was erected there in 1859 after the foundering five years earlier of the steamship SS *Nile*, which hit the Stones, a submerged reef beyond the island, and sank with the loss of all 40 passengers and crew. On 30 January 1649, on the very day Charles I was executed, a ship called the *Garland*, carrying the King's wardrobe and personal effects to France, was driven onto the rocks of Godrevy Island and sank, with the loss of all on board save for one man, one boy and a dog who all survived.

WEST CORNWALL

With Hal-An-Tow! Jolly Rumble O!
For we are up as soon as any day. O!
And for to fetch the summer home,
The Summer and the May, O!
For Summer is a-come, O!
And Winter is a-gone, O!

From the Helston Furry Dance

St Ives

St Ives

ST IVES WAS founded in the 6th century by St Ia, an Irish princess who floated across from Ireland on a leaf and built an oratory where St Ia's parish church now stands. The current church dates from the reign of Henry V (1413–22) and has remained pretty much unchanged since then. Old St Ives lies sandwiched between two wide sandy beaches, leaving no room for expansion, thus it has kept its ancient allure and its picturesque maze of colourful sea-blown cobbled streets. This colour and charm, along with the light reflected off the Cornish sea, has long attracted artists like J.M.W. Turner, James McNeill Whistler and Walter Sickert, and since 1928 when local artist Alfred Wallis and his contemporaries founded the St Ives School colony of artists, has been considered a major centre for British art.

It may look like a film set today, but St Ives was once a tough, rugged fishing port, forever battling with the sea and the storms. The glorious setting and the work of the many artists has softened and colour-washed the hard edges of the town, although a certain rigour is still required to fight one's way along the heaving narrow streets and alleyways at the height of summer.

In 1920 BERNARD LEACH, the '*Father of British Studio Pottery*', and Japanese potter SHOJI HAMADA, with whom Leach had studied pottery in Japan, founded the LEACH POTTERY in St Ives, combining the pottery skills of East and West for which Leach became famous. In 1922 Leach and Hamada invited TSURONOSUKE MATSUBAYASHI, an engineer and kiln specialist from the Asahi pottery family of Kyoto, to come to St Ives to design and build a triple-chambered kiln in the traditional Japanese manner, THE FIRST JAPANESE CLIMBING KILN IN THE WESTERN WORLD. The Leach Pottery is considered the global birthplace of studio pottery and potters, students and apprentices still come to St Ives from across the world to train and study.

Sculptor BARBARA HEPWORTH moved to St Ives from her native Yorkshire in 1939 and created a studio in a lovely house on the hill behind the parish church. She died there in a fire in 1975 and her studio was opened as a museum in her memory the following year, in 1976. Barbara drew her inspiration from the stark Cornish landscape and many of her favourite pieces can be seen amongst the flowers and palms in the garden. I am not always a fan of modern sculpture but there is one piece in the garden that frames a view of the town and the sea beyond that is perhaps the most beautiful vision of Cornwall to be found anywhere. I hope they never move it.

The BARBARA HEPWORTH MUSEUM has been managed since 1980 by the Tate, who opened their own gallery in St Ives in 1993 to showcase local artists.

A battery built to defend the town from Napoleon and a simple 14th-century chapel dedicated to the patron saint of sailors, ST NICHOLAS, enjoy panoramic views from the promontory called the Island, at the north end of the town. During the 18th century, excisemen would hide in the chapel waiting to spring out on any passing smugglers, though they never had much success because the leader of the smugglers was an eccentric fellow called JOHN KNILL who also happened to be the Mayor of St Ives and the local customs collector.

Knill clearly collected a lot of customs fees because he had his own 50-foot (15 metres) monument, a granite obelisk resembling a church steeple, built on a hill overlooking St Ives. Intended as a mausoleum, it was designed for him by John Wood the Younger, the architect of the Royal Crescent in Bath. Knill also set aside funds for a ceremony to be held every five years on the Day of St James the Apostle whereby the Mayor of

Krill Monument

St Ives, a custom's officer and a vicar, accompanied by a fiddler playing the Furry Dance and ten young dancing girls dressed in white from the 'families of fishermen', set off from the Guildhall and dance through the streets of St Ives to the Knill Steeple. Although it was meant to commemorate him after his death, John Knill lived another ten years and attended the first ceremony in person. And he never got to take up residence in his mausoleum, being buried in St Andrew's Holborn in London instead. Nevertheless, the Knill Steeple provides a handy navigational aid for shipping and Knill's ceremony is still held every five years to this day.

Down on the harbour front, THE SLOOP INN has been around since 1312, one of the oldest inns in Cornwall. The present building is 17th century.

Zennor Mermaid

Zennor

At the end of the alphabet and at the end of the world, storm-lashed ZENNOR sits 300 feet (91 metres) above the sea in a bleak and extraordinarily beautiful landscape of small rock-strewn fields separated by thick granite walls. It is all too easy in this mysterious place to believe the story illustrated on the Mermaid Chair, a carved medieval wooden chair that stands by the altar in the church of St Senara after whom Zennor is named. The carving shows a rather Rubenesque mermaid holding a mirror and a comb, and the story goes that a beautiful young woman called Morveren who never seemed to age would attend mass in the church from time to time, sitting in that very chair listening to the choir boys sing, and then disappear. She became smitten by the pure singing voice of one particular choir boy called Matthew Trewhella and lured him down to Pendour Cove under the high cliffs of Zennor Head and out to sea. The two of them were never seen again. Although sometimes, on warm summer nights, they can be heard singing of their love together across the waves. It is said that if their voices are high the sea will be calm, while if their voices are low then rough seas can be expected.

St Just

ST JUST IS ENGLAND'S MOST WESTERLY TOWN and is possibly named after St Justus, the 4th Archbishop of Canterbury. Inside the church can be found a stone dating from the 6th century bearing the Latin inscription '*Selus Ic Iacet*,' meaning 'Selus lies here'. Selus is thought to be the brother of St Justus.

At the centre of town lies a *plain-an-gwary*, Cornish for 'a place for plays' – a round amphitheatre where Cornish mystery plays were performed in the 16th and 17th centuries. Later it was used for Cornish wrestling, an ancient sport for which Cornishmen have been renowned for centuries: at the Battle of Agincourt, soldiers from Cornwall marched behind a banner depicting two wrestlers.

St Just's oldest pub, the 18th century STAR INN, with its flagstone floors and old beams, just serves drinks, no food other than a bag of crisps, and is sometimes called the last proper pub in Cornwall.

Tin Mining

St Just was an important centre for the mining of copper and tin and lies within the CORNISH MINING WORLD HERITAGE SITE. Tin and copper mining in Cornwall dates back to prehistoric and Roman times, and by 1800 Cornwall was the world's largest producer of copper. With the discovery of copper deposits elsewhere in the world, the Cornish copper industry collapsed but tin mining was revived for a time, although this too ceased by the end of the 19th century. Scattered along the coastline near St Just are the starkly derelict buildings of old tin and copper mines.

The tunnels of the BOTALLACK MINE, which closed in 1895, went far out under the sea and the miners could hear the pebbles being scraped along the seabed above their heads by the tide. What remains is a picturesque grouping of old mine buildings perched on the edge of the cliff that is often used for filming – including the BBC television series *Poldark*. The site is owned by the National Trust.

Also owned by the National Trust is the LEVANT MINE where you can see THE ONLY WORKING STEAM-POWERED CORNISH BEAM ENGINE IN SITU IN THE WORLD. It was built in 1840 and was fitted with an early sort of lift called a man engine (see page 173). The idea for man engines came from Germany and the

first one in Britain was installed at the Tresavean Mine at Gwennap near Redruth in 1842. At the Levant Mine it took about 30 minutes to descend the main shaft via 130 platforms. In 1919 the mine, whose main shaft was 2,000 feet deep, with levels reaching out more than a mile under the Atlantic Ocean, was the scene of a devastating accident when the man engine broke and 31 miners died falling down the shaft. The Levant man engine was the last surviving such lift and was closed after the accident.

The nearby GEEVOR MINE, also now owned by the National Trust, closed in 1990 after 300 years, the last but one Cornish tin mine to close and THE LAST SURVIVING EXAMPLE OF A COMPLETE 20TH-CENTURY CORNISH TIN MINE as well as THE LARGEST PRESERVED MINE SITE IN BRITAIN. It now houses the Tin Mining Museum and visitors can take a guided underground tour of an 18th-century mine.

Across the moor to the northeast of St Just, high on a hill with glorious views towards Penzance, are the three remaining engine houses of CORNWALL'S OLDEST MINE: THE DING DONG MINE, named after the bells of nearby MADRON CHURCH which would ring out to signal the miners' last shift. Ding Dong was the first mine where Richard Trevithick tried out his steam engine for pumping water out of mines, which eventually made deeper mines possible, leading to the expansion and greater profitability of the mining industry – a significant step in the story of the Industrial Revolution. The remains of the Count (Account) House from where he worked can be seen nearby.

Sennen

Sennen, a scattered community set high above the sea overlooking a deep cove and a long sandy beach popular with surfers, is THE MOST WESTERLY VILLAGE IN MAINLAND BRITAIN. The 13th-century church of St Sennen's stands aloof across fields to the south, and is BRITAIN'S MOST WESTERLY CHURCH, its squat turreted tower facing across the ocean to America.

In September 1497, the good folk of Sennen found themselves mixed up in politics when pretender to the throne of Henry VII, PERKIN WARBECK, who claimed to be Richard

Duke of York, younger son of Edward IV and one of the Princes in the Tower, landed in Sennen Cove and persuaded some of the local fishermen to join him in the march against Henry. They were open to such persuasion because Henry had raised taxes to fight a war against Scotland and, at the same time, after disagreements over new regulations, suspended the operation and privileges of the Cornish mining industry leading to much hardship. Many disgruntled Cornishmen and much of the Cornish gentry joined Warbeck and they got as far as Taunton before Warbeck deserted them and fled, leaving them forced to surrender. The ringleaders were executed and the rest fined.

First and Last

Just past the church, for those heading south towards Land's End, is the last inn in England. Just before the church, for those heading north away from Land's End, is the first inn in England. To avoid confusion the sign over the front door says THE FAMOUS FIRST AND LAST. This wonderful old inn, dating from 1620, was once the headquarters of Sennen's smuggling and shipwrecking industry and 'the resort of all the idle blackguards in the county'. The wreckers were far from idle though, keeping themselves busy by luring unsuspecting ships onto the rocks off Land's End and relieving them of their cargo which they would stash in the First and Last, carrying the loot through a series of

tunnels dug between the inn and the coast. The entrance to one of these tunnels, known as ANNIE'S WELL, can still be seen in the inn, now covered by a sheet of glass.

Who Was Annie?
Well, at the end of the 18th century the inn was owned by a wealthy farmer called DIONYSIUS WILLIAMS, who was also head of the smuggling operation run from the First and Last. He leased the pub to a couple called JOSEPH AND ANNIE GEORGE who acted as his smuggling agents. There's no honour amongst thieves, however, and Annie decided to blackmail their landlord and stop paying the rent. When Williams tried to evict them, Annie shopped him to the authorities and Williams was arrested and sentenced to a long jail sentence. This ploy worked so well that Annie began to sneak on the other smugglers in the village, until eventually they turned on her and took her down to the cove, where they staked her to the rocks covered in fishing nets to be left until she drowned. They then carried her body back to her bedroom at the inn to await burial in an unmarked grave in the churchyard next door.

Guests at the First and Last can stay in ANNIE'S ROOM should they so wish, but those who have done so tell of nightmares where they find themselves trapped in a net and slowly drowning ...

Land's End

At LAND'S END, THE MOST WESTERLY AND SOUTH-WESTERLY POINT ON THE ENGLISH MAINLAND, England falls dramatically 200 feet (61 metres) down granite cliffs into the sea. Here,

more than anywhere else in England, you can feel you are unmistakably at the End. The best time to savour the view out to the Longships Lighthouse and experience the mysterious atmosphere of this ancient place is at dawn or dusk, when the crowds are absent and the only sounds are the cries of the gulls and the roar of the Atlantic rising up out of the Celtic mist. Then it is truly possible to believe in a Cornwall of giants and wizards and magic.

During the day, Land's End is occupied by a theme park, with children's playgrounds, interactive displays, a cinema, a gift and souvenir shop in the First and Last House, a small animals farm and a hotel.

But perhaps the most iconic attraction is the Land's End Signpost, erected in the 1950s and made famous by a million photos. The Signpost informs us that the furthest point of mainland Britain from Land's End – John O' Groats in Scotland, the north-westernmost point of Britain – is 874 miles away, the Longships Lighthouse one and a half miles, the Scilly Isles, which can be seen from the cliff top on a clear day, are 28 miles away and, beyond that, nothing but ocean for 3,147 miles to New York.

Scilly Isles

THE SCILLY ISLES, considered a part of Cornwall, are said to be all that is left of the lost kingdom of Lyonesse and the burial place of King Arthur. The first English land to taste the Atlantic breakers, the islands nonetheless bask in the warm currents of the Gulf Stream and grow fruit and flowers earlier and for longer than the rest of Britain.

St Mary's

ST MARY'S is the largest and most populous of the Scilly Isles, while Hugh Town on St Mary's is the largest settlement and unofficial capital. The Council of the Isles of Scilly meets at the Isles of Scilly Town Hall in Hugh Town. Prime Minister Harold Wilson liked to spend his holidays on St Mary's and is buried on the island in St Mary's Old Town Churchyard, in a peaceful setting by the sea overlooking Old Town Bay.

Tresco

TRESCO, the second largest Scilly Isle, is considered the most beautiful of the islands. It was transformed into a garden island by a 19th-century squire called AUGUSTUS SMITH who leased the island from the Duchy of Cornwall, built himself a house called the Abbey, and laid out a beautiful subtropical garden around the ruins of the old abbey which became world-famous and attracted much-needed tourism to the Scilly Isles. He also introduced THE FIRST COMPULSORY EDUCATION IN BRITAIN for the children of Tresco, 30 years before it was introduced on the mainland. His descendants, the Dorrien-Smiths, retain the lease to Tresco to this day.

St Martin's
ST MARTIN'S is the northernmost populated island and has the least light pollution, so hosts the Scilly Isles community observatory. St Martin's is considered the best place in England from which to view the Milky Way.

St Agnes
ST AGNES is the southernmost Scilly Isle and THE SOUTHERNMOST POINT OF BOTH ENGLAND AND THE UNITED KINGDOM. The island's Troy Town Farm is THE SOUTHERNMOST SETTLEMENT IN BRITAIN. St Agnes Lighthouse, built in 1680, was the second lighthouse to be established by Trinity House, the authority for lighthouses in England, Wales, the Channel Islands and Gibraltar, after the Lowestoft lighthouses in 1609.

The settlements on BRYHER are THE WESTERNMOST IN ENGLAND and Bryher's only hotel, the HELL BAY HOTEL, IS THE MOST WESTERLY HOTEL IN ENGLAND.

The jagged rocks off the Scilly Isles lured many a ship to its doom, especially in the days before any accurate means of navigation were invented. In 1707 the flagship of ADMIRAL SIR CLOUDESLEY SHOVELL, HMS *Association*, leading the fleet returning from the siege of Toulon in thick fog, hit the rocks west of Scilly and sank. The Admiral, barely alive, was washed ashore on St Mary's Island where he was found by a poor island woman who suffocated him by pushing his face into the sand, then buried him and made off with his emerald ring. She confessed on her deathbed 30 years later, gave up the ring and revealed where the Admiral's body was buried. He was reburied in Westminster Abbey and the site of Sir Cloudesley Shovell's temporary grave, at Porth Hellick, is now marked by a quartz block. The loss of the *Association* prompted the government to offer a huge prize for anyone who could devise a means of determining longitude and it was won, in 1761, by John Harrison, who invented the marine chronometer.

In 1967 the Scilly Isles was the scene of the world's first supertanker

disaster when the *Torrey Canyon* hit the Seven Stones Reef, seven miles off the Scilly Isles, and sank, spilling 120,000 tonnes of oil. At the time this was THE BIGGEST SHIP EVER TO BE WRECKED IN HISTORY, THE WORLD'S MOST EXPENSIVE SHIPWRECK and is still THE WORST EVER OIL SPILL OFF THE COAST OF ENGLAND.

Mount's Bay

Mount's Bay stretches from Gwennap Head, south of Land's End, to Lizard Point and is CORNWALL'S BIGGEST BAY, with a coastline stretching 40 miles in length. It takes its name from St Michael's Mount in the north of the bay.

Porthcurno Cove

Porthcurno Cove, three miles east of Land's End, was once known as 'the centre of the universe', for here came ashore the submarine telegraph cables connecting Britain to its empire and the rest of world, along the world's first international telegraph system. The first cable, the link to India, was landed here in 1870 and for the next 100 years the PORTHCURNO CABLE OFFICE was at the centre of Britain's international cable network. Between the World Wars, Porthcurno was THE LARGEST SUBMARINE CABLE STATION IN THE WORLD, operating 14 international cables. During World War Two, tunnels were dug into the granite hillside to house the sensitive telegraphy equipment and protect it from bomb attack; these tunnels can now be visited as part of the Porthcurno Telegraph Museum. The telegraphy facility at Porthcurno finally closed in 1970, 100 years after it first began operations.

The Minack Theatre

Carved out of the granite cliffs high above Porthcurno Cove and set against a sublime backdrop of turquoise sea, the MINACK THEATRE is internationally famous as one of the world's most spectacular open-air theatres.

The Minack was built by hand by ROWENA CADE at the bottom of her garden, with the help of her gardener Billy Rawlings and local craftsman Charles Angove, and over the winter of 1931 they fashioned out of the rock a stage and a rough terrace of seating to create a venue for local drama enthusiasts. The new theatre opened in 1932 with a performance of *The Tempest*, with stage lighting provided by batteries and car headlights.

Rowena Cade continued to build up and improve the theatre every winter until her death in

1983, even constructing a dressing room out of wooden beams that she personally removed one by one from a Spanish ship wrecked on the beach at Porthcurno. She was never charged with theft because the police refused to believe that such a slender soul could have carried the beams up the cliffs on her own.

Performances at the theatre are attended by up to 100,000 people every year and to watch a play here on a warm summer's evening, with the wind and waves setting the mood, the moon and stars as the lighting, the ocean as the backdrop, sometimes with dolphins or basking sharks featuring as extras, is one of life's great experiences. Just one warning – no umbrellas are allowed, and it takes a truly horrendous storm to stop a performance, so come prepared ...

Mousehole

MOUSEHOLE, said the poet Dylan Thomas, is '*the loveliest village in England*'. He spent his honeymoon in 'Mowzull', as it is pronounced, staying at the LOBSTER POT INN with his new wife Caitlin after they had got married at Penzance Registry Office in 1937. The picturesque narrow streets and stone cottages are no older than the 17th century, for in 1595 the Spanish sailed into Mount's Bay and sacked Mousehole, along with Newlyn and Penzance, leaving only one building standing, the KEIGWIN ARMS, now a private house. Mousehole was Cornwall's main fishing port for many years before it lost its position to Newlyn, and it was not that long ago that the women of Mousehole would come down to the quay to help the men land their catch while singing Cornish songs.

DOLLY PENTREATH, THE LAST KNOWN PERSON TO HAVE SPOKEN ONLY CORNISH, lies in the churchyard at PAUL, a village in the hills above Mousehole. She died in 1777, possibly at the age of 102, and in 1860 a monument was erected there in her honour by the Emperor Napoleon's nephew Prince Louis-Napoleon Bonaparte, who was born and raised in England and had a love for languages.

Newlyn

NEWLYN, THE LARGEST FISHING PORT IN ENGLAND,

was so pretty that in the 1880s it began to attract its own colony of artists, the Newlyn School, drawn by the natural light and the opportunity to paint outdoors (plein air). In 1937 the planners demolished much of the old fishing quarter that had appealed to the artists, and they began to drift away to St Ives or LAMORNA COVE a few miles west, but their legacy lived on and in 2011 the NEWLYN SCHOOL OF ART was formed to provide art courses given by established artists living in Cornwall.

On 16 August 1620 the MAYFLOWER stopped off at Newlyn to take on water, making Newlyn the *Mayflower*'s last port of call in England.

Newlyn also has a special significance to those of us who love maps – the heights on all Ordnance Survey maps are measured from the Mean Sea Level at Newlyn between 1915 and 1921.

Since 1983 Newlyn has been the home of the PENLEE LIFEBOAT station, which before that was situated south of the town at Penlee Point. On the evening of 19 December 1981, in one of the worst lifeboat disasters of modern times, the entire eight-man crew of the lifeboat *Solomon Browne* was lost while trying to rescue the crew of the vessel *Union Star*, adrift in Mount's Bay in heavy seas after its engines had failed. There were no survivors from either vessel and altogether 16 men perished. The pilot of the rescue helicopter overhead described the actions of the *Solomon Browne*'s crew that night as *'the greatest act of courage I have ever seen'*.

Penzance

PENZANCE, CORNWALL'S FIRST RESORT TOWN AND THE ONLY CORNISH TOWN TO HAVE A PROMENADE, is as far west as the railway dares to go nowadays. A ferry takes you further west to the Scilly Isles,

as does a scheduled helicopter service. Dominating the narrow streets of the town centre is the domed MARKET HALL, now Lloyds Bank, built in 1838 to house the town market and guildhall. Outside is a statue of the town's most famous son, SIR HUMPHRY DAVY, born at 4 Market Jew Street in Penzance in 1778. He is depicted holding the miner's safety lamp he invented in 1815, which saved the lives of countless Cornish miners. In 1783, Penzance was also the birthplace of MARIA BRANWELL, mother of the Brontë sisters.

In Chapel Street, which winds its way up into the town from the harbour, is the colourful EGYPTIAN HOUSE, one of only two such houses in Britain, both of which were built by JOHN FOULSTON at a time when Egypt was being opened up by European explorers and the Egyptian aesthetic was all the rage. This one was built for a local businessman in 1835. Originally the subject of some derision, the house is now a much-loved symbol of Penzance, today owned by the Landmark Trust and used for holiday lets.

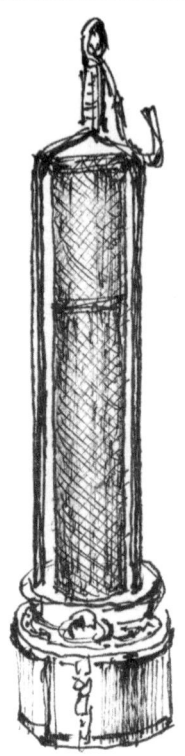

Davy Lamp

Sir Humphry Davy (1778–1829)

The young HUMPHRY DAVY, described as a genius by his schoolmates, was a very fine poet and painter – in the words of Samuel Coleridge, '*had he not been the first chemist, he would have been the first poet of his age*' but it was science that really caught his imagination. His speciality was experimenting with the effect of gases on humans, an interest that nearly killed him more than once, as he always used himself as a guinea pig. His research on nitrous oxide, a recent discovery of Joseph Priestley's, led

Davy to label it 'laughing gas' and he was the first to spot its potential as an anaesthetic. He is best remembered, however, for the safety lamp.

At that time, a naked flame was the only way of illuminating mines and in 1812, 92 miners were killed by a horrific gas explosion in a mine near Sunderland. Davy, as the acknowledged expert on the subject, was asked to design a safety lamp that could prevent such a disaster happening again. His solution was to cover the flame with a gauze that allowed air in to feed the flame but kept out the dangerous gases.

A giant Davy Lamp stands in the middle of the roundabout at the entrance to Sunderland Football Club's Stadium of Light in honour of the importance of the safety lamp to the local mining industry, and the stadium is so named after the light it brought to miners' lives.

Davy was also a founder of the ZOOLOGICAL SOCIETY and LONDON ZOO and in later life became PRESIDENT OF THE ROYAL SOCIETY. His laboratory assistant Michael Faraday would go on to enhance Davy's work and become the inventor of the electric motor.

St Michael's Mount

ST MICHAEL'S MOUNT, which lies half a mile offshore of Marazion, was granted to the Benedictine monks of Mont Saint-Michel, an almost identical

island off the coast of Normandy in France, by Edward the Confessor in the 11th century. They built a priory and church there, to which a castle was added in the 14th century. It was on the top of the church tower that the first beacon was lit to warn of the approach of the Spanish Armada in 1588. In 1659 the island was bought by the St Aubyn family who have lived there ever since, today under a 999-year lease from the National Trust. Queen Victoria visited the island in 1846, and a brass inlay of her footstep is at the top of the landing stage. It is also possible to see the remnants of a railway built in 1900 to carry goods up the steep hill to the castle in place of the pack horses previously used. The castle is open to the public and can be reached along a causeway from Marazion at low tide or by boat at high tide.

Godolphin House

Ramshackle GODOLPHIN HOUSE, which lies a few miles north-west of Helston, is one of Cornwall's loveliest and most romantic houses, a Tudor and Jacobean manor house that sits on a hill inhabited since Neolithic times and surrounded by tin mines. The Godolphin family acquired the site and started their rise to prominence in the 13th century. Two hundred years later, by now wealthy from the proceeds of their tin mines and a judicious smuggling and 'wrecking' business, they began to build the manor house on the hill, parts of which we can still see there today. At the height of its glory in the 17th century, the house had over 100 rooms, and the distinctive Palladian north front with its grand colonnade of giant Tuscan pillars which Godolphin

presents to the approaching visitor dates from that time. The house is surrounded by Elizabethan gardens, perhaps the most important such gardens in England.

The Godolphins flourished under Henry VIII and were Royalists during the Civil War. In 1646 Sir Francis Godolphin sheltered the future Charles II in the house during his flight from Falmouth to the Scilly Isles, and later went with Charles into exile in France, leaving the new additions to the house unfinished. Their fortune restored after the Restoration, Sir Sydney became Lord Treasurer to Queen Anne and his son Francis married the Duke of Marlborough's daughter while Sir Sydney was named 1st Earl of Godolphin. Francis Godolphin's daughter Mary married the 4th Duke of Leeds and so Godolphin House became the property of the Dukes of Leeds, although they never lived there and the house was instead occupied by a succession of tenant farmers and became much neglected.

In 1937 the American painter Sydney Schofield, a member of SPAB, the Society for the Protection of Ancient Buildings, who had spied Godolphin through a gap in the hedge while on holiday in Cornwall several years earlier and fallen in love with it, bought Godolphin and devoted the rest of his life to restoring both house and garden. In 2007 the estate was purchased by the National Trust who are continuing the restoration work and Godolphin is now part of the UNESCO Cornwall and West Devon World Heritage Site. The house is now open to visitors for the first week of every month. For the other three weeks Godolphin is available to let as a somewhat superior 'holiday cottage'.

Helston

Helston is the most southerly town on mainland Britain, just over a mile further south than Penzance. It was also

THE MOST SOUTHERLY POINT IN ENGLAND EVER REACHED BY THE RAILWAYS, but the branch line to the town closed in 1963 and today the nearest station is Redruth.

Helston was once an important port, until the 13th century when a bar of sand and shingle called the LOE BAR formed across the mouth of the River Cober to the west and Helston was forced to move its port activities a few miles east to Gweek, on the Helford River.

Helston was also a stannary town, as recalled by the name of the main street: Coinagehall Street. The COINAGE HALL occupied an old chapel of ease in the middle of the street at the bottom end and was where tin was brought to be tested and taxed by the Duchy of Cornwall. Wealthy tin mine owners the Godolphins, of Godolphin House, had a fine town house in the same street from which to carry out their business at the Coinage Hall. Dating from the 1540s, that house is now the Angel Hotel.

Coinagehall Street drops down from the imposing Victorian Town Hall to the distinctive, granite GRYLLS MONUMENT at the bottom of the hill, which forms a rather grand entrance to the town bowling green, believed to be the site of Helston Castle, a 13th-century fortified manor house built by the Earl of Cornwall of which there is now no trace. The Grylls Monument was erected in 1834 to honour the memory of HUMPHRY MILLET GRYLLS, a Helston banker who persuaded the banks to keep the local Wheal Vor mines open at a time of recession, saving the jobs of over 1,000 people.

Loe Pool

A pleasant 15-minute walk heading south through woods from Helston brings you to LOE POOL, formed in the 13th century when the River Cober estuary was cut off from the sea by the ever shifting Loe Bar. Covering 120 acres, Loe Pool is THE LARGEST NATURAL FRESHWATER LAKE IN CORNWALL and is encircled by a scenic six-mile trail. A culvert now takes the overflow from the lake out into Mount's Bay but before that was built, those with homes by the lake that were liable to flooding had to ask the local lord of the manor if they could cut a trench through the bar. According to Alfred, Lord Tennyson the Loe is the lake into which King Arthur's sword Excalibur was thrown by Sir Bedivere and then taken down into the depths by the hand of the Lady of the Lake (see Dozmary Pool on page 242).

The people of Helston, if asked, will tell you that the name Helston comes from 'Hell's Stone', nothing so boring as a combination of '*hen lys*', Cornish for 'old court' and '*ton*', the Saxon for 'manor'. No, apparently, Satan was flying over Cornwall carrying a huge boulder when he was spotted by St Michael (to whom the parish church is dedicated) and battle ensued, during which Satan dropped his boulder which hit the ground with a mighty crash at the spot that became known as Hell's Stone, eventually Helston. In the meantime, St Michael vanquished Satan and the people below were so overjoyed they all began dancing and have been dancing ever since.

The Furry Dance

The famous HELSTON FURRY DANCE is a Cornish May Day festival that celebrates the end of winter and the coming of spring. With origins in pre-Christian pagan times, it is one of the oldest of all the English folk festivals. The name 'furry' comes from the old Cornish word '*feur*' meaning 'a feast' or 'festival' and it is always held on 8 May, except when that is a Sunday or Monday, in which case it takes place the previous Saturday.

Helston prepares for its big day for weeks beforehand. Houses and public buildings are decorated with spring foliage: bluebells, gorse, sycamore, hazel and laurel; gardens are tied up; school children rehearse. Then at 7am on the day, the Town Band strikes up and the Early Morning Dance begins, with dancers bedecked with the town flower, lily-of-the-valley, pirouetting in and out of people's houses and gardens. This is followed at 8am by Hal-An-Tow, when English folk heroes such as Robin Hood, Friar Tuck, St Michael and St George move through the town re-enacting battles where good triumphs over evil, while singing the traditional Hal-An-Tow song:

With Hal-An-Tow! Jolly Rumble O!
For we are up as soon as any day. O!
And for to fetch the summer home,
The Summer and the May, O!
For Summer is a-come, O!
And Winter is a-gone, O!

The Children's Dance starts at 10am when over 1,000 children, all dressed in white, dance through the town, and then at noon the Furry Dance itself begins. This is by invitation only. The Mayor, in all his finery, leads the procession along the streets, in and out of shops and houses, banishing winter and welcoming in summer. All the ladies wear long dresses with hats and gloves and the men are in full morning dress, complete with top hats. Then at 5pm, it is time for the final event, the Evening Dance, when everyone, locals and visitors alike, is invited to dance and the whole town rocks. Don't expect to get much peace on Furry Dance Day in Helston ...

Helston's Heroes

In 1807 a frigate called the HMS *Anson* was driven on to the Loe Bar and more than 100 men lost their lives within sight of the shore. One of those watching helplessly as the tragedy unfolded was Helston resident HENRY TRENGROUSE (1772–1854), who was so affected by the sight of the men drowning almost within touching distance of safety that he went away determined to find some way to prevent such a thing happening again. Inspired by watching a fireworks display in Helston to celebrate the birthday of George III, he devised a rocket system that could be fired from the shore to carry a lifeline out to a ship in distress. This was secured by a barbed anchor and a chair run along it to haul the men ashore. His device, now known as a breeches buoy, is still used today, albeit with some improvements. Trengrouse also invented an early form of life jacket and his inventions over the years have saved many thousands of lives. He lived in Helston all his life and is buried in St Michael's churchyard, also remembered in the naming of one of Helston's main thoroughfares, Trengrouse Way.

BOB FITZSIMMONS (1863–1917), THE FIRST BOXER TO BE CHAMPION IN THREE DIVISIONS, was born in a thatched cottage at the top of Wendron Street, a continuation of Coinagehall Street, indicated by a plaque above the door. A middleweight, light heavyweight and heavyweight champion, Bob ranked third in the greatest heavyweights of all time and was considered THE GREATEST POUND-FOR-POUND KNOCKOUT PUNCHER IN THE HISTORY OF BOXING. His most celebrated triumph was defeating the American champion heavyweight boxer Gentleman Jim Corbett, the only man ever to beat the American John L. Sullivan.

WELL, I NEVER KNEW THIS ABOUT

WEST CORNWALL

Author ROSAMUNDE PILCHER (1924–2019) was born in Lelant, just outside St Ives, and she set her best-selling novel *The Shell Seekers* in St Ives and the surrounding countryside. When the book was made into a TV mini-series in 2006, starring Vanessa Redgrave as the lead character Penelope Keeling, it was filmed at various locations in Cornwall including Lamorna Cove, Port Isaac, St Michael's Mount and Prideaux Place in Padstow.

D.H. LAWRENCE wrote much of *Women in Love* while living in Zennor during World War Two. He was forced to leave eventually because he and his German wife Frieda were suspected of being pro-German and signalling German submarines off the Cornish coast.

On moorland above the village of Zennor is ZENNOR QUOIT, dating from the Bronze Age and THE LARGEST SURVIVING CHAMBERED TOMB IN BRITAIN. It is the best preserved of several similar quoits unique to this part of Cornwall, which include Sperris Quoit and the restored Lanyon Quoit.

CAPE CORNWALL IS THE ONLY CAPE IN ENGLAND, a cape being a headland where two bodies of water meet, which here are the Atlantic Ocean and the English Channel. The cape lies one mile west of St Just, and until the first Ordnance Survey in the early 19th century Cape Cornwall was thought to be the most westerly point in England. There was a tin mine on the Cape which operated between 1838 and

Heinz Monument

1883 and the mine's chimney, erected up on the point in 1864, has been kept as an aid to navigation. In 1987 the mine was bought by the American food company H.J. Heinz, who gave it to the nation, while the chimney was christened the Heinz Monument.

Across the bay from the Minack Theatre, perched 100 feet (30 metres) up on top of the cliffs near Treen, the LOGAN ROCK rocks no more. Once upon the time the naturally balanced 65-tonne boulder, when given the lightest of touches, would rock or 'log' gently in such a delightful manner that it became a popular tourist attraction. In 1824, however, Lieutenant Hugh Goldsmith, nephew of the poet Oliver Goldsmith, and a number of men from a Royal Navy cutter, *Nimble*, decided to see if they could move the rock and managed to heave it into the sea. Naturally, the locals complained, and the Admiralty ordered Goldsmith to recover the rock and put it back in position at his own expense. He succeeded, although the operation almost bankrupted him and, alas, he wasn't able to balance the rock as nature had done and consequently the Logan Rock no longer rocks.

In 1638 the CHURCH OF ST BURYAN introduced THE FIRST PEAL OF EIGHT BELLS IN CORNWALL and since then has rung out THE HEAVIEST PEAL OF FOUR IN THE WORLD AND THE THIRD HEAVIEST PEAL OF FIVE IN THE WORLD. Today the Church of St Buryan can boast THE HEAVIEST PEAL OF SIX IN THE WORLD.

AUGUSTUS SMITH (1804–72), Victorian Lord Proprietor of the

Isles of Scilly, is buried in the churchyard of St Buryan, at the foot of the tower. He was able to see the great tower of St Buryan shimmering in the early morning sun through a telescope from his home on Tresco and asked to be buried there at six o'clock in the morning as the sun lit up the tower.

The Merry Maidens Stone Circle near St Buryan is the most complete stone circle in Cornwall. Two hundred yards to the north-east are two more standing stones known as the Pipers. At 10 feet (3 metres) tall these are the largest surviving standing stones in Cornwall. Legend has it that these stones were pipers who were playing music for nineteen maidens when they heard the St Buryan church clock strike midnight and ran away as they realised they were breaking the Sabbath. It didn't do them any good and they were turned to stone, as were the maidens who had gone on dancing. A similar tale is told of the Nine Maidens stone circle on Dartmoor.

The Tater-du Lighthouse, on the clifftop half a mile south of Lamorna Cove, became operational in 1965 and is Cornwall's newest lighthouse, as well as being Britain's first fully automatic lighthouse.

Waste tips on the east side of Lamorna Cove are all that is left of the quarries that were worked from 1849 to 1911 and produced granite for the construction of the Thames Embankment.

Poldark Mine at Wendron near Helston is the only complete underground tin mine open to the public. The original ancient mine of Wheal Roots was lost in the 19th century and rediscovered in the 1960s when it was developed as a tourist attraction and heritage centre, offering underground tours through the ancient mine workings. The mine was renamed the Poldark Mine after Winston Graham's novels and many of the underground scenes from the BBC television series *Poldark* were filmed here. The Poldark Mine is temporarily closed for financial reasons but is expected to reopen in 2026.

SOUTH CORNWALL

Report to Falmouth for orders.

Instructions to ships arriving in England from all over the world in the 17th and 18th centuries

St Germans Priory

The Lizard

THE SOUTHERNMOST PART of the British mainland, THE LIZARD gets its name from the Cornish '*lis*' meaning 'palace' and '*ard*' meaning 'high'. There have been more shipwrecks off these rockbound shores than anywhere else on the Cornish coastline, hence there were once three lifeboat stations within a six-mile stretch of the Lizard coastline, more than anywhere else in Britain. The old lifeboat station at Mullion Cove was, for more than 40 years, home to Cornwall's biggest lifeboat.

CORNWALL'S FIRST LIGHTHOUSE was built on LIZARD POINT in 1619, much to the annoyance of the local populace who made a hearty living from 'wrecking' – helping themselves to the cargoes of the many ships that ran aground and wrecked on the Lizard's treacherous rocks. This was replaced in 1752, with a twin-towered affair which in 1903 was fitted with what at the time was the most powerful single beam in the world.

Gunwalloe

GUNWALLOE, on the west Lizard coast three miles south of Helston, is but a smattering of houses and a farm by the sea, but holds a significant place in Cornish history: it incorporates Winnianton Manor, THE FIRST PLACE IN CORNWALL THAT APPEARS IN THE DOMESDAY BOOK. At the time the book was written most of Cornwall belonged to William the Conqueror through his half-brother Robert, Count of Mortain, 1st Earl of Cornwall, and

Winnianton was then a large and important manor for the King.

A mile south down a narrow lane, the name is kept alive by Winnianton Farm and 200 yards beyond that, tucked amongst the dunes away from the sea storms by a rocky headland, with just the top of the tower peeping above the trees, is the first of the Lizard's two ST WINWALOE churches. This one was THE FIRST CORNISH CHURCH TO APPEAR IN THE DOMESDAY BOOK. Known as the Church of Storms, it is THE ONLY INTACT CHURCH IN CORNWALL ACTUALLY LOCATED ON A BEACH and the churchyard has to be constantly swept clear of sand. The church consists of three gabled aisles from the 15th century and a detached tower with a pyramid cap embedded in the side of the cliff, which survives from an earlier 13th-century church. Inside there are sections of a 15th-century rood screen which local legend says was recovered from a Portuguese treasure ship that was wrecked on the coast at Gunwalloe in 1527, although this is unsubstantiated. The view from the porch of St Winwaloe, of sea and sand and sky, is sublime.

Poldhu

A stone monument on the bare cliffs above POLDHU, west of Mullion, marks the very spot where the age of radio began. It was from here that the world's first high-powered radio transmitter sent THE FIRST TRANSATLANTIC RADIO SIGNAL over 2,000 miles to Newfoundland, where it was received by the man whose invention had made it all possible, the *'father of radio'*, GUGLIELMO MARCONI. A permanent radio station was later set up at Poldhu, where ship-to-shore radio communications were pioneered. In 1912 the station at Poldhu was the first to receive the news about the sinking of the *Titanic*. Nothing is left of the original radio station save for the foundations but along with the memorial there is a museum where the story of Poldhu's significance to the world

Marconi Monument

of communications, television and the internet is told.

A little way inland is the GOONHILLY EARTH SATELLITE STATION, where THE FIRST INTERCONTINENTAL PICTURE TRANSMISSIONS were received from the United States via satellite in 1962.

Lizard Point and Village

LIZARD POINT is THE SOUTHERNMOST POINT OF MAINLAND BRITAIN and LIZARD VILLAGE the MOST SOUTHERLY SETTLEMENT, THE ONLY VILLAGE IN MAINLAND BRITAIN TO LIE SOUTH OF THE 50TH PARALLEL. East of the Point is Pen Olver, the cliff from which the Spanish Armada was first sighted in 1588.

St Wynwallow's, Landewednack

At Church Cove on the Lizard's east coast, a little way east of Landewednack, which is now part of Lizard village, is the second of the Lizard's St Winwalloe churches, sometimes spelt Wynwallow to differentiate it from the one at Gunwalloe. ENGLAND'S MOST SOUTHERLY CHURCH lies in a hollow embowered in trees bent to the wind. To the west is England's most southerly village, Lizard. To the south and east there is only sea. The sounds and smells of the ocean are all around. In the churchyard is a memorial to Cornishmen lost at sea. Tombstones are carved with seagulls. The rest of the world seems very far away. It is said that THE LAST SERMON PREACHED

in the Cornish tongue was spoken here, in 1674.

A wooden church was established here in about AD 600 and dedicated to St Winwaloe (460–532), a Celtic saint of Cornish ancestry who spent much of his life in Brittany. The stone church was begun by the Normans and enlarged in the 13th and 14th centuries.

The result is a very beautiful little church. The sturdy tower features an irregular patchwork of granite bricks and massive, rough-hewn blocks of grey, blue and dark green serpentine, a local stone found only on the Lizard. The whole is flecked with golden lichen.

The gabled south transept throws a protective arm around the tiny embattled square porch, which shelters a 15th-century doorway sitting underneath the oldest remaining feature of the building, a mossy Norman arch carved out with crosses, rings and chevrons.

The interior is simple and unpretentious but has a strange ambulatory (covered walkway), supported by a round pillar, running between the transept and the chancel, which gives the church a rather endearing lopsided appearance. There are some interesting carvings on the chancel seats. One of the church bells was cast in c.1456, making it one of the oldest church bells in Cornwall.

The square font, made of serpentine, sits on four legs and bears the inscription '*Master Richard Bolham made me*'. He was rector here in the early 15th century.

Helford River

The Helford River on the Lizard's east coast is a beautiful estuary of seven creeks. Frenchman's Creek on the south side, overhung with trees and lush vegetation, is a mysterious, silent place that might be a swamp in Louisiana, and was immortalised by Daphne du Maurier in her novel of the same name. She spent her honeymoon here on her new husband's yacht *Ygdrasil* in 1932.

On the north side, Porth Navas is the site of the Duchy of Cornwall's oyster beds and at one time produced a quarter of Britain's oysters. Unlike today, oysters were once considered food for the poor. As Sam Weller remarked in Charles Dickens's *The Pickwick Papers*, '*poverty and oysters always seem to go together.*' Not these days.

Gweek, at the head of the estuary, is home to Britain's largest seal sanctuary.

Carrick Roads

Falmouth

Falmouth is Cornwall's largest town and largest port. It sits at the entrance to the Carrick Roads, which forms the deepest natural harbour in western Europe and the third deepest in the world. Four hundred years ago there was just one modest manor house here, Arwenack House, home of the Killigrews, which still stands at the heart of the town it spawned.

At the Restoration Sir Peter Killigrew built a parish church for the rapidly growing new town of Falmouth and dedicated it to King Charles the Martyr. In 1688 Falmouth became the communication centre for the growing British Empire when it was chosen to be the Royal Mail's first packet station from where mail was sent out across the world by fast, lightly armed sailing vessels referred to as 'Falmouth Packets'. When ships arrived in England from anywhere in the world they would *'report to Falmouth for orders'*. It took far less time to send dispatches to London overland by horse from Falmouth than by ship beating up the Channel against the wind – indeed, Falmouth was the first place in England to learn of Nelson's victory at the Battle of Trafalgar in 1805.

Pendennis Castle

Pendennis Castle, which was there long before Falmouth, was

Pendennis Castle

built by Henry VIII in 1539–45 as part of the largest coastal defence programme since Roman times to defend the Carrick Roads and its two original ports, Penrhyn and Truro, from threats by Catholic Europe. It stands high above the town on the headland at the mouth of the harbour and the circular design takes advantage of the all-round view of the town, the harbour, Carrick Roads and the Channel. Indeed, the view from the castle is as breathtakingly panoramic and commanding today as it was then. Charles I's queen, Henrietta Maria, spent her last day in England before escaping to France in 1644 in Pendennis Castle, THE LAST ROYALIST STRONGHOLD TO SURRENDER to Oliver Cromwell during the Civil War, after withstanding a six-month siege in 1646.

St Mawes Castle

St Mawes Castle, built to guard the eastern approach to Carrick Roads, is the most memorable and best preserved of all Henry VIII's artillery castles along the south coast of England. It was completed in 1542, two years before its sister castle Pendennis at whom it gazes across the estuary. Together these two fortresses could create a crossfire that made the entrance to the harbour in Carrick Roads almost impregnable. St Mawes is larger than Pendennis and while Pendennis is circular, St Mawes is constructed in a most satisfying clover leaf shape with a tall, almost round

St Mawes Castle

central tower and three protruding round bastions used for the gun platforms. Unlike Pendennis, the garrison of St Mawes capitulated to Cromwell's forces in 1646 without a shot being fired – largely because all the guns face out to sea. Both Pendennis and St Mawes remained operational until after World War Two, ready for action against the Spanish Armada in 1588, the French and the Americans during the War of Independence, the French again during the Napoleonic Wars and the Germans during the two world wars.

St Just-in-Roseland

'*And did those feet, in ancient times, walk upon England's mountains green ...*' If they did, they would probably have landed here at ST JUST-IN-ROSELAND, across Carrick Roads from the Pandora Inn. Once you have experienced the magical atmosphere of the lovely 13th-century church of St Just-in-Roseland, enveloped in subtropical gardens beside a dazzling blue creek, you may well find yourself open to the idea that Jesus did indeed set foot on England's pleasant pastures right here while accompanying Joseph of Arimathea in search of Cornish tin – pastures don't come more pleasant. Indeed, there is a stone down by the water on to which Jesus is said to have stepped while coming ashore. I defy anyone not to feel a frisson ...

St Just-in-Roseland

Caerhays Castle

CAERHAYS CASTLE is a vast castellated mock Gothic mansion overlooking a sandy bay near Mevagissey. It was built near the site of a previous manor house in 1808 to the design of John Nash, architect of the Prince Regent's Brighton Pavilion, and is in every way as fantastical as that extravagant pleasure palace. Indeed, so extravagant that it bankrupted the owner, the one-time High Sheriff of Cornwall and MP JOHN BETTESWORTH-TREVANION (1780–1840), and he was forced to flee to Paris to get away from his creditors. (The story of John Bettesworth-Trevanion and his flight to Paris is told in *Bella Poldark,* the last of Winston Graham's *Poldark* novels.) The house was left empty for a decade before it was finally purchased from the creditors by MICHAEL WILLIAMS in 1854. It then passed down generations of Williams to JOHN CHARLES WILLIAMS who inherited in 1879. A keen gardener, he collected plants from around the world to create a magnificent garden of some 120 acres full of plants that thrive in the mild climate at Caerhays, which lies in a hollow protected from the west winds. It is especially renowned for its magnolias and rhododendrons.

Mevagissey

MEVAGISSEY is Cornwall's second largest port and has an inner harbour from 1774 and an outer harbour from 1888. The town grew rich on pilchards and claims to be THE FIRST PLACE IN CORNWALL TO BE LIT BY ELECTRICITY when a small plant powered by pilchard oil was built on the quay in 1895 to power the new cast iron lighthouse on the end of the pier – THE FIRST LIGHTHOUSE IN ENGLAND TO BE LIT BY ELECTRICITY.

ANDREW PEARS, inventor of PEARS SOAP, the first transparent soap, was born in Mevagissey in 1770. His great-great-grandson, Thomas Pears (1882–1912), who was travelling first class, went down with the *Titanic* when it sank on its maiden voyage in 1912. His wife Edith was rescued.

The Lost Gardens of Heligan

The gardens at Heligan, a mile west of Mevagissey, were begun by the Tremayne family at the end of the 18th century and built up by several generations of Tremaynes throughout the 19th century to become one of the finest Victorian gardens in Britain. At the outbreak of World War One in 1914 the family and the workforce went off to fight in the trenches, with many of them never returning. Heligan House was leased out and eventually sold, minus the gardens, for apartments in the 1970s and during this time the gardens fell into decay and were lost to brambles and weeds. They were rediscovered in 1990 and restored in their original Victorian form to become THE LARGEST GARDEN RESTORATION PROJECT IN ALL OF EUROPE. The restored gardens, which were opened to the public in 1992, cover some 200 acres and include an Italian garden, a subtropical area filled with tree ferns known as the Jungle and THE ONLY PINEAPPLE PIT LEFT IN EUROPE.

sistible draw for any number of film and television companies seeking an authentic 18th-century maritime backdrop, the most recent examples being the 1998 TV film of Daphne du Maurier's *Frenchman's Creek* and the 2015 BBC *Poldark* series.

Charlestown

CHARLESTOWN is a virtually unchanged Georgian harbour designed at the end of the 18th century by the harbour engineer John Smeaton for CHARLES RASHLEIGH, a local mine owner. The harbour operated as a port for St Austell and was used for the export of copper and china clay, Cornwall's 'white gold', but by the mid-20th century, because of its tortuous entrance, the harbour had grown unsuitable for larger vessels. St Austell's trade shifted to deeper ports such as Par and Fowey, and Charlestown was left frozen in time. Today the harbour is owned by Square Sail, a company that manages a fleet of tall ships, one or two of which can normally be seen anchored at Charlestown, adding to the harbour's old-world charm. As the BEST-PRESERVED GEORGIAN HARBOUR IN ENGLAND, Charleston's film-set quality has proved an irre-

St Austell

For centuries ST AUSTELL was a small village slumbering in the shadow of the impressive 90-foot (27 metres) tower of the 15th-century parish church of Holy Trinity, making a living from the numerous tin mines dotted all around. Then, in 1755, a Quaker called WILLIAM COOKWORTHY arrived. He was the first person in Britain to discover how to make the hard paste porcelain and he came to Cornwall in search of minerals similar to those used in its manufacture in China. He found CHINA CLAY in great quantities around St Austell. His discovery laid the foundations for the English Bone China and fine porcelain industry and made Britain THE WORLD'S LARGEST PRODUCER OF CHINA CLAY with St Austell at its centre. The landscape was transformed as well, with the huge white spoil tips left by the china clay industry known as the CORNISH ALPS surrounding St Austell and visible for miles.

Eden Project

Occupying a disused china clay pit three miles north of St Austell is THE EDEN PROJECT, an enterprise aimed at reconnecting people with the natural world. Opened in 2001, the project consists of a series of structures called biomes that are made from inflatable plastic cells supported by steel frames which act as green houses, allowing for the creation of artificial climates where tropical and desert plants are able to flourish. The largest biome houses THE LARGEST INDOOR RAINFOREST IN THE WORLD with tropical plants and fruits, such as rubber trees, giant bamboo, banana and coffee plants, while the second largest emulates a Mediterranean climate suitable for such things as olives and grapevines.

There is also an outdoor botanical garden where plants from temperate regions can grow such as lavender, hops, hemp and sunflowers, all mixed with an ever-changing series of exhibitions and art installations.

In 2002 the Eden Project was used as a location for the James Bond film *Die Another Day* and since that year has hosted the Eden Sessions, a series of concerts by artists who have included Gary Barlow, Texas, Diana Ross, Bryan Adams, the Pet Shop Boys, Manic Street Preachers, Liam Gallagher and Kylie Minogue.

Two Famous St Austell Mines

Polgooth

It is thought that tin has been mined at POLGOOTH, two miles south-west of St Austell, for hundreds if not thousands of years and was possibly even traded with the Phoenicians, although

first records date from the 16th century. By the 18th century Polgooth was the richest tin mine in Britain and known as *'the greatest tin mine in the world'*. Discovery of tin elsewhere in the world in the 19th century sent tin prices tumbling and Polgooth became unviable, closing in 1894.

Carclaze

Like Polgooth, CARCLAZE, on the northern edge of St Austell, is thought to have supplied tin to the Phoenicians some 3,000 years ago. By the 19th century it was the world's largest open cast tin mine and when the tin market collapsed later that century it moved on to china clay extraction. The mine covers 12 acres, is 150 feet deep and has a circumference of more than a mile, making it one of the largest man-made pits in the world, rivalling nearby Delabole (see page 175).

CHINA CLAY

China clay, officially known as kaolin, is a soft, white clay mineral. Although famously used to make porcelain, it also has many other properties and is used in the manufacture of paper, beauty products, and paint, as well as potentially for batteries and water purifying.

Menabilly

'*Last night I dreamt I went to Manderley again. It seemed to me I stood by the iron gate leading to the drive ...*' These lines from Daphne du Maurier's *Rebecca* are amongst the most famous and evocative opening lines in English literature. Anyone can go to Manderley today but only as far as the iron gate, for Manderley is MENABILLY, a small, early Georgian house surrounded by woodland and set in glorious countryside above the Gribben cliffs of East St Austell Bay, not far from Fowey. Menabilly has been the seat of the powerful Rashleigh family since the 16th century, and the present house incorporates parts of the original Elizabethan house. CHARLES RASHLEIGH was the builder of Charlestown and during the late Victorian era the

Rashleighs were the biggest landowners in Cornwall.

Daphne du Maurier discovered Menabilly in 1927, when it had been neglected for a number of years and was in a parlous state, and used it in her 1938 novel *Rebecca* as the model for Manderley. Menabilly even has its own small beach, as featured in *Rebecca*. In 1943, using the proceeds from the success of *Rebecca*, du Maurier leased Menabilly from the Rashleighs and restored it, living there for 25 years before handing it back to the Rashleighs in 1969. After her death, du Maurier's ashes were scattered on the cliffs near Menabilly. Today, Menabilly is the home of Sir Richard Rashleigh, 6th Baronet, and his family.

Fowey

Described by the poet Robert Bridges as '*the most poetic-looking place in England*', Fowey is one of the oldest towns in Cornwall with '*the narrowest streets I ever saw in England*' tumbling down '*perpendicular hills*' into the river, according to Queen Victoria. The Fowey estuary provides a deep, safe harbour and Fowey has thrived on fishing and trade, particularly china clay, as attested to by the many fine houses in the town.

In medieval times Fowey sailors had a reputation for being unruly and audacious, which made them perfect recruits during the Hundred Years' War with France, and in 1346 Fowey was made the assembly point for the ships embarking on the Siege of Calais. When the war was over, the Fowey men, known as Fowey Gallants, continued to conduct raids on the French coast until in 1457 the French struck back, sailing into the river and setting fire to the town. The defence of the town was organised by the redoubtable DAME ELIZABETH TREFFRY who took the townsfolk into her fortified tower house, PLACE HOUSE, just behind the church, and poured molten lead over the attackers. After a fruitless six-week siege, the French gave up and went home. Like Fowey, Place House survives, although somewhat remodelled, and can be viewed on occasion.

In August 1644, as Charles I was standing above Bodinnick surveying the retreating Roundheads trapped in the Fowey valley after the Battle of Lostwithiel, he escaped death by a whisker when he turned away and a Roundhead

Fowey Hall

bullet hit a sailor who had taken his place.

Fowey also has an unsurpassed literary heritage. Bodmin-born SIR ARTHUR QUILLER-COUCH (1863–1944) was a professor, critic and editor of *The Oxford Book of English Verse*, who wrote under the pseudonym 'Q' and lived in THE HAVEN, a fine house on the Esplanade, from 1892 until his death in 1944. Q was a great friend of author KENNETH GRAHAME, who got married in Fowey parish church while staying at the Haven and also honeymooned in Fowey. Q was the inspiration for the talkative 'Ratty' in Grahame's *The Wind in the Willows*, while the Victorian FOWEY HALL, a splendid pile built above the town for politician SIR CHARLES HANSON in 1899 is said to have inspired Toad Hall.

Grahame inscribed a first edition of *The Wind in the Willows* to Q's daughter Foy Quiller-Couch. Foy meanwhile became great friends with DAPHNE DU MAURIER, whose parents had a house at nearby Bodinnick, and it was when the two of them went riding on Bodmin Moor that du Maurier got the idea for her novel *Jamaica Inn*.

Another writer who honeymooned in Fowey thanks to his friendship with Q was the

playwright J.M. BARRIE. Q is buried in the churchyard of the parish church St Fimbarrus and there is a granite memorial to him overlooking Fowey harbour.

Bodinnick

A short ferry ride across the Fowey river takes you to the fishing village of BODINNICK where Daphne du Maurier lived in a big white-washed house with blue-painted window frames called FERRYSIDE located, appropriately enough, beside the slipway where the ferry comes in. Her family bought the property as a second home in 1926 and Daphne wrote her first novel there, *The Loving Spirit*, published in 1931. She moved out to Menabilly in 1943 but her sister Angela continued to live at Ferryside until her death in 2002.

The Bodinnick Ferry was first recorded in 1344 although it is more than likely that there was a crossing here long before that, as it avoids a difficult six-mile round trip to the nearest bridge at Lostwithiel. For a long time the ferry was run from the Old Ferry Inn just up from the slipway. The villagers and visitors from all over the world were stunned and angered when the inn, the heart of the community for 600 years, closed in August 2025.

St Germans

ST GERMANS, once the seat of the Bishops of Cornwall, is one of those places that takes your breath away at first sight. Here, beside a big stone lychgate and a battlemented gateway, is CORNWALL'S BIGGEST AND MOST IMPRESSIVE NORMAN CHURCH set on a slope below the road, with the stately PORT ELIOT house beyond resting amongst glorious gardens laid out by Humphry Repton that run down to the creek where ST GERMANUS landed in the 5th century and founded a church and monastery.

Over 1,000 years ago during the reign of King Athelstan, the church was rebuilt and became the cathedral seat of the first Bishops of Cornwall, until the middle of the 11th century when the bishopric moved to Devon.

The present Norman church was begun in 1161 but was such a massive enterprise that it took 100 years to complete, finally being consecrated in 1261. The glory of the Norman building is the west front which remains almost entirely as the Normans built it. The south-west tower is square with small Norman windows and THE ONLY EXTERNAL NORMAN STAIRCASE IN CORNWALL, while the north-west tower begins square and rather cleverly becomes octagonal halfway up, finishing with a 13th-century octagon at the top. Between the two towers is THE FINEST NORMAN DOORWAY IN CORNWALL, if not in ENGLAND. It is huge, with the door deeply recessed behind seven orders of arches carved with traditional Norman zig-zag decoration. The west front of St Germans is, in many people's opinion, THE FINEST EXAMPLE OF NORMAN ARCHITECTURE IN CORNWALL.

Port Eliot

The great house next to the church stands on the site of the priory founded by St Germanus, which survived until the Dissolution of the Monasteries in 1538. Not long afterwards it became the home of the Eliots, later made Earls of St Germans by George III, and kinsmen of the poet T.S. Eliot. They renamed the priory PORT ELIOT and have lived there ever since. The 13th-century undercroft of the priory survives, as does the refectory which now serves as the main hall of the house. The present classical-style house was built around this 12th- and 13th-century core in 1806, mostly to the designs of Sir John Soane, and having been lived in for over 1,000 years Port Eliot has a plausible claim to be THE OLDEST CONTINUALLY INHABITED DWELLING IN BRITAIN.

Moyle Almshouses

In the village of St Germans there is an unusual and very attractive set of gabled almshouses built by SIR WILLIAM MOYLE in 1583, consisting of 12 one-room apartments, 6 on the ground floor and 6 on the first floor, the latter opening on to a gallery with stairs at either end. They were converted into four separate dwellings by the National Association of Almshouses in 1967.

Cornwall's Viaducts

St Germans railway station, which opened in 1859, is considered THE BEST-PRESERVED VICTORIAN RAILWAY STATION IN CORNWALL and sits at the western end of one of Cornwall's more spectacular viaducts. The St Germans Viaduct crosses the River Tiddy at a height of 106 feet (32 metres) on 17 arches and with an overall length of 978 feet (298 metres).

Due to the topography of the county, the Cornwall Railway running east to west from Plymouth to Truro, which opened in 1859, had to cross a considerable number of north–south river valleys which required viaducts, 42 of them, all originally made of timber to save on costs. Designed to be temporary, some of these rickety looking wooden structures remained in service for over 70 years until the 1930s, although all have now been rebuilt in stone.

Rame Peninsula

Known as 'Cornwall's Forgotten Corner', the Rame Peninsula is often by-passed by those on their way in or out of Cornwall across the Tamar Bridge further to the north and, indeed, a part of it was actually in Devon until the 19th century.

RAME HEAD, at the southernmost tip of the peninsula, is crowned by the 14th-century chapel of St Michael, which used to show a beacon to guide ships into Plymouth Harbour. This job is now done by the Eddystone Lighthouse.

The twin smuggling villages of KINGSAND and CAWSAND are attractive to artists as a less crowded version of St Ives. Kingsand, which is known for its clock tower erected to celebrate the coronation of George V, was in Devon until boundary changes in 1844. Cawsand to the south, meanwhile, was in Cornwall, and the old county boundary is marked by a house called Devon Corn, on which there is plaque. Kingsand was the home of JOHN POLLARD, the man who shot the French sniper who killed Lord Nelson at the Battle of Trafalgar, Arthur Ransome's daughter TABITHA, and ANN DAVISON, who in 1953 became THE FIRST WOMAN TO SAIL SINGLE-HANDEDLY ACROSS THE ATLANTIC.

Both villages are in the MOUNT EDGCUMBE NATIONAL PARK, THE OLDEST LANDSCAPED GARDENS

in CORNWALL, consisting of 885 acres of gardens and woodland created by the Edgcumbe family in the 18th century. The park includes England's NATIONAL CAMELLIA COLLECTION. At the centre of the park stands Mount Edgcumbe House, rebuilt in its original Tudor style after being bombed in 1941. Since 1987 the house and park have been publicly owned and are open to visitors.

The village of CREMYLL sits at the gates to the park and from here there is a foot passenger ferry to Stonehouse in Plymouth, following an ancient ferry route dating back to the 11th century.

WELL, I NEVER KNEW THIS ABOUT

SOUTH CORNWALL

THE PANDORA INN on beautiful RESTRONGUET CREEK, on the west coast of the Carrick Roads near Falmouth, dates from the 13th century and is a claimant to be CORNWALL'S OLDEST INN. It is named after HMS *PANDORA*, the ship that was sent to Tahiti to find and arrest the mutineers of the *Bounty*, who set their captain,

William Bligh, adrift in the South Pacific in 1789. Sad to say, the *Pandora* sank on the Great Barrier Reef in 1791 with the loss of many of the crew and mutineers. The ship's CAPTAIN EDWARDS was court-martialled when he got back to Cornwall, subsequently left the Navy, and consoled himself by becoming the landlord of what is now the Pandora Inn.

KENNETH GRAHAME began the series of letters to his son that would become *The Wind in the Willows* while staying at the elegant 17th-century GREENBANK HOTEL on the waterfront at Falmouth.

Falmouth is the home of THE WORLD'S FIRST POLYTECHNIC, THE ROYAL CORNWALL POLYTECHNIC SOCIETY, founded in 1833 by the Quaker FOX FAMILY of Falmouth to provide further education for the workers at their foundry in Perran, a few miles north of the town.

One of Falmouth's most celebrated attractions is JACOB'S LADDER, a set of 111 steps leading from the Moor, the town's main square, up to a small street of houses, Vernon Place. They were built by Falmouth businessman JACOB HAMBLEN in the 1840s as a way of getting from the harbour, where his business was, to his home.

The 1990s Channel 4 TV drama *The Camomile Lawn*, adapted from Mary Wesley's novel of the same name, was filmed at BROOM PARC, a stunning Georgian house perched on the cliff top near Veryan.

The bells of the church at ST VEEP, three miles inland from Fowey, make up THE ONLY 'VIRGIN' OR 'MAIDEN' PEAL OF BELLS IN ENGLAND. A maiden peal is a set of bells that are perfectly in tune when they are cast. The bells at St Veep were cast in the churchyard by bell caster JOHN PENNINGTON in 1770. He is said to have leapt for joy when he tapped the bells with his tuning fork and found them to be the most perfect bells he had ever cast.

POLPERRO is the least spoiled fishing village and smugglers' haunt on Cornwall's south coast, with tight narrow lanes streaming down the valley to the sea, rows of solid old fishermen's cottages and a pretty harbour. Born in Warren Cottage in 1789 was JONATHAN COUCH, who for 60 years served as Polperro's doctor. He rarely left Polperro

Woolly monkey

and died there in 1870 aged 81. He had three sons with his wife, a member of Polperro's Quiller family, and they all took the name Quiller Couch. Jonathan Couch was the grandfather of the writer Arthur Quiller-Couch, known as 'Q' (see Fowey, page 218).

The two separate ancient towns of EAST AND WEST LOOE are joined by a Victorian 7-arched bridge, which replaced a medieval bridge that had 13 arches and a small chapel dedicated to St Anne in the middle. A little further along the coast is the WILD FUTURES MONKEY SANCTUARY, which was set up in 1964 by Len Williams, father of guitarist John Williams, to rescue woolly monkeys from the pet trade. It was THE FIRST CENTRE IN THE WORLD TO SUCCESSFULLY BREED WOOLLY MONKEYS.

ANTONY HOUSE was built in 1724 for Sir William Carew, whose family have owned the estate since the 16th century. The grounds were landscaped by Humphry Repton and include the NATIONAL COLLECTION OF DAY LILIES. Antony is famous for its portraits, with a number by Sir Joshua Reynolds and a portrait of Rachel Carew that inspired Daphne du Maurier's *My Cousin Rachel*. The Carews still live at Antony, although the house and gardens were given over to the National Trust in 1961 and are open to the public during the summer months.

MID CORNWALL

Onan hag Oll
'One and All'

Duchy of Cornwall's motto, signifying unity

Truro Cathedral

Cornwall's Capitals

CORNWALL'S CAPITAL HAS been a moveable feast for 700 years or more and there is still a degree of rivalry between Truro and Bodmin for the title of county town of Cornwall. The concept of county town is ill-defined but is usually taken to mean where the chief administrative or judicial offices are located. In Cornwall's case the capital was wherever the Earl of Cornwall chose to make it, and that was usually where the most powerful castle happened to be. Interestingly, Cornwall's capital, or what became the county town, has moved further west on each occasion as the Earldom, now the Duchy, extended its reach deeper into the county. What is certain is that each capital or county town has been and still is central, rather than north or south. Thus Launceston, the Gateway to Cornwall, was the first town to be fortified by the Earl of Cornwall and hence his first capital. A later Earl moved west to Lostwithiel to take advantage of the powerful new castle at Restormel, but Lostwithiel developed more slowly than Launceston, which for a while regained the crown. For a few years of the 19th century Bodmin, right at the heart of Cornwall, became the county town as the judicial courts took advantage of Bodmin gaol, the premier gaol in the county. Bodmin then lost out to Truro with its new cathedral status and Truro is now generally accepted as the county town, although it was never officially made so. Bodmin and, to a degree Launceston, still maintain a faint claim. Each is, in its own way, worthy of the title but it seems the cathedral is Truro's trump card.

Launceston

Known as the Gateway to Cornwall, LAUNCESTON sits just one mile west of the River Tamar which here forms the border between Devon and Cornwall.

St Stephen's

Launceston means 'estate of the church of St Stephen' (Lanstefan-ton) and while there was most probably a Celtic settlement here, the Launceston of today began life as a Saxon monastery dedicated to St Stephen that stood on the north bank of the River Kensey, near the present 13th-century church of St Stephen. Cornwall's first mint was established at Launceston around 935 during the reign of King Athelstan and Cornwall's earliest coin, one of the rarest coins in existence, is thought to be a silver penny from the reign of Ethelred II (the Unready) that was minted here. Only two of these coins still exist, with one in the British Museum and the other recently bought at auction by an unknown buyer.

In 1127 an Augustinian priory was built on the other side of the River Kensey which, by the time of the Dissolution of the Monasteries in the 1500s, had grown into the biggest and richest religious house in Cornwall. The priory was demolished after the Dissolution and the stones used for building elsewhere in Launceston, but some remnants of the priory church were rediscovered and excavated in the 19th century which can be seen today. The huge Norman font from the priory, at 12 feet (3.6 metres) in diameter the largest Norman font in Cornwall, can be found in St Thomas church which sits on the priory site. The priory's richly carved Norman doorway now forms the main entrance to the White Hart Hotel in the town centre. The beautiful little packhorse bridge that crosses the river here dates from the 15th century and is known as the Prior's Bridge.

Launceston Castle

In 1070 ROBERT, COUNT OF MORTAIN AND EARL OF CORNWALL, half-brother to William the Conqueror, built a timber motte and bailey castle on top of the natural rocky outcrop across the river in what was then known as Dunheved, meaning 'hilltop', from where he could watch over both his domain and the ford across the River Tamar, which was at that time the most important crossing place into Cornwall from

Devon. The view from the top of the keep is breathtaking.

After the castle was built, the market at St Stephen's was moved to the safety of the castle's outer bailey and the settlement that subsequently grew up around the castle took over the name Launceston. In the 13th century, Henry III's younger brother Richard, made Earl of Cornwall by the King, rebuilt the castle in stone and added the tall central round tower, creating what was, at the time, Cornwall's most powerful castle. South of the castle stands the Southgate Arch, the only surviving gate from the town walls which Richard put around the town, making Launceston CORNWALL'S ONLY WALLED TOWN. Now well protected, Launceston became the Earldom's administrative centre and Cornwall's first capital until Richard's son Edmund moved his seat to the luxurious new castle of Restormel at Lostwithiel, which then became Cornwall's second capital.

Launceston continued to be Cornwall's judicial centre, with the castle maintaining its role as the Earldom's main courthouse and gaol – in 1656 Quaker founder George Fox was imprisoned in the castle for eight months for distributing subversive literature around Launceston – and this would eventually lead to Launceston winning back its status as Cornwall's county town, a position it held until the county assizes moved to Bodmin in 1838.

Castle Street, running away

from the castle walls to the west, displays the finest collection of Georgian red-brick houses in the West Country, one of the best being LAWRENCE HOUSE of 1753 which now houses the town museum.

St Mary Magdalene

Apart from the castle, which dominates the town from every direction, Launceston possesses a number of fine buildings, the pick of which is the unique church of ST MARY MAGDALENE, sitting amongst a maze of narrow lanes under the castle walls to the north. Only the tower is still standing of the original 14th-century church; the rest was built in the early 16th century by local squire SIR HENRY TRECARREL, twice Mayor of Launceston. What makes the church unique in England is that, apart from the tower, every inch of the granite walls, and even the pinnacles of the buttresses, are covered in carvings, not just of the Trecarrel coat of arms but of saints, animals, flowers, biblical texts and all manner of foliage. Although crude, the carvings are remarkably unweathered, the granite being hard enough to survive even the storms that drove the Spanish Armada to destruction. The carvings were meant for Sir Henry Trecarrel's new mansion a few miles away at Trecarrel near St Neot on Bodmin Moor, but in 1511 his son was drowned in the bath and the boy's mother died shortly afterwards of shock. Distraught, Sir Henry turned his attention to the new church, leaving the house unfinished with just the Great Hall and chapel completed. Both still stand, amongst the best-preserved domestic Tudor buildings in the country.

Lostwithiel

Cornwall's second royal capital after Launceston, LOSTWITHIEL is located at the highest tidal point on the River Fowey and served as the port for Restormel Castle from where the Duchy could export its tin to the Mediterranean. In 1292 Edmund, 2nd Earl of Cornwall, built the Stannary or Duchy Palace in Lostwithiel, later used by the Black Prince who placed the Prince of Wales's plume of feathers on the roof of the Exchequer Hall where they can still be seen. In 1495 Lostwithiel was confirmed as Cornwall's chief stannary town and administrative capital when Henry VII, directed that *'the standard weights for Cornwall to be kept at Lostwithiel'*. The

offices of the Duchy of Cornwall can still be found in Lostwithiel.

Lostwithiel is also noted for its marvellous 15th-century bridge across the Fowey and for St Bartholomew's church, which dates from the 13th century and boasts a distinctive octagonal broach spire that was added to the tower in the 14th century – the way that the square tower transforms seamlessly into an octagonal spire is pure genius, one of the glories of Cornwall. The stained glass of the great Perpendicular east window, 90 feet (27 metres) high and one of the most magnificent in Cornwall, was replaced in 1886 with Victorian glass of the highest quality telling the story of the Crucifixion. The old octagonal font, which probably dates from the same time as the spire, sits on five shafts and is exuberantly carved with animals as well as a hunter blowing a horn and a bishop sprouting foliage from his mouth. During the Civil War, Royalists christened a horse at this font with the name of Charles.

Bodmin

BODMIN, the only large Cornish town mentioned in the Domesday Book, became Cornwall's third county town in 1838 when the county assizes moved there from Launceston. In 1889 the newly formed Cornwall County Council decided to base itself in the new cathedral town of Truro and in 1988 the main courthouse followed, more or less destroying Bodmin's faint hopes of remaining the county town. Bodmin is dominated by the 15th-century ST PETROC'S CHURCH, the largest church in Cornwall, which stands on the site of a monastery founded by St Petroc in AD 530. Church treasures include a wonderful richly carved 12th-century Norman font standing on pillars with capitals of winged angels and figures engaged in the fight between good and evil. On display in the south aisle is the 12th-century painted ivory 'Bodmin Casket' which once held the relics of St Petroc.

Bodmin's grim gaol, said to be Britain's most haunted, was built in 1779 and was THE FIRST BRITISH PRISON TO HOLD PRISONERS IN INDIVIDUAL CELLS. During World War One it provided a safe haven for the Domesday Book as well as other important state papers and records. It closed as a prison in 1927, leaving Cornwall with no prison at all, and has since been converted into a hotel and tourist attraction.

Truro

TRURO sits at the head of one of the many arms of the River Fal, where the Kenwyn and Allen join to form the River Truro. It is CORNWALL'S ONLY CITY AND THE SOUTHERNMOST CITY IN BRITAIN. When, in 1889, the newly constituted Cornwall County Council chose Truro over the then county town of Bodmin for its headquarters, Truro became for all intents and purposes the county town of Cornwall, a status that was only consolidated when the main county court moved from Bodmin to Truro in 1988, although even today the position is debated.

An important port and stannary town in the Middle Ages, Truro was granted a charter 800 years ago by King John and was Cornwall's earliest municipality. It lost much of its trade to Falmouth after the Civil War but regained at least its social standing in the 18th and 19th centuries, when the rich merchants and mine owners chose Truro for their town houses over the somewhat disreputable and workaday port of Falmouth.

Today, as a result, Truro boasts some of the finest Georgian architecture in the country. Georgian Truro's social life revolved around the splendid ASSEMBLY ROOMS of 1780, located outside the West Door of the cathedral on High Cross, the tiny cobbled plaza that marks the birthplace of Truro. The rooms were used for balls and as a theatre. Beautiful LEMON STREET, funded by tin merchant and MP SIR WILLIAM LEMON, was completed in 1830 and would do Bath proud – indeed, it is known as the 'Pride of Truro'. WALSINGHAM PLACE, constructed in 1837, is an almost perfect small Georgian crescent that was, unbelievably, threatened with demolition in the 1960s until John Betjeman, who was touring Cornwall researching for his Shell Guide, put a stop to the madness, as he so often did.

Lander's Monument

At the top of Lemon Street, the explorer RICHARD LANDER gazes out over Truro from the top of one of Cornwall's grandest monuments, a Doric column known as Lander's Monument. Standing at 70 feet (21 metres) from the base to the top of the statue's head, the monument was built in 1835 by Devonport-born architect PHILIP SAMBELL who designed a number of buildings in Truro, his talent being all the more remarkable in that he was born deaf and non-verbal. Richard Lander was born in Truro in 1804, as was his brother John two years later, and together they charted the true course of the River Niger in West Africa in 1830, the first Europeans to discover that the Niger drained into the Atlantic. In 1832 Richard became THE FIRST WINNER OF THE ROYAL GEOGRAPHICAL SOCIETY'S FOUNDER'S MEDAL '*for the encouragement and promotion of geographical science and discovery*'. He died from gangrene on a later expedition along the Niger in 1834 after sustaining a gunshot wound.

Truro Cathedral

Dominating Truro and rising majestically above the rooftops and the narrow streets, with no close or spreading lawns to keep it aloof from the town, is Truro Cathedral, THE FIRST ANGLICAN CATHEDRAL AFTER ST PAUL'S TO BE BUILT SINCE THE REFORMATION AND THE FIRST ANGLICAN CATHEDRAL TO BE BUILT ON A NEW SITE IN ENGLAND SINCE SALISBURY CATHEDRAL IN 1220. It is THE SOUTHERNMOST CATHEDRAL IN ENGLAND AND ONE OF ONLY TWO ENGLISH CATHEDRALS WITH THREE SPIRES, the other being Lichfield.

The cathedral is the mother church of the Diocese of Cornwall which, with backing from Prime Minister Benjamin Disraeli, separated from the Diocese of Devon in 1876 while the first Bishop of Truro, EDWARD BENSON, was consecrated in St Paul's Cathedral in 1877. The foundation stone of the cathedral was laid by the Earl of Cornwall, later Edward VII, in 1880.

Often described as the perfect cathedral in miniature, Truro was designed in Early English Gothic Revival style by leading architect of the day J.L. Pearson and completed by his son, and is regarded as an outstanding example of Victorian high art. It stands on the site of Truro's original 16th-century parish church of St Mary, the south aisle of which has been seamlessly incorporated into the cathedral and still serves as Truro's parish church.

The 250-foot (76 metres) central tower was completed in 1905 while the two western towers, each 220 feet (61 metres) high, were the last part of the cathedral to be finished in 1910. They were dedicated to the recently deceased Edward VII and his wife Queen Alexandra, of whom there are statues, along with Queen Victoria and Bishop Edward Benson, over the West Door. The central tower is known as the Victoria Tower in honour of the Queen who granted Truro city status in 1877.

Highlights of the cathedral include the intricately carved reredos by Nathaniel Hitch behind the high altar and the stained-glass windows which narrate the story of the Church, starting with the birth of Christ and finishing with the building of Truro Cathedral. The windows are by Clayton and Bell and are regarded as amongst the finest examples of Victorian stained glass in England. If you stand at the west door and look down the length of the cathedral, you may notice that the nave and the choir are not perfectly aligned. This is because the site allotted for the cathedral was extremely cramped and irregular so that the nave and choir had to be designed along slightly different axes.

In the early years, while the cathedral was being built, Bishop Edward Benson conducted services from a wooden hut beside the building site and it was there that he held THE FIRST SERVICE OF NINE LESSONS AND CAROLS, a service he devised and which is now a traditional part of Anglican Christmas Eve church services across the world.

Bodmin Moor

BODMIN MOOR is wild and bleak, brown and boggy, but somehow romantic with a desolate, granite beauty. Covering some 80 square miles in the heart of Cornwall, most of the moor is a plateau over 800 feet high dotted with tors, and one of the densest concentrations of Bronze Age and Neolithic sites in Europe. The moor boasts Cornwall's two highest points, ROUGH TOR at 1,313 feet (400 metres) and BROWN WILLY at 1,378 feet (420 metres). The latter's name is a corruption of the Cornish 'Bron Ewhella' meaning 'highest hill'.

The views from both range across Cornwall from the Atlantic to the Channel and even into Devon, with the little church at far-off Brentor on the edge of Dartmoor seen glinting in the sun on a fine day.

Just one main road, the A30, crosses the moor, and to appreciate the rugged beauties of the landscape you must mostly leave the car and walk, although Bodmin's most celebrated attraction actually lies beside the road, right in the middle of the moor.

Jamaica Inn

Named in honour of Lord of the Manor Sir William Trelawny (1722–72) who had been a Governor of Jamaica, and also because it did a good trade in Jamaican rum, this atmospheric old inn in the tiny hamlet of Bolventor was made famous by Daphne du Maurier's best-selling 1936 novel, *Jamaica Inn*, which tells the story of a murderous innkeeper mixed up in smuggling and wrecking and was written after du Maurier stayed at the inn in 1930.

Standing alone on the empty moor midway between Launceston and Bodmin, the real Jamaica Inn was built in the 1750s as somewhere travellers and passenger coaches making their gruelling way across the moor could change horses and rest awhile. By saving the long trek around the north of the moor, the inn quickly became popular with the Royal Mail carrying mail between London, Exeter and Falmouth, then the port for international mail. The last Royal Mail coach to call at Jamaica Inn was in 1851 after Falmouth lost the Royal Mail contract to Southampton, and for the next half a century the inn suffered a catastrophic decline in trade. It was rescued by the introduction of the car, bringing a resurgence of traffic across the moor and, in 1930, the visit of Daphne du Maurier, whose inspiration ensured that Jamaica Inn would flourish evermore. The Daphne du Maurier Museum at the inn, which opened in 1990, contains memorabilia including her original writing desk and typewriter.

For a few years in the 1960s, Jamaica Inn was owned by thriller writer Alistair MacLean.

Bodmin's Moorland Villages

Cornwall's two highest points, Brown Willy and Rough Tor, are both mentioned in the novel *Jamaica Inn* as is the moorland village of Altarnun.

Altarnun
A cheerful sight after the grey emptiness of the moor, the gaily painted cottages of ALTARNUN, 'the altar of St Non', sit in a shelter of trees beside a fast-running stream crossed by an old packhorse bridge. The village sits at the centre of the largest parish in Cornwall and boasts a huge church to match. Known as the Cathedral of the Moor, the Church of St Nonna (mother of St David, patron saint of Wales) is 15th-century and renowned for its superb Norman font, grand waggon roof and fine carved bench ends dating from between 1510 and 1530, showing jesters,

griffins, angels and even a bagpipe player, far from home. There is also a rare 'vernicle' or image of Jesus, as seen on the veil used by St Veronica to wipe his face of sweat and blood when she encountered him on the Via Dolorosa on his way to the Crucifixion.

Elsewhere, John Wesley watches from above the door of the Georgian meeting house, as a bust by NEVILL BURNARD (1818–78), who sculpted the statue of Richard Lander atop Lander's Monument in Truro and who was born in Altarnun.

Blisland

Of all the country churches of the West that I have seen, I think that Blisland is the most beautiful.

Sir John Betjeman

The gorgeous Norman church of ST PROTUS AND ST HYACINTH in BLISLAND is the only church in England with such a dedication. St Protus and St Hyacinth were brothers who were martyred in Rome for their Christian faith during the persecution of the Emperor Valerian in the 3rd century. The church possesses a glorious 15th-century barrel-vaulted roof with painted bosses and carvings of angels, amongst the best in any English church, and a magnificent rood screen richly coloured in reds, greens and golds that was the work of F.C. EDEN who was responsible for restoring the church in 1894.

The lovely tree-bedecked village green, one of only three in all of Cornwall, is fringed with Georgian stone cottages, the award-winning Blisland Inn and a beautiful Tudor manor house with a fine gabled porch.

Lavethan
Just outside the village is LAVETHAN, 'the house in the meadow', one of the oldest houses in Cornwall, which began life as a typical Cornish longhouse with rooms below for animals and the upper rooms for the human occupants and was then expanded in the 13th century by the Kempe family. Although there were further additions in the 17th and 18th centuries, much of the 13th-century core of the house survives. Today the house and outbuildings are used for concerts, events and residential courses.

Prehistoric Remains
Blisland lies below HAWKSTOR DOWN, one of Bodmin's highest hills, which is scattered with

prehistoric sites including two Neolithic stone circles, the TRIPPET STONES and the STRIPPLE STONES, considered the most impressive of the moor's many prehistoric remains.

Jubilee Rock

Up on the moor not far from Blisland is the JUBILEE ROCK, considered to be the oldest stone on Bodmin Moor. It was decorated in 1810 with the Falmouth coat of arms on one side and the Molesworth coat of arms on the other to celebrate George III's Golden Jubilee. Inscriptions honouring the Golden Jubilees of Queen Victoria and Elizabeth II were added later.

Minions

At 980 feet (300 metres) above sea level, MINIONS, on the eastern flank of Bodmin Moor, is THE HIGHEST VILLAGE IN CORNWALL. The village found fame in 2015 with the release of the animated comedy film *Minions*, which brought an influx of tourists wanting to be photographed next to the village road sign donated by the film company showing a group of Minions characters urging motorists to drive carefully.

One mile north-west of Minions is the CHEESEWRING, a distinctive natural rock outcrop

The Cheesewring

of volcanic slabs resembling a stack of cheeses. Below is DANIEL GUMB'S CAVE where stonemason Daniel Gumb lived with his wife and children to avoid paying taxes.

St Breward

At 700 feet (213 metres) above sea level, ST BREWARD, on the western edge of Bodmin Moor, is another of the highest villages in Cornwall and can boast CORNWALL'S HIGHEST CHURCH AND CORNWALL'S HIGHEST PUB, THE OLD INN, which dates from the 11th century (as does the church), and has been trading as a pub since the 15th century.

King Arthur's Hall

Two miles to the north-east of St Breward is KING ARTHUR'S HALL, a rectangular Neolithic stone enclosure thought to have been used for ceremonial purposes. This is another of the sites on Bodmin Moor supposed to have been frequented by King Arthur (see Dozmary Pool, page 242), hence the name.

De Lank Quarries
East of St Breward on the De Lank River are the famous DE LANK GRANITE QUARRIES, source of the world's finest silver-grey granite, the building blocks for many London landmarks including London Bridge, Tower Bridge and the Thames Embankment. The De Lank River itself is a favourite haunt of otters.

Devil's Jump
Three miles north of St Breward, two mighty granite crags guard the entrance to a deep ravine. Called the DEVIL'S JUMP, they stand 300 yards (275 metres) apart on either side of the valley, one of Bodmin Moor's more spectacular sites.

St Neot
Set in a beautiful wooded valley on the southern slopes of Bodmin Moor, ST NEOT, named after a 9th-century saint who was related to Alfred the Great, is a quiet village gathered around a large 15th-century church spectacularly sited against a hill. The village was firmly Royalist in the Civil War and on Oak Apple Day, 29 May, which celebrates Charles II's restoration to the throne, an oak branch is placed on top of the church tower to express their historic loyalty to the Crown.

This is not why people come to St Neot from far and wide, however; they do so to gaze in wonder at one of the finest collections of medieval stained-glass windows in any church in England. There are 17 windows, some donated by local families, with about 350 figures representing various scenes from the lives of saints such as St Neot and St George and stories from the Bible such as Noah, the Last Supper and the Resurrection.

When the church was being restored in the 1820s some of the medieval glass was found to be missing or broken and this was carefully replaced by new glass, so most of the windows are a mix of original and restored work. The finest and least restored window is the Creation Window which is said to date from 1199, making it one of the oldest stained-glass windows in Britain.

To see the interior of St Neot's church when the sun is shining through the south windows and all is dappled in rich colours and the figures seem to move and sway is one of the unmissable sights of Cornwall.

St Clether

ST CLETHER'S WELL in the less-visited north of Bodmin Moor is the largest and best-preserved holy well in Cornwall, a county renowned for its holy wells. St Clether was one of the many children of the Welsh king Brychan who appear in Cornwall and here his well springs from the rocks in the wild and beautiful valley of the River Inny. It is reached through an arch protected by a huge pointed roof from where it flows underground into a recess in the medieval chapel next to it.

Not far away is one of Cornwall's oldest and most secretive houses, the early 14th-century BASILL MANOR, its name unchanged since 1302. The house is set around a courtyard and includes a great hall, a spiral staircase and, above one of the doors, a coat of arms granted to the owners, the TREVELYANS, by Edward I for service during the Crusades.

A visit to this hidden corner of Cornwall, with Basill Manor and St Clether's Holy Well and Chapel untroubled by modernity, transports you right back to the early 13th century, the days of chivalry and saints, a magical place.

Warleggan

Known as the loneliest place in Cornwall, WARLEGGAN is tucked away down a narrow lane in the heart of Bodmin Moor a few miles west of St Neot. Tiny cottages climb away from a rocky stream towards a 15th-century church on a hill that looks out across miles of rugged moorland. Few people wept when the Rector of Warleggan, the REVEREND FRANCIS DENSHAM, died alone in the Rectory in 1953. Rev Densham was renowned as the rudest clergyman in Cornwall and on taking up the post in 1931 he closed the Sunday school, painted the interior of the church in bright colours and fitted the windows and doors of the church with locks. He was so abusive to his parishioners that for ten years they refused to attend church services, as attested to in one church register: 'No fog. No wind. No rain. No congregation.'

Unbothered, he made himself a congregation of cardboard figures, which he propped up in the pews and on Sundays would harangue them with fiery sermons. Thought to survive on a diet of nettles and gruel, he got rid of all his furniture in case it was stolen and, just to be doubly sure, surrounded the Rectory with barbed wire and a pack of dogs. There was another side to him, however. He would take flowers to the villagers in spring and milk to parishioners who were ill. He even built a playground for the village children in his garden, although few came, and gave slide shows that some of the villagers remember going to when they were young. Unorthodox, maybe, eccentric without doubt. But he certainly put tiny Warleggan on the map.

Daphne du Maurier is believed to have based the mad vicar in *Jamaica Inn* on Rev Densham.

River Fowey

One of the most picturesque of Cornwall's many picturesque rivers, the RIVER FOWEY rises on the slopes of Brown Willy, Cornwall's highest point, and flows south for 27 miles past a variety of interesting places to reach the English Channel at Fowey.

Half a mile east of the River Fowey, set in a stone enclosure beside a narrow country lane near St Cleer, sits the 9th-century KING DONIERT'S STONE, three sides carved with an intricate interlacing pattern and the fourth side bearing the inscription *'Doniert Rogavit pro anima'* which translates as *'Doniert begs prayers for the sake of his soul'*. Doniert is thought to be King Dumgarth, the last King of Cornwall, who drowned in the River Fowey in AD 875.

After coming off the moor, a little further on from King Doniert's Stone, the Fowey flows through ancient oak woodland down a spectacular series of cascades known as GOLITHA FALLS.

The river is then joined by a tributary fed by COLLIFORD LAKE, the largest inland lake in Cornwall, covering some 900 acres. Colliford Lake is, in turn, fed by Dozmary Pool.

Dozmary Pool

A mile south from Bolventor, the hamlet that grew up around Jamaica Inn, DOZMARY POOL is said to be bottomless and to have never dried up. Alas, it is actually no more than nine feet (2.7 metres) deep and it did dry up in 1899 – but this need not detract from the legend that tells us it was here that King Arthur rowed out to receive his sword Excalibur from the Lady of the Lake, and that it was to here that Arthur's knight Bedivere returned Excalibur after Arthur was slain at the Battle of

Camlann. After Bedivere flung the sword into the lake a woman's arm, clad in white, rose out of the water, clasped the sword and sank down beneath the surface. Excalibur apparently lies in Dozmary Pool still, although the black, lifeless water does not entice you to dive in and look for it.

JAN TREGEAGLE – CORNWALL'S FAUST

When the wind moans across the moor or howls across the clifftops, Cornish folk are wont to say *'Tis the crying of Tregeagle'*. Legend has it that Jan Tregeagle was an evil lawyer and land agent for the Duchy of Cornwall in the 17th century who robbed his tenants, murdered his wife and sold his soul to the Devil in return for becoming fabulously rich. When he died, he was buried in St Breock church near Wadebridge but, tormented by his sins, his soul was unable to rest easy and so he begged the local priests to save him from the hounds of hell in return for his ill-gotten fortune. The priests decided their only option was to set him a series of tasks that would keep him busy until Judgement Day and the first of these tasks was to bale out Dozmary Pool (then thought to be bottomless) using a limpet shell with a hole in it. If he faltered, the hounds would pounce ... Other tasks included spinning ropes out of sand and carrying bags of sand across the River Cober near Helston, one of which he spilled across the mouth of the river, thus forming Loe Bar (see page 198).

Respryn Bridge

Having flowed west for a few miles, the Fowey then ripples under the lovely 15th-century RESPRYN BRIDGE, which replaced an earlier 13th-century bridge, which in turn replaced a chapel where travellers could pray for a safe crossing. It was said that too many times their prayers were not answered and they didn't make it to the other side, which is hard to fathom when you see the innocent-looking slow-running stream that burbles under the bridge today. However, this was a key crossing place on the old

Lanhydrock House

track from Bodmin to Looe and one of the most important strategic points in Cornwall, hence the need for a bridge. Respryn Brigde came into its own again during the Civil War as it lay between Lanhydrock and Boconnoc which were on opposite sides, and the bridge was used more than once by Charles I in 1644.

Lanhydrock House

A glorious avenue of beech trees leads from the bridge through parkland to Lanhydrock's striking battlemented and turreted gatehouse of 1651.

LANHYDROCK HOUSE itself is considered by many to be Cornwall's loveliest old house. It was built between 1620 and 1642, originally around a courtyard, by the ROBARTES family. Despite these wool and tin merchants from Truro being known as 'the Wealthiest of the West', the house was neglected over the years by the family who lived mostly in London. The east wing was demolished in 1780 and then, between 1857 and 1864, the house was modernised and remodelled by Sir George Gilbert Scott for owner THOMAS JAMES AGAR-ROBARTES (1808–82), MP for East Cornwall. Much of this work was destroyed by fire in 1881 and restored and extended again to the same design by Scott's assistant Richard Coad.

The only part of the 17th-century house that survives is the North Wing which contains the highlight of Lanhydrock, the tunnel-vaulted Long Gallery of c.1650, 116 feet (35 metres) long with a sensational plaster ceiling illustrating scenes from the Old Testament.

Restormel Castle

Restormel Castle

At Lanhydrock the Fowey turns south and after three miles flows past the remarkable RESTORMEL CASTLE, the best preserved of the 71 round shell keeps in England and Wales. Perched on a high mound and surrounded by a dry moat, Restormel is an almost perfect ring of stone set within a ring of trees.

Originally a wooden motte and bailey castle built around 1100 to command a key crossing point on the Fowey, Restormel was rebuilt in the 13th century, with the external wooden palisade replaced by a stone wall, while the inner bailey was filled with domestic buildings curved to fit within the circular walls. Water was supplied through a well in the courtyard and also via an early kind of pressurised water system that used gravity to pipe water from a spring further up the hill along a lead conduit into the castle. All this was done to provide luxurious accommodation for Edmund, the Earl of Cornwall, grandson of King John, who made Restormel his major residence and the administrative centre of his Cornish estates. The castle was made into an even more sumptuous palace for the BLACK PRINCE, 1ST DUKE OF CORNWALL, who enjoyed two long stays at Restormel in 1354 and 1362. After this the castle fell into decay and, except for a brief moment in the Civil War when it was occupied by Royalist forces under Sir Richard Grenville, Restormel was allowed to disintegrate until taken into the care of the state in 1925. While still officially owned by the Duchy of Cornwall, Restormel is now cared for by English Heritage.

The Fowey now flows on through Cornwall's ancient royal capital Lostwithiel (see page 231) and ripples past the lonely but lovely riverside church of St Winnow, originally Norman but rebuilt in the 15th century. Boasting an Elizabethan pulpit, 16th-century rood screen and exotically carved 16th-century bench ends, the church sits next to the ST WINNOW BARTON FARM MUSEUM which showcases Cornish farming equipment from the last 100 years.

Next the Fowey is joined by the River Lerryn, really just a wooded tidal creek that glides past ETHY WOODS, where Kenneth Grahame wandered while honeymooning in Fowey, and are said to be the inspiration for the Wild Wood in *The Wind in the Willows*. Then on to the impossibly pretty village of Lerryn with its pre-16th-century bridge mentioned by Elizabeth I as needing restoration. If the tide is out, you can cross the river here on stepping-stones.

Boconnoc House

BOCONNOC HOUSE, four miles east of Lostwithiel, is a beautifully situated Georgian mansion that was the home of the PITT family, who produced two British prime ministers, for much of the 18th century. The site had been occupied since Norman times and the present house was begun in 1579 on the site of a medieval tower house by Sir William Mohun, a member by marriage of the Courtenay family, later Earls of Devon.

In 1717, THOMAS PITT, Governor of Madras, bought Boconnoc with the proceeds from the sale of a diamond he had purchased while in India. He became known as DIAMOND PITT, while the diamond became known as the Pitt Diamond. Pitt bought the diamond for the equivalent of £4 million today and sold it to the Duke of Orleans, Prince Regent of France, for the equivalent of £26 million. It then became known as the Regent Diamond and was inserted into the coronation crowns of Louis XV and Louis XVI; the latter then gave it to his wife, Marie Antionette. By divers means the diamond came to be in the possession of the Louvre in Paris where it is on display today and is thought to be worth some £60 million at today's prices, making Boconnoc House one of the best bargains ever. Thomas 'Diamond' Pitt was the grandfather of Prime Minister William Pitt the Elder and great-grandfather of Prime Minister William Pitt the Younger, cousin of Prime Minister William

Grenville, and whose mother was the sister of Prime Minister George Grenville. That's the way they did things in those days.

Boconnoc House eventually passed by marriage to the FORTESCUE family, who still own it today and run the estate as a wedding and holiday venue. The ancient deer park at Boconnoc House is ONE OF THE MOST IMPORTANT SITES IN EUROPE FOR LICHENS.

Cotehele

COTEHELE, the second home of the Edgcumbe family of Mount Edgcumbe, sits in a secluded wooded valley on the west bank of the River Tamar. It was built by Sir Richard Edgcumbe in 1485 around an earlier medieval house and funded by the rewards of fighting for Henry VII at the Battle of Bosworth. The only way to get to the house was by boat from Plymouth and because it was so remote and difficult to access, the Edgcumbes rather neglected the house, with the result that it is ONE OF THE BEST-PRESERVED AND LEAST-ALTERED TUDOR HOUSES IN ENGLAND. In 1947 Cotehele was handed over to the National Trust, the first house to be given to the Trust in lieu of death duties. It is famous for the finest collection of tapestries in England.

The grounds go down to the quay on the river where the Edgcumbes and their guests would arrive from Plymouth. The National Trust has renovated the quayside warehouses and docks to give an idea of how it would have looked in the Edgcumbes' time.

Nearby is a small chapel on a low promontory. In the days

before the Battle of Bosworth, Richard III had sent men to Cotehele to arrest Sir Richard Edgcumbe, a known supporter of Henry Tudor, but he fled down to the river, threw his cap into the water and hid behind a low promontory. His pursuers assumed Sir Richard had drowned and they departed. When he returned triumphant after the battle, he built the chapel on the promontory in thanks for his escape.

WELL, I NEVER KNEW THIS ABOUT

MID CORNWALL

Pride of place in the ROYAL CORNWALL MUSEUM in Truro is the TREWINNARD COACH, built in 1700, the first coach ever seen in Cornwall and one of the earliest in all of England. A status symbol, it was built for the Spanish ambassador and later came into the possession of wealthy lawyer Christopher Hawkins (1694–1767) who would use it to go to church with his wife Mary. The coach was last used in 1780 to transport Mary Hawkins to St Erth Church for her burial.

Hidden in a green hollow at the foot of a steep hill and embowered in trees is COME-TO-GOOD, a tiny hamlet a few miles south of Truro. The name comes from the Cornish 'Cwm Ty Quoit' which means 'house in a wooded

combe'. Beside the road sits one of the quaintest houses in Cornwall, a simple, straw-thatched, white-painted cob hut built in 1710: one of the oldest Quaker meeting houses in England. The windows came from an older building and date from 1640 while inside is all wood panelling, with plain wooden benches lining the walls and facing a table at the centre. There is a small gallery, supported on wooden pillars, from where the meeting is addressed. Quaker ministers have been known to preach for three hours or more by which time the benches, which have no cushions, must be quite uncomfortable – which, of course, is what they are meant to be. The Meeting House has been in regular use since it was built and still hosts meetings every Sunday.

In 2017 Bodmin Moor was designated an International Dark Sky Landscape, where there is little or no artificial light pollution to interfere with observation of the night sky.

Born at Lidcott Farm in Laneast, west of Launceston, JOHN COUCH ADAMS (1819–92) predicted the existence of Neptune by calculating that anomalies in the orbit of Uranus indicated an eighth planet beyond it. While the farmhouse where he was born has been rebuilt, the little schoolroom beside the church where he studied mathematics and first saw a meteor shower, the Leonid meteor shower of 1833, still stands. This event inspired Adams to study meteor showers for the rest of his life and he was the first person to discover that meteor showers are caused by debris trails left by comets. The Adams Prize, awarded each year by St John's College, Cambridge, to a UK-based mathematician for distinguished research in mathematical sciences, is named in his honour.

CORNWALL'S OLDEST BRIDGE, and the only Cornish bridge to feature stone ribs in the vaults underneath, is YEOLM BRIDGE, which spans the River Ottery some two miles north of Launceston. Comprised of two pointed arches, the bridge was built in 1350 when the Ottery here formed the boundary between Cornwall and Devon, making Yeolm Bridge one of the earliest bridged crossing points between the two counties. The bridge gives its name to the village of YEOLMBRIDGE and is still in use.

CAMELFORD means 'ford over the twisting river' from the Cornish

word *'kammel'* meaning 'crooked'. Since it sounds like the animal, the town has adopted the camel as a symbol. There is a golden camel sitting atop the cupola of the town hall as a weathervane and a camel can be seen on the town coat of arms. Camelford is one of a number of places in the West Country that claims to be King Arthur's Camelot and possibly the site of the 6th-century Battle of Camlann at which King Arthur was mortally wounded. This ties in nicely with the legend of Dozmary Pool, where Arthur's sword Excalibur was returned by the knight Bedivere, which lies only ten miles away on Bodmin Moor.

The church at DAVIDSTOW, a small village on the northern edge of Bodmin Moor some three miles from Camelford, is thought to have been founded in the 6th century by the patron saint of Wales, St David, while on a visit to his mother St Nonna at Altarnun. Today the village is known as the site of BRITAIN'S LARGEST CHEESE PRODUCER, DAVIDSTOW, which uses water from St David's Holy Well to make Davidstow Cheddar and Cathedral City cheeses.

GAZZETTEER

Interesting locations and places open to the public.

(NT) National Trust
(EH) English Heritage

Exeter

St Nicholas Priory
The Mint, Exeter, Devon, EX4 3BL
https://nicholaspriory.com

Tuckers Hall
140 Fore Street, Exeter, EX4 3AN
Tel: 01392 302 109
https://tuckershall.org.uk/

Exeter Custom House
46 The Quay, Exeter, EX2 4AN
Tel: 01392 271 611
https://exetercustomhouse.co.uk/

Exeter Cathedral
https://www.exeter-cathedral.org.uk/

Underground passages
2 Paris St, Exeter, EX1 1GA
Tel: 01392 665 887
https://exeter.gov.uk/leisure-and-culture/our-attractions/underground-passages/visitor-information/

East Devon

Tiverton Castle
Park Hill Tiverton Devon, EX16 6RP
Tel: 01884 253 200
https://www.tivertoncastle.com/history.htm

Old Blundell's (NT)
Station Road, Tiverton,
Devon, EX16 4LB https://www.heritageopendays.org.uk/submission-event/old-blundell-s.html

Knightshayes Court (NT)
Bolham, Tiverton, Devon, EX16 7RQ
Tel: 01884 254 665
https://www.nationaltrust.org.uk/visit/devon/knightshayes

Bickleigh Mill
Bickleigh, Tiverton, EX16 8RG
Tel: 01884 855 419
https://www.bickleighmill.com/

Devon Railway Centre
The Station, Bickleigh, Tiverton,
EX16 8RG
Tel: 01884 855 671
https://devonrailwaycentre.co.uk/contact-us/

Bickleigh Castle
Bickleigh, Tiverton, EX16 8RP
Tel: 01884 855 363
https://bickleighcastle.com/contact/

A La Ronde (NT)
Summer Lane, Exmouth, Devon, EX8 5BD
Tel: 01395 265 514
https://www.nationaltrust.org.uk/visit/devon/a-la-ronde

Gazzetteer

Branscombe Forge (NT)
Branscombe, Seaton, EX12 3DB
Tel: 01297 680 481
https://www.branscombeforge.com/

Seaton Tramway
Harbour Rd, Seaton, EX12 2WD
https://www.tram.co.uk/

Beer Quarry Caves
Quarry Ln, Beer, Seaton, EX12 3AS
Tel: 01297 680 282
https://www.beerquarrycaves.co.uk/

Cadhay House
Ottery St Mary, Devon, EX11 1QT
Tel: 01404813 511
https://cadhay.org.uk/contact/

Old Shute House (NT)
Shute, near Axminster, Devon, EX13 7PT
https://www.nationaltrust.org.uk/visit/devon/shute-barton

North Devon

Lundy Island (Landmark Trust)
Tel: 01271 863 636
https://www.landmarktrust.org.uk/lundyisland/contact-us/

Clovelly
Tel: 01237 431 781
https://www.clovelly.co.uk/

Hartland Abbey
Hartland, Bideford, EX39 6DT
Tel: 01237 441 496
https://www.hartlandabbey.com/

Chambercombe Manor, Ilfracombe
https://chambercombemanor.org.uk/

Dartmoor and West Devon

Okehampton Castle (EH)
Castle Ln, Okehampton, EX20 1JA
https://www.english-heritage.org.uk/visit/places/okehampton-castle/

Finch Foundry (NT)
Sticklepath, Okehampton, EX20 2NW
Tel: 01837 840 046
https://www.nationaltrust.org.uk/visit/devon/finch-foundry

Canonteign Falls
Lower Ashton, Nr Exeter, Devon, EX6 7RH
Tel: 01647 252434
https://www.canonteignfalls.co.uk/

Castle Drogo (NT)
Drewsteignton, near Exeter, Devon, EX6 6PB
Tel: 01647 433 306
https://www.nationaltrust.org.uk/visit/devon/castle-drogo

Lydford Gorge (NT)
Lydford, near Tavistock, Devon, EX20 4BH
Tel: 01822 820 320
https://www.nationaltrust.org.uk/visit/devon/lydford-gorge

Dartmoor Prison Museum
HMP Dartmoor, Princetown, Devon, PL20 6RR
Tel: 01822 322 130
https://www.dartmoor-prison.co.uk/

Morwellham Quay
Tavistock, Devon, PL19 8JL
Tel: 01822 832 766
https://www.morwellham-quay.co.uk/

Buckfast Abbey
Buckfastleigh, Devon, TQ11 0EE
Tel: 01364 645 500
https://www.buckfast.org.uk/

Buckland Abbey
Yelverton, Devon, PL20 6EY
Tel: 01822 853 607
https://www.nationaltrust.org.uk/visit/devon/buckland-abbey

Dart Valley Railway
https://www.southdevonrailway.co.uk/

South Devon

Dartmouth Castle (EH)
https://www.english-heritage.org.uk/visit/places/dartmouth-castle/

Greenway (NT)
Greenway Road, Galmpton, near Brixham, Devon, TQ5 0ES
Tel: 01803 843 235
https://www.nationaltrust.org.uk/visit/devon/greenway

Totnes Castle (EH)
https://www.english-heritage.org.uk/visit/places/totnes-castle/

Dartington Hall
Dartington, Totnes, Devon, TQ9 6EL
Tel: 01803 847000
https://www.dartington.org/

Torre Abbey
The King's Drive, Torquay, TQ2 5JE
Tel: 01803 293 593
https://www.torre-abbey.org.uk/

Kents Cavern
Cavern House, 91 Ilsham Road, Torquay, Devon, TQ1 2JF
Tel: 01803 215 136
https://www.kents-cavern.co.uk/

Compton Castle (NT)
Marldon, Paignton, Devon, TQ3 1TA
Tel: 01803 843 235
https://www.nationaltrust.org.uk/visit/devon/compton-castle

Powderham Castle
Powderham Estate, Exeter, EX6 8JQ
Tel: 01626 890 243
https://www.powderham.co.uk/

Plymouth

Royal Citadel (EH)
https://www.english-heritage.org.uk/visit/places/royal-citadel-plymouth/

Devonport Column
Ker St, Devonport, Column, Plymouth, PL1 4EL
Tel: 01752 395 028
https://www.visitplymouth.co.uk/things-to-do/devonport-guildhall-p2942623

Saltram House (NT)
Plympton, Plymouth, Devon, PL7 1UH
Tel: 01752 333 500
https://www.nationaltrust.org.uk/visit/devon/saltram

North Cornwall

Hawker's Hut (NT)
Morwenstow, Nr Bude
Tel: 01208 863 046
https://www.nationaltrust.org.uk/visit/cornwall/morwenstow/hawkers-hut-walk

Bude Castle
The Wharf, Bude, EX23 8LG
Tel: 01288 357 300
https://www.thecastlebude.co.uk/

Museum of Witchcraft and Magic
The Harbour, Boscastle, PL35 0HD
https://museumofwitchcraftandmagic.co.uk/

Tintagel Castle (EH)
https://www.english-heritage.org.uk/visit/places/tintagel-castle/

Old Post Office
Fore Street, Tintagel, Cornwall, PL34 0DB
Tel: 01840 770 024
https://www.nationaltrust.org.uk/visit/cornwall/tintagel-old-post-office

Prideaux Place
Padstow, Cornwall, PL28 8RP
Tel: 01841 532 411.
https://prideauxplace.co.uk/

Murdoch House
7 Cross Street, Redruth, Cornwall, TR15 2BU
Tel: 01209 213 807
https://murdochhouse.org.uk/

West Cornwall

Leach Pottery
Higher Stennack, St Ives, Cornwall, TR26 2HE
Tel: 01736 799 703
https://www.leachpottery.com/history

Barbara Hepworth Museum
Barnoon Hill, St Ives, TR26 1AD
Tel: 01736 796 226
https://www.tate.org.uk/visit/tate-st-ives/barbara-hepworth-museum-and-sculpture-garden

Botallack Mine (NT)
Nr St Just, Cornwall, TR19 7QQ
Tel: 01736 786 934
https://www.nationaltrust.org.uk/visit/cornwall/botallack

Levant Mine (NT)
Trewellard, Pendeen, Nr St Just, Cornwall, TR19 7SX
Tel: 01736 786 156
https://www.nationaltrust.org.uk/visit/cornwall/levant-mine-and-beam-engine

Geevor Tin Mine
Pendean, Penzance, Cornwall, TR19 7EW
Tel: 01736 788 662
https://geevor.com/

Land's End
Sennen, Penzance, TR19 7AA
Tel: 01736 871 501
https://landsend-landmark.co.uk/

Scilly Isles
https://www.visitislesofscilly.com/

Porthcurno Telegraph Museum
Eastern House, Porthcurno, Penzance, TR19 6JX
Tel: 01736 810 966
https://pkporthcurno.com/

Minack Theatre
Porthcurno, Penzance, TR19 6JU
Tel: 01736 810 181
https://minack.com/

St Michael's Mount (NT)
Marazion, Cornwall, TR17 0EG
Tel: 01736 887 822
https://www.nationaltrust.org.uk/visit/cornwall/st-michaels-mount

Godolphin House (NT)
Godolphin Cross, Helston, Cornwall, TR13 9RE
Tel: 01736 763 194
https://www.nationaltrust.org.uk/visit/cornwall/godolphin

Poldark Mine
Trenear, Helston, TR13 0ES
Tel: 01326 573 173
http://www.poldarkmine.org.uk/

South Cornwall

Pendennis Castle (EH)
Castle Dr, Falmouth, TR11 4LP
https://www.english-heritage.org.uk/visit/places/pendennis-castle/

St Mawes Castle (EH)
Castle Dr, St Mawes, Truro, TR2 5DE
https://www.english-heritage.org.uk/visit/places/st-mawes-castle/

Caerhays Castle
Gorran, St Austell, Cornwall, PL26 6LY
Tel: 01872 501 310
https://visit.caerhays.co.uk/

Lost Gardens of Heligan
Pentewan, St Austell, PL26 6EN
Tel: 01726 845 100
https://www.heligan.com/

Eden Project
Bodelva, Par, PL24 2SG
Tel: 01726 811 972
https://www.edenproject.com/

Port Eliot
St Germans, Saltash, PL12 5ND
Tel: 01503 230 211
https://www.porteliot.co.uk/

Mount Edgcumbe
Torpoint, Cornwall, PL10 1HZ
Tel: 01752 822 236
https://www.visitplymouth.co.uk/things-to-do/mount-edgcumbe-house-and-country-park-p1373933

Monkey Sanctuary
Murrayton House, St Martin, Looe, Cornwall, PL13 1NZ
Tel: 01503 262 532
https://www.monkeysanctuary.org/

Antony House (NT)
Torpoint, Cornwall, PL11 2QA
Tel: 01752 812 191
https://www.nationaltrust.org.uk/visit/cornwall/antony

Mid Cornwall

Launceston Castle (EH)
Castle Dyke, Launceston, PL15 7DR
https://www.english-heritage.org.uk/visit/places/launceston-castle/

Bodmin Jail
Berrycoombe Rd, Bodmin, PL31 2NR
https://www.bodminjail.org/

Lanhydrock House
Bodmin, Cornwall, PL30 4AB
Tel: 01208 265 950
https://www.nationaltrust.org.uk/visit/cornwall/lanhydrock

Restormel Castle (EH)
Restormel Rd, Lostwithiel, PL22 0HN
Tel: 01208 872 687
https://www.english-heritage.org.uk/visit/places/restormel-castle/

Boconnoc House
Boconnoc, Lostwithiel, PL22 0RG
Tel: 01208 872 507
https://boconnoc.com/

Cotehele (NT)
St Dominick, near Saltash, Cornwall, PL12 6TA
Tel: 01579 351 346
https://www.nationaltrust.org.uk/visit/cornwall/cotehele

INDEX OF PEOPLE

Abbot, William 59
Adam, Robert 147–8
Adams, John Couch 249
Agar-Robartes, Thomas James 244
Albert, Prince 50, 116, 132
Alexandra, Queen 235
Alfred the Great 3, 73
Amundsen, Roald 135
Angove, Charles 191
Anne of Cleves 19
Arthur, King 159, 161, 198, 242–3, 250
Arthur, Prince 127
Astor, Nancy 147
Athelstan, King 2, 3, 48, 221
Austen, Jane 59

Babbage, Benjamin 102
Babbage, Charles 23, 102
Bacon, Richard 171
Ball, Nicolas 103–4
Barnes, Djuna 80
Barrie, J.M. 220
Barron, Richard 68
Beacon, Belisha 131
Beatles 94, 116
Becket, St Thomas 6
Bedford, Earl of 13
Bedivere, Sir 198, 242–3
Benson, Edward, Bishop of Truro 235, 236
Beornwynn of Shaftesbury, Lady 104
Betjeman, Sir John 156, 163, 176, 233, 238
Bettesworth-Trevanion, John 213
Bickford, William 171
Binyon, Laurence 162
Black Prince 133, 231, 245

Blackmore, R.D. 19, 45
Blake, Admiral Robert 129
Bligh, Captain William 129–30, 135, 225
Blundell, Peter 19
Blyton, Enid 59
Bodley, Thomas 104
Boehm, Sir Joseph 127
Bolham, Richard 209
Bonaparte, Prince Louis-Napoleon 192
Bonville, Cecily 30, 39
Bonville, Sir William 39
Boone, Daniel 36
Boone III, George 36
Branwell, Maria 194
Bridges, Robert 218
Britten, Benjamin 108
Brooke, Charles 83
Brooke, Charles Vyner 83
Brooke, James 83
Brunel, Isambard Kingdom 118–19, 132
Brutus 99–100
Brychan (Celtic king) 150, 176, 241
Burges, William 20
Burgess, Guy 131
Burke, Edmund 146
Burnard, Nevill 238
Burton, Sir Richard 114–15
Bute, Marquess of 20
Butterfield, William 29, 30
Byron, Ada 23
Byron, Lady 23
Byron, Lord 23

Cabell, Richard 79, 85
Cade, Rowena 191–2
Cameron, David 176

[256]

Index of People

Cameron, Samantha 176
Camilla, Duchess of Cornwall 62
Campbell, Ivar 17–18
Carew, Dorothy 19
Carew family 17, 21, 22
Carew, Rachel 226
Carew, Sir William 226
Carew, Tom Daniel 19
Cary family 56, 114
Catherine of Aragon 127, 129, 133
Cavell, Edith 111
Cavendish family 119
Cavendish, William 119, 120
Chambers, Sir William 145
Chamond, Sir John 156
Champernowne, Catherine 117
Champernowne family 106
Champernowne, Sir Arthur 106
Chantrey, Sir Francis 136
Chapin, Samuel 111
Charles I, King 13, 21, 141, 156, 177, 218, 244
Charles II, King 1, 97, 127, 197, 240
Charles III, King 62, 98
Charlotte, Queen 35
Chichester, Sir Francis 61, 134
Christian, Fletcher 135
Christie, Archibald 115
Christie, Dame Agatha 71, 94–5, 99, 114, 115–16
Christie, Rosalind 99
Churchill, Winston 94
Churston, Lord 121
Clarkson, Thomas 136
Clerke, Charles 135
Coad, Richard 244
Coleman, Charlotte 107
Coleridge, James 30
Coleridge, Reverend John 30
Coleridge, Samuel Taylor 15, 30, 194
Colleton, Sir John 22–3
Collins, Ben 19

Compton family, de 116
Compton, Joan de 116
Cook, Captain James 133–4, 135
Cook, John Douglas 160
Cook, Peter 116
Cookworthy, William 215
Corbett, Jim 200
Cornwall, Duchy of 74, 76, 227, 232, 245
Cornwall, Earls of 74, 159, 228, 230, 231, 245
Cott, Johannes 105
Couch, Jonathan 225–6
Courtenay family 21, 46, 67, 119, 119–20, 246
Courtenay, Henry 67
Courtenay, Hugh 8
Courtenay, William 16, 119
Coverdale, Miles 112
Coward, Noel 94
Cowley, Hannah 20
Crediton, Bishop of 37, 63
Cromwell, Oliver 30, 102, 211, 212
Curry, William 107

Darwin, Charles 134
Davis, Steve 7
Davison, Ann 223
Davy, Sir Humphry 194–5
Day, John 146
Defoe, Daniel 32, 101
Denham, Reverend Francis 241–2
Devon, Earls of 16, 18, 67, 68, 119–20, 142
Dickens, Charles 13, 56
Disraeli, Benjamin 235
Dobson, Henry Austin 138
Doyle, Sir Arthur Conan 76, 79, 80, 147
Drake, Lady Fuller 127
Drake, Sir Francis 10, 27, 52, 54, 81, 88–90, 99, 110, 117, 126–7, 127, 129, 133, 134

Index of People

Drewe, Adrian 72
Drewe, Frances 72
Drewe, Julius 71–2
Dumgarth, King 242
Duncan, Isadora 112
Dutfield, Harry 36
Dyer, John 10

Eastlake, Charles Locke (architect) 137–8
Eastlake, Sir Charles Lock (painter) 136, 137, 143
Eden, F.C. 238
Edgcumbe family 247
Edgcumbe, Sir Richard 247, 248
Edmund, 2nd Earl of Cornwall 231
Edmund, Earl of Cornwall 245
Edward, Duke of Kent 31
Edward IV, King 39
Edward the Black Prince 133, 231, 245
Edward the Confessor 22, 73, 196
Edward VII, King 116, 235
Edward VIII, King 94
Edwards, Captain 225
Edwulf, Bishop of Crediton 63
Elford, Mary 76
Elizabeth I, Queen 26, 27, 28, 38, 89, 99, 117, 134
Elizabeth II, Queen 98, 134, 167, 239
Elmhirst, Leonard and Dorothy 80, 106, 108
English Heritage 18
Ethelred II (the Unready) 229
Exeter, Bishop of 82
Eyre, Richard 61

Fairfax, Sir Thomas 16–17, 30, 82, 102
Faraday, Michael 195
Farrand, Beatrix 109
Finch, William 68
Fitz Martin family 104
FitzGilbert, Baldwin 67
Fitzsimmons, Bob 200

Foot, Michael 139
Foreman, Freddie 78
Fortescue family 247
Fortescue, Sir John 60
Fortibus, Isabella de, Countess of Devon 8
Foulston, John 130, 194
Fowey Gallants 218
Fowler, Charles 101
Fox, George 230
Francis, Trevor 139–40
Freud, Clement 107
Freud, Lucien 107
Frobisher, Martin 127–8, 129
Froude, James 110
Froude, Margaret 109
Froude, Richard 109
Froude, Robert 109
Froude, William 109–10

Gainsborough, Thomas 43
Gandhi, Mahatma 111
Garfunkel, Art 21
Gay, John 49
Geoffrey of Monmouth 100, 159, 161
George III, King 35, 145, 239
George, Joseph and Annie 187
George V, King 98, 139
George VI, King 98
Georgina, Duchess of Bedford 81
Gibbons, Grinling 19
Gibbons, Stanley 147
Giffard family 59
Gifford, Emma 159
Gifford, Sir Robert 88
Gilbert, John 116
Gilbert, Sir Humphrey 26, 99, 117–18, 128, 147
Gilbert, Sir Jeffrey 116
Gladstone, William 139
Glanvill, Joseph 136
Godolphin family 196–7, 198

Index of People

Godolphin, Mary 197
Godolphin, Sir Francis 197
Godolphin, Sir Sydney 197
Goldsmith, Lieutenant Hugh 202
Goodwin, Ron 139
Gordon, General 6
Gordon of Khartoum, General 24
Graham, Winston 165, 203
Grahame, Kenneth 219, 225, 246
Grandisson, John, Bishop of Exeter 29–30
Gray, Charles, 2nd Earl Gray 136
Greenway, John 18, 19
Grenville family 52, 53–4
Grenville, George 247
Grenville, Roger 53, 88
Grenville, Sir Richard 10, 27, 53, 54, 88, 90, 117, 128, 157, 245
Grenville, William 246–7
Grey, Thomas 39
Grylls, Humphry Millet 198
Guggenheim, Peggy 80
Gurney, Sir Goldsworthy 153, 154–5
Gytha 3, 4, 5

Haigh, John 78
Hamada, Shoji 180
Hamblen, Jacob 225
Hamlyn, Christine 56
Hamlyn, Zachary 56
Hamlyn-Williams, James 57
Hansom, Joseph 132
Hanson, Sir Charles 219
Hardy, Thomas 159
Harrison, John 189
Harry, Prince 176
Harward family 25
Harward, Reverend Charles 25–6
Hawker, Robert 139
Hawker, Robert Stephen (grandson) 139, 151–2
Hawkes, Chesney 7

Hawkins, Christopher 248
Hawkins, Lady Judith 120
Hawkins, Mary 248
Hawkins, Sir John 10, 52, 117, 120, 134–5
Hawkins, Sir Richard 120
Hawley, John 97
Hayden, Robert 38
Haydon, Benjamin 136–7, 143
Haydon, John 37–8
Hearder, John Nash 130–1
Heathcoat-Amory, Sir John 20
Heathcoat, John 16, 20
Heenan, Hammersley 109
Hele, Elize 143
Henrietta Maria of France 21, 211
Henrietta, Princess 13, 21
Henry III, King 12, 38, 74
Henry VI, King 127
Henry VII, King 186, 247
Henry VIII, King 38, 48, 53, 59, 88, 141, 197, 211, 231
Hepworth, Barbara 180–1
Hickson, Joan 37
Hillier, Joseph 148
Hirst, Damien 48
Hitch, Nathanial 235
Hitler, Adolf 18
Holand, John 105
Holms, John 80
Hope, Alan 91
Hore-Belisha, Leslie 131
Howard, Admiral 54
Howland, John 146
Hudson, Thomas 145

Incledon-Bury, Penelope 51–2

James I, King 28, 119
James, John 20
Jekyll, Gertrude 73
John, King 73
Johnson, Amy 94

Index of People

Johnson, Dr Samuel 145
Juhel of Totnes 101

Keats, John 118, 137
Kellawy, John 33
Kellond, Waltert 102
Kemp, Edward 20
Kempe family 238
Killigrew, Sir Peter 210
Kingsley, Charles 54, 56, 152
Kipling, Rudyard 54–5
Knill, John 181–2
Kray, Reggie 78
Kray, Ronnie 78

Lander, John 234
Lander, Richard 234
Lane, Sir Allen 58, 62
Lang, Kirsty 107
Langtry, Lily 116
Lawrence, D.H. 201
Lawrence, Gertrude 94
Le Carré, John 59
Leach, Bernard 108, 180
Leach, William Elford 137
Lemon, Sir William 233
Lescaze, William 107
Ley, George 45
Licinius 160
Loam, Michael 173
Lodge, Sir Oliver 166
Lombard, Fleur 163
Lorimer, Sir Robert 125
Louis IX of France, King 12
Louis XV of France, King 246
Louis XVI of France, King 246
Lovelace, Ada 102
Lovelock, James 108
Lutyens, Edward 71, 73
Lyall, Kate 57
Lyte, Henry Francis 110–11

Mably, Alice 163
Mably, John 163
MacArthur, Ellen 134
MacCarthy, Sir Desmond 138
Maclean, Alistair 237
Mallowan, Max 115
Marchant, Chesten 177
Marconi, Guglielmo *207*
Margaret of Anjou 127, 133
Marie Antoinette 246
Marsh, John 26
Martin, Chris 176
Marwood, Thomas 32
Mary, Queen 127
Matilda, Empress 142
Matsubayashi, Tsuronosuke 180
Matthew the Miller 5
Maufe, Sir Edward 125
Maurier, Angela du 220
Maurier, Daphne du 59, 215, 218, 219, 220, 236, 237, 242
McVitie, Jack 'Jack the Hat' 78
Millais, Sir John Everett 26
Milne, Christopher 98–9
Mitchell, Frank 'The Mad Axemen' 78
Mitchell, R.J. 94
Mohun, Sir William 246
Molland, Alice 4
Monk, General 25
Monk, Nicholas 25
Moore, Dudley 116
Moore, Henry 109
Moresby, Sir Fairfax 23
Morpurgo, Clare 62
Morpurgo, Michael 62
Mountbatten, Lord 94
Moyle, Sir William 222
Mullally, Sarah 37
Murdoch, William 169, 170
Murnaghan, Dermot 61
Musser, Rev Christine 158

Index of People

Nash, John 213
Neele, Nancy 115
Nelson, Lady Frances 'Fanny' 23
Nelson, Lord 23, 32, 210, 223
Nesbit, Kate 140
Nettlefold, Archibald 94
Newcomen, Thomas 98
Newnes, Sir George 44, 60
Newton, Andrew 50
Nisbet, Josiah 23
Northcote, James 136, 143, 146
Norton, Mary 58

Oates, Captain Lawrence 135–6
Orleans, Duke of 13, 246
Owen, David 145
Oxenham family 70

Pajowska, Joanna 134
Parker, John 147
Parker, Lady Catherine 147
Parminter, Jane 24
Parminter, Mary 24
Parnell, Anna 47
Passmore, George 108, 139
Paulet, William 38
Pearce, Tom 69
Pears, Andrew 214
Pears, Thomas 214
Pearson, J.L. 235
Pellew, Captain 71
Pentreath, Dolly 192
Philip II of Spain, King 89, 127, 133
Philip, Prince 98
Pilcher, Rosamunde 59, 201
Pitt family 246
Pitt the Elder, William 246
Pitt the Younger, William 246
Pitt, Thomas 'Diamond' 246
Plantagenet, Katherine 16
Pollard, John 223
Poulett, Sir Amias 38
Prideaux family 164

Prior, Edward 36
Pritchard, Gerry 86
Prout, Samuel 136
Pugh, Lewis 136

Quaker Fox family 225
Quiller-Couch, Foy 219
Quiller-Couch, Sir Arthur 'Q' 219–20, 226
Quiller family 226

Raleigh, Sir Walter 10, 26–8, 52, 53, 82, 99, 117, 128
Randall, Tom 57
Ransome, Tabitha 223
Rashleigh, Charles 215, 217–18
Rashleigh family 217, 218
Rawdon, General 43
Rawlins, Billy 191
Reay, Samuel 19
Red Cross 162
Redvers, Baldwin de, 1st Earl of Devon 142
Redvers family, de 18, 119
Redvers, Richard de 16, 142
Rendel, Stuart, 1st Baron Rendel 139
Rennie, John 124
Rennie, Sir John (son) 124
Repton, Humphry 81, 99, 221, 226
Reynolds, Samuel 145
Reynolds, Sir Joshua 136, 142, 143, 144, 145–6, 226
Rich, Edmund 52
Richard, Earl of Cornwall 74, 159, 230
Richard II, King 105
Richard III, King 12–13, 248
Richard Strode of Newnham 74, 141, 142
Richard the Lionheart 96
Robartes family 244
Robert, Count of Mortain 206, 229
Rook, David 71

Index of People

Roscarrock, Nicholas 176
Rous, John 56
Rubinstein, Arthur 108
Ruskin, John 47, 136
Russell, Bertrand 107
Russell, John 81
Russell, John 'Jack,' the 'Sporting Parson' 19, 51–2, 98, 143

Sambell, Richard 234
Savery, Thomas 98
Saxons 2
Schmidt, Bernard 19
Schmidt, Christian 19
Schofield, Sydney 197
Scott, George Gilbert 11
Scott, Norman 50
Scott, Robert Falcon 131, 135–6
Scott, Sir George Gilbert 59, 244
Selassie, Haile 58
Sellers, Peter 48
Shackleton, Ernest 134
Shakespeare, William 12
Shelley, Harriet 43
Shelley, Percy Bysshe 41, 43
Shovell, Admiral Sir Cloudesley 189
Sickert, Walter 180
Simon, Paul 21
Simpson, Mrs 94
Sinden, Donald 138
Singer, Isaac 112
Singer, Isabella 112
Singer, Paris 112
Slee, George 19
Sleep, Wayne 139
Smart, Richard, Rector of Plymtree 25
Smeaton, John 126, 215
Smith, Augustus 188–9, 202–3
Smith, George 171
Smith, Herchel 139
Soane, Sir John 222
Southey, Robert 44–5

Spanish Armada 10, 27, 50, 53, 54, 89–90
Squire, Sir John Collings 138
St Aubyn family 196
St Boniface 63
St Clether 241
St David 250
St Edmund 6
St Edmund of Canterbury 52
St Endelienta 176
St Germanus 221, 222
St Hyacinth 238
St Ia 180
St Justus 183
St Michael 199
St Morwenna 150
St Nicholas 48, 181
St Petroc 232, 233
St Piran 166–7
St Protus 238
St Stephen 228
St Veronica 238
St Winwaloe 209
Stafford, Henry 39
Stafford, Humphrey and Isabel 25
Stein, Rick 164
Stephen, King 142
Stravinsky, Igor 108
Strode, Richard 74, 141, 142
Strode, Richard (son) 141
Strode, Sir William 141
Strong, Leonard 138
Stucley, William 59
Suffolk, Duke of 61
Sultan of Oman 23
Susan, Lady Exmouth 71

Tennyson, Lord Alfred 53, 54, 113, 152, 159, 198
Thomas, Dylan 192
Thompson, Flora 98
Thorpe, Jeremy 50
Throckmorton, Elizabeth 28

Index of People

Throckmorton family 45–6
Thunberg, Greta 134
Tolpuddle Martyrs 134, 147
Treby, George (son) 142
Treby, Sir George 142
Trecarrel, Sir Henry 231
Treffry, Dame Elizabeth 218
Tregeagle, Jan 243
Trelawny, Sir William 236
Tremayne family 214
Trengrouse, Henry 200
Trevelyan family 241
Trevithick, Richard 'Cornish Giant' 154, 170–1, 185
Tudor, Henry, Earl of Richmond 13
Turner, J.M.W. 180
Turner, William 60
Tyrwhitt, Thomas 76–7

Valera, Éamon de 77
Victoria, Princess 31
Victoria, Queen 32, 116, 196, 235, 239

Wadham, Joan 33
Wadham, Nicholas 33
Wadham, Sir John 33
Waldron, John 19
Wallis, Alfred 180
Warbeck, Perkin 185–6
Warden, Lord 172
Warelwast, William, Bishop of Exeter 11, 140
Waugh, Evelyn 91
Webb, Sir Aston 97
Welsford, Giles 101

Welshe, Robert 6
Wesley, John 20, 238
Wesley, Mary 225
Wesley, Samuel 20
Westcott, Blagdon 32
Westcott, Mrs 32
Whistler, James McNeill 180
White, John 27
Whitty, Thomas 34–5, 36
Wilberforce, William 23
Wildy, Mary 10
William II, King 96
William of Orange 5, 12, 110, 120–1
William, Prince 98, 176
William the Conqueror 3, 4, 5, 49, 206–7
Williams, Dionysius 187
Williams-Ellis, Susan 107
Williams, John Charles 213
Williams, Len 226
Williams, Michael 213
Williamson, Cecil 158
Wills, William 101
Wilson, Harold 188
Wonnacott, Tim 61
Wood the Younger, John 181
Woodville, Elizabeth 39
Wordsworth, William 137
Wren, Sir Christopher 142
Wyattville, Jeffry 81
Wynard, William 7
Wyndham, John 19

Yogge, Thomas 130
Young, Michael (Lord Young of Dartington) 107

INDEX OF PLACES

A La Ronde, Exmouth 24
Agatha Christie Mile, Torquay 116
Agatha Christie Potent Plants Garden, Torquay 114
Albert Clock, Barnstaple 50
All Saints Church, Brixham 110
All Saints Church, Clovelly 56
Altarnun 237–8
Annie's Tunnel, Sennen 187
Antony House, Polperro 226
Arwenack House, Falmouth 210
Ashburton 66, 82, 92
Assembly Rooms, Truro 233
Athelstan's Tower, Exeter 2, 3
Axminster 34–6
Axmouth 33–4

Baker's Pit, Pridhamsleigh Cavern 86
Barbara Hepworth Museum 181
Barbican, Plymouth 127–8
Barnstaple 48–50, 61
Barras Nose 160
Barry Head lighthouse, Torbay 121
Basilica of San Vitale 24
Basill Manor, St Clether 241
Bayard's Cove, Dartmouth 97
Beacon Tower, Lynmouth 43
Bedford House, Exeter 13
Beer 37
Beer Heights Light Railway 37
Beers Head 33
Belstone 70–1
Belstone Tor 70
Bickleigh, Exe Valley 21
Bickleigh Castle 21–2
Bickleigh Chapel 22

Bickleigh Mill 21
Bideford 52–5
Bishops Throne, Exeter 12
Black Friar's Distillery, Plymouth 129
Black Friar's Monastery, Plymouth 129
Black Torrington 52
Blackpool Mill Cottage, Hartland Quay 62
Blickling Hall, Norfolk 35
Blisland 238
Blisland Inn 238
Blue Ball Inn, Countisbury 42
Blue Boar Inn, Exeter 7
Blue Hills Mine, St Agnes 167
Blundell's School, Tiverton 19, 51
Boat Float, Dartmouth 97, 98
Boconnoc House, Lostwithiel 246–7
Bodinnick 219, 220
Bodinnick Ferry 220
Bodmin 228, 232–3
Bodmin gaol 233
Bodmin Moor 236–42, 249
Bolventor 236, 242
Boscastle 157–8
Botallack Mine 184
Branscombe 33
Braunton 61
Braunton Burrows 61
Braunton Marsh 61
Breakwater Fort, Plymouth 125
Brentor 87–8
Britannia Royal Navy College, Dartmouth 97
Brixham 110–11
Brook Manor, Buckfastleigh 79, 85
Broom Parc, Veryan 225

Index of Places

Brown Willy, Bodmin Moor 236, 237, 242
Brutus Stone, Totnes 100
Bryher, Scilly Isles 189
Buckfast Abbey, Buckfastleigh 84–5
Buckfastleigh 79, 85, 86, 91, 92
Buckland Abbey, Dartmoor 88, 89, 90
Bude 153–4
Bude Canal 153–4
Bude Castle *149*, 153, 155
Budleigh Salterton 26–8
Burgh Island *93*, 94–5, 115–16
Burgh Island Hotel 94
Burrator Reservoir, Dartmoor 91
Bush Inn, Morwenstow 152
Butchers Row, Barnstaple 50
Butterwalk, Totnes 97, 104
Byron Court, Exmouth 23

Cabell Mausoleum, Buckfastleigh 85
Cadhay House, Ottery St Mary 37–8
Caerhays Castle 213
Camborne 169–70
Camborne Hill 170
Camborne Library 170
Camelford 249–50
Camelot Castle, Tintagel 160
Canonteign 71
Canonteign Barton 71
Canonteign House 71
Cape Cornwall 201–2
Carclaze Mine, St Austell 217
Carrick Roads, Falmouth 210, 211
Castle Drogo, Dartmoor 71–3, *72*, 90
Castle Mound, Barnstaple 49
Castle Street, Launceston 230–1
Cathedral Church of Saint Mary and Saint Boniface, Plymouth 132
Cathedral Close, Exeter 8–9
Cathedral of North Devon, Stoke 58
Cawsand 223
Chagford 66
Chambercombe Manor, Ilfracombe 60–1

Chapel of St Lawrence, Ashburton 82
Chapel Street, Penzance 194
Chapman Barrows, Exmoor 46
Charles Church, Plymouth 139
Charlestown 215
Cheesewring, Bodmin Moor 239, *239*
Cherub Inn, Dartmouth 97
Church of St Buryan, St Buryan 202, 203
Church of St Mary, Molland 45–6
Church of St Mary, Plympton 140–1
Church of St Mary Steps, Exeter 5
Church of St Mary, Totnes 103
Church of St Nonna, Altarnun 237–8
Church of St Pancras, Exeter 4–5
Clovelly *41*, 55–7
Clovelly Court 56
Coinage Hall, Helston 198
Coinagehall Street, Helston 198
Coleridge Way, Lynmouth 42
Colleton Barton 52
Colleton Manor 51–2
Colliford Lake 242
Combe Martin 45
Come-to-Good hamlet 248–9
Come-to-Good Quaker Meeting House 249
Compton Castle, Marldon 116–18
Cornish Mining World Heritage Site 184
Cornwall and West Devon Mining Landscape 172
Cornwall and West Devon World Heritage Site 197
Cornwall County Council 232, 233
Cornwall Railway 223
Cotehele 247–8
Cott Inn, Dartington 105
Council Chamber, Exeter 7
Count (Account) House, St Just 185
Countess Weir 8
Countisbury 42
Crazy Kate's Cottage, Clovelly 57

Index of Places

Creation Window, St Neot Church 240
Crediton 63
Cremyll 224
Crowndale Farm, Tavistock 81
Custom House, Exeter 8, 10

Daniel Gumb's Cave, Cheesewring 239
Daphne Du Maurier Museum 237
Dartington 104–10
Dartington College of Arts 108
Dartington Hall 105–9
Dartington Hall Gardens 109
Dartington Hall School 106–7
Dartington Pottery 108
Dartmoor 65–6, 90–2
Dartmoor Brewery 91
Dartmoor National Park 68
Dartmoor Prison 74, 76–8, 80
Dartmoor Prison Museum 78
Dartmouth 96–9
Dartmouth Castle 96–7
Davidstow 250
De Lank Quarries, Bodmin Moor 240
De Lank River 240
Delabole 175
Delabole Quarry 175
Delabole Wind Farm 175
Devil's Bellows, Boscastle 157
Devil's Cauldron, Lydford Gorge 74
Devil's Jump, Bodmin Moor 240
Devil's Steps, Buckfastleigh 85
Devon Corn house, Kingsland 223
Devon Railway Centre 21
Devonport, Plymouth 125, 130–1
Devonport Column, Plymouth 130
Devonport Guildhall, Plymouth 130
Ding Dong Mine, Madron 185
Diocese of Cornwall 235
Diocese of Devon 235
Dolcoath Mine, Camborne 173
Dolphin Hotel, Plymouth 147
Doom Bar, Padstow 163–4
Door of Unity, Plymouth 130

Dorset Aisle, St Mary's 30, 39
Dozmary Pool, Bodmin Moor 242–3, 250
Drewsteignton 71–2
Duchy Hotel, Princetown 80
Duchy Palace, Lostwithiel 231
Duke of York Inn, Iddesleigh 62

East Looe 226
East Lyn River 42, 43
Easton Court Hotel, Chagford 91
Ebbingford Manor, Bude 175
Eddystone Lighthouse 125–6, 223
Eden Project, St Austell 216
Egyptian House, Penzance 194
Elberry Cove, Torbay 116, 121
Elizabethan House, Plymouth 128
Endsleigh Cottage (later Hotel Endsleigh), Tavistock 81
Ethy Woods 246
Exeter 1–13, 118
Exeter Astronomical Clock 13
Exeter Cathedral *1*, 5, 10–12, 13
Exeter College 51
Exeter Guildhall 7
Exeter Ship Canal 8
Exmoor 42, 43
Exmouth 22–4

Falmouth 210, 225, 233
Falmouth University 108
Ferryside, Bodinnick 220
Finch Foundry, Sticklepath 68–9
Fingle Bridge, Dartmoor 91
First and Last Inn, Sennen 186–7
Fisherman's Cot, Bickleigh 21
Fistral Beach, Newquay 166
Fordmoor Farm, Plymtree 25
Fore Street, Plympton 143–4
Fosse Way 2, 33
Four Village Trail, Dartmoor 69–71
Fowey 218–20
Fowey Hall 219, *219*

[266]

Index of Places

Fox Tore Mire, Dartmoor 80–1
Foxholes Hill, Exmouth 36
Frenchman's Creek, Helford River 209

Gaiety Theatre, Ilfracombe 48
Geevor Mine, Pendeen 185
Geevor Tin Mining Museum, Pendeen 185
Globe Theatre, Plymouth 131
Godolphin House, Godolphin Cross 196–7
Godrevy Island 177
Godrevy Point 177
Golitha Falls, Bodmin Moor 242
Goodwin Crescent, Plymouth 139
Goonhilly Earth Satellite Station 208
Grand Hotel, Torquay 116
Great Field, Braunton 61
Great Hall, Dartington 104, 105–6, 108
Great Hangman, Combe Martin 45
Greenbank Hotel, Falmouth 225
Greenway, Dartmouth 99
Greenway Chapel, Tiverton 18
Grimspound 81
Grylls Monument, Helston 198
Guildhall, Totnes 102
Guildhall Shopping Centre, Exeter 4
Gunwalloe 206–7
Gweek 209
Gwennap 173
Gwithian 177

Hamoaze, Plymouth 130, 133
Harbour Bookshop, Dartmouth 99
Hartland Abbey 58–9
Hartland Point 57
Hartland Quay 57
Hatherleigh 62
Haven, Tintagel 160
Hawker Memorial Window, St Morwenna's Church 151
Hawker's Hut, Morwenstow 152
Hawkstor Down, Bodmin Moor 238–9

Hayes Barton, Budleigh 26
Hayford Hall 'Hangover Hall,' Buckfastleigh 79–80
Haytor, Dartmoor *65*, 66
Headland Hotel, Newquay 166
Heath's Court, Ottery St Mary 30
Heavitree, Exeter 4
Heinz Monument, Cape Cornwall *201*, 202
Helford River 209
Heligan House, Mevagissey 214
Helston 197–200
Helston Castle 198
Helston Furry Dance 199–200
Helston River 198
Henna Cliff, Morwenstow 152
High Cliff, Crackington Haven 175
High Cross House, Dartington 107
High Street, Exeter 9
High Willays, Dartmoor 66
Hobby Drive, Clovelly 57
Holy Trinity Church, Buckfastleigh 85
Holy Trinity Church, Ilfracombe 47
Honiton 31–2, 38
Honiton Fair 38–9
Hooken Cliffs, Branscombe 33
Horwood Almhouses, Barnstaple 50
House of Cards, Ashburton 82
Huer's Hut, Newquay 165–6
Hugh Town, Scilly Isles 188

Iddesleigh 62
Ilfracombe 47–8
Illogan 176–7
Imperial Hotel, Torquay 116
Island House, Plymouth 128

Jacka Bakery, Plymouth 129
Jacob's Ladder, Falmouth 225
Jamaica Inn, Bodmin Moor 236–7
Joint Mitnor Cave, Pridhamsleigh Cavern 86
Jubilee Rock, Blisland 239

Index of Places

Keigwin Arms, Mousehole 192
Kents Cavern, Torquay 114, 116
King Arthur's Hall, St Breward 239–40
King Doniert's Stone, St Cleer 242
King Edward VI Grammar School, Totnes 101–2
Kingsand, Rame Peninsula 223
Kingsley's Cottage, Clovelly 56
Kingswear Castle, Dartmouth 96–7
Kipling Tors, Westward Ho! 55
Kirkham Chantry, Paignton 111
Kirkham House, Paignton 111
Knightshayes Court, Tiverton 20
Knill Steeple, St Ives 182, *182*
Knowstone Manor, Knowstone 18

Lady Exmouth Falls, Canonteign 71
Lamorna Cove, Newlyn 203
Lander's Monument, Truro 234
Landmark Theatre 'Madonna's Bra,' Ilfracombe 48
Land's End 187–8
Land's End Signpost 188
Lanhydrock House 244, *244*
Lantern Hill, Ilfracombe 47–8
Lanyon Quoit, Madron 201
Launcells 156–7
Launceston 228–31
Launceston Castle 229–30
Lavethan house, Blisland 238
Lawrence House, Launceston 231
Leach Pottery, St Ives 180
Lemon Street, Truro 233
Lerryn 246
Levant Mine, St Just 173, 184, 185
Lidcott Farm, Laneast 249
Littleham 23
Lizard Point 206, 208
Lizard Village 208
Lobster Pot Inn, Mousehole 192
Loe Bar, River Cober 198, 200, 243
Loe Pool 198–9

Logan Rock, Treen 202
Long Bridge, Barnstaple 49
Long Bridge, Bideford 52
Longships Lighthouse, Land's End 188
Lostwithiel 228, 231–2, 245–6
Lundy Island 55
Lustleigh 91
Lustleigh Cleave 91
Lydford 73–4
Lydford Castle 73–4
Lydford Gorge 74
Lyme Bay 96
Lynmouth 42–4
Lynton 44–5
Lynton and Barnstaple Railway 60
Lynton and Lynmouth Cliff Railway 44

Madron Church 185
Magnolia Centre, Exmouth 23
Magnolia Walk, Exmouth 23
Manor of Rill, Exmouth 23
Marazion 195, 196
Marchant's Cross, Sheepstor 91–2
Marconi Monument, Poldhu 207, *207*
Marwood House, Honiton 32
Mayflower Steps, Plymouth *123*, 128–9
Medieval Exeter 6–12
Meldon Dam, Dartmoor 68
Meldon Viaduct 68
Menabilly, East St Austell Bay 217–18, 220
Merlin's Cave, Tintagel 160
Mermaid Chair, Zennor 183
Mermaid Inn, Ashburton 82
Merry Maidens Stone Circle, St Buryan 203
Mevagissey 214
Miles Coverdale Tower, Paignton 112
Minack Theatre, Porthcurno Cove 191–2, *191*
Minions 239
Minstrel's Gallery, Exeter Cathedral 12

Index of Places

Mirimar, Exmouth 24
Molland 45–6
Mol's Coffee House, Exeter 9–10
Morwellham Quay 81–2
Morwenna's Well, Morwenstow 152
Morwenstow 150–2
Mount Edgcumbe House 224
Mount Edgcumbe National Park 223–4
Mount's Bay 190
Mousehole 192
Moyle Almshouses, St Germans 222
Mullion Cove lifeboat station 206
Murdoch House, Redruth 168–9
Museum of Witchcraft and Magic, Boscastle 157–8
Music Room, Powderham Castle 35

National Marine Aquarium, Plymouth 148
National Park Visitor Centre, Princetown 76
Nelson House, Exmouth 23
Newlyn 192–3
Newlyn School 193
Newlyn School of Art 193
Newquay 165–6
Nine Maidens Stone Circle, Belstone 70, 203
Norman Exeter 3–5
North Devon Crematorium 61
North Devon Heritage Coast 61
North Street, Ashburton 82
Northernhay Gardens, Exeter 2
Nutcracker Rock, Dartmoor 91

Odd Fellows Hall, Plymouth 131
Okehampton 67
Okehampton Castle 67–8
Old Court House, Bickleigh Castle 22
Old Exe Bridge, Exeter 5, 6
Old Exeter Inn, Ashburton 28, 82
Old Ferry Inn, Bodinnick 220
Old Palace Yard 28

Old Plymouth 124
Old Post Office, Tintagel 160, *160*
Old School House, Plympton 143, 145
Old Shute House, Axminster 39
Old Town Bay, Scilly Isles 188
Oldway Mansion, Paignton 112–13
1 Execliff, Exmouth 23
Orcombe Point, Exmouth 36
Ottery St Mary Church *15*, 28–30, 37–8, 38
Oxenham Arms, South Zeal 70

Pack o' Cards Inn, Combe Martin 45
Padstow 163–5
Paignton 111–13
Pandora Inn, Restronguet Creek 224, 225
Pannier Market, Barnstaple 50
Parliament Cottage, Longcombe 120–1
Parracombe 46–7
Parson and Clerk, Teignmouth 118–19
Paul (village) 192
Pen Olver cliff 208
Pendennis Castle, Carrick Roads 210–11, *211*, 212
Penhale Beach, Perranporth 166
Penlee Lifeboat station, Newlyn 193
Penrhyn port 211
Penrose's Almshouses, Barnstaple 49–50
Penzance 193–5
Perranporth 166
Pilchard Inn, Burgh Island 95
Pipers (standing stones), St Buryan 203
Place House, Fowey 218
Plymouth 123–48
Plymouth Dock 130
Plymouth Gin 129
Plymouth Hoe 89, 125–7
Plymouth Naval Memorial 125
Plymouth Rock, New World 124
Plymouth Sound 124–5, 133, 137, 146, 147
Plymouth Synagogue 147

[269]

Index of Places

Plympton 66, 124, 140–6
Plympton Grammar School *141*, 142–3
Plympton Guildhall 144
Plympton House 142
Plympton St Mary 140–2
Plympton St Maurice 142–4
Plymtree 24–6
Plymtree Manor 25
Poldark Mine, Wendron 203
Poldhu 207–8
Polgooth Mine, St Austell 216–17
Polperro 225–6
Polperro Mine 167
Polzeath 162–3, 176
Port Eliot, St Germans 221, 222
Port Isaac 175–6
Port of Plymouth Sailing Regatta 147
Porth Navas 209
Porthcurno Cable Office 190–1
Porthcurno Cove 190–1
Porthcurno Telegraph Museum 191
Postbridge 91
Powderham Castle 67–8, 119–20
Prideaux Place, Padstow 164–5
Pridhamsleigh Cavern 86
Primrose Cottage, Exmouth 22
Princetown 76–9, 80
Prior's Bridge, Launceston 229
Priory of St Peter and St Paul,
 Plympton St Mary 140–1
Prysten House, Plymouth 130

Quayside, Exeter 8
Queen Anne's Walk, Barnstaple 50

Rame Head 223
Rame Peninsula 223–4
Rectory, Plympton 144
Red Lion Hotel, Clovelly 57
Red Mound, Exeter 3
Redruth 168–9
Reed's Cave, Buckfastleigh 85, 86
Respryn Bridge 243–4

Restormel Castle, Lostwithiel 228, 230, 231, 245–6, *245*
Restronguet Creek 224, 225
River Axe 33, 34
River Camel 163
River Cober 198, 243
River Dart 96, 99, 100
River Exe 16, 42, 119
River Fal 233
River Fowey 231, 242–6
River Inny 241
River Jordan 158
River Kensey 228, 229
River Lerryn 246
River Loman 16
River Lyd 74
River Ottery 249
River Plym 124
River Tamar 3, 63, 130, 132, 133, 228, 229–30
River Tavy 81
River Taw 48, 49, 68, 70
River Teign 71, 72, 90
River Tiddy 223
River Torridge 52, 63
River Truro 233
River Valency 158
Rock 176
Roman Exeter 2
Roscarrock farm, St Endellion 176
Rougemont Castle, Exeter 3, 4
Rougemont Castle Gatehouse, Exeter 3–4
Rougemont Gardens, Exeter 2
Rough Tor, Bodmin Moor 236, 237
Royal Albert Bridge, Plymouth 132–3
Royal Albert Hall 36
Royal Citadel, Plymouth Hoe 127
Royal Clarence Hotel, Exeter 10
Royal Cornwall Museum, Truro 248
Royal Cornwall Polytechnic Society, Falmouth 225
Royal Glen Hotel, Sidmouth 31
Royal Marine Barracks, Plymouth 131

Index of Places

Royal Pavilion 35
Royal Seven Stars, Totnes 101

Saltram House, Plymouth 35, 147–8
Sarawak 83–4
Saunton Sands 61
Saxon Exeter 3
Saxon Minster, Crediton 63
Saxon Minster, Exeter 11
Schumacher College, Dartington 108–9
Scilly Isles 188–90
Seaton 33–4
Seaton Tramway 34
Sennen 185–7
Sennen Cove 186
Sheeps Tor, Dartmouth 91
Shelley's Hotel, Lynmouth 43
Sidbury 36
Sidmouth 31
Slapton Ley 95
Slapton Sands 95–6
Smeaton's Tower, Plymouth Hoe *125*, 126
Society for the Protection of Ancient Buildings (SPAB) 25
South Crofty Mine, Pool 173
South Devon Railway 91–2
South Gate, Exeter 7
South Molton 51
South Tawton 70
South West Coast Path 42
South Zeal 70
Southgate Arch, Launceston 230
Spanish Barn, Torquay 114
Sperris Quoit, Zennor 201
Squeezy Belly Alley, Port Isaac 176
St Agnes 167–8
St Agnes Lighthouse, Scilly Isles 189
St Agnes, Scilly Isles 189
St Andrew's Church, Plymouth 129–30
St Anne's Chapel, Barnstaple 49
St Austell 215–16

St Bartholomew's Church, Lostwithiel 232
St Breock Church, Wadebridge 243
St Breward 239
St Buryan 202, 203
St Clether 241
St Clether Holy Well Chapel 241
St David's Holy Well, Davidstow 250
St Edmund Hall 52
St Endellion 176
St Enodoc Church 163
St Erth Church 248
St Fimbarrus Church 220
St George's Church 20
St Germans 221–2
St Germans Priory Church *205*, 221–2
St Germans railway station 223
St Germans River 133
St Germans Viaduct 223
St Giles Church, Sidbury 36–7
St Ia's Parish Church, St Ives 180
St Ives 179–82, *179*
St Ives School 180
St James Church, Swimbridge 50–1
St John the Baptist Church, Plymtree 24–5
St John's College, Cambridge 249
St Juliot 159
St Just 183–4
St Just-in-Roseland Church 212
St Leonard's Church, Sheepstor 83–4
St Margaret and St Andrew's Church, Littleham 23
St Martin's Church, Exeter 9
St Martin's, Scilly Isles 189
St Mary Arches Church, Exeter 5
St Mary Magdalen Church, Launceston 231
St Mary Old Town Church, Scilly Isles 188
St Mary the Virgin Church, Bickleigh 22
St Mary's Chapel, South Zeal 70
St Mary's Church, Truro 235
St Mary's Old Church, Dartington 105

Index of Places

St Mary's, Scilly Isles 188
St Materiana Church, Tintagel 160
St Maurice House, Plympton 144
St Mawes Castle, Carrick Roads
    211–12, *212*
St Michael de Rupe Church, Brentor
    87–8, 236
St Michael's Chapel, Rame Head 223
St Michael's Church, Axmouth 34
St Michael's Church, Paignton 111–12
St Michael's Church, Princetown 79
St Michael's Island, Plymouth 125
St Michael's Mount 195–6
St Michael's Parish Church, Honiton 32
St Morwenna's Church, Morwenstow
    150–2, *150*
St Nectan's Church, Stoke *57*, 58
St Nectan's Church, Welcombe 62–3
St Neot 240–1
St Neot Church 240–1
St Nicholas Chapel, Ilfracombe 47–8
St Nicholas Priory, Exeter 4, 5
St Olave's Church, Exeter *3*, 5
St Pancras Church, Dartmoor 75–6
St Peter and St Paul Church,
    Holsworthy 62
St Peter's Church, Barnstaple 49
St Peter's Church, Tiverton 16, 18–19
St Petrock's Church, Exeter 9
St Petrock's Church, Parracombe 46–7
St Petroc's Church, Bodmin 232–3
St Petrox Church, Dartmouth 97
St Piran's Oratory, Perranporth 166–7
St Protus and St Hyacinth Church,
    Blisland 238
St Saviour's Church, Dartmouth 97
St Sennen's Church 185
St Stephen's Church, Launceston
    228–9, 230
St Swithin's Church, Launcells 156–7
St Swithin's Well, Launcells 157
St Thomas 6
St Thomas Church, Exeter 6

St Thomas Church, Launceston 229
St Veep Parish Church 225
St Winifred's Church, Branscombe 33
St Winnow 246
St Winnow Barton Farm Museum 246
St Winnow Church 246
St Winwaloe Church, Gunwalloe 207
St Wynwallow Church, Landewednack
    208–9
Star Inn, St Just 183
Starcross 119
Stepcote Hill 5
Sticklepath 69–70
Stippy Stappy, St Agnes 168
Stockton and Darlington Railway 169
Stonehouse, Plymouth 131–2
Stripple Stones, Bodmin Moor 239
Summerleaze Beach, Bude 153
Sutton, Plymouth 124, 127
Sutton Pool, Plymouth 127
Swimbridge 50–1

Tamar Suspension Bridge 132–3, 223
Tarka Trail 42, 61
Tater-Du Lighthouse, Lamorna Cove 203
Tavistock 66, 81–2
Tavistock Canal 81
Teignmouth 118–19
Theatre Royal Plymouth 148
The Chanter's House, Ottery St Mary 30
The Haven, Fowey 219
The House in the Sea, Newquay 166
The House That Moved, Exeter 5, 6
The Jack Russell, Swimbridge 51
The Kraken, Hartland Quay 57
The Lizard 206
The Lost Gardens of Heligan,
    Mevagissey 214–15
The Mansion, Totnes 101
The Old Inn, St Breward 239
The Sloop Inn, St Ives 182
The Valiant Soldier, Buckfastleigh 86
Tinner's Rabbits, St Pancras Church 75

[272]

Index of Places

Tinside Lido, Plymouth 147
Tintagel 159–61
Tintagel Castle 159–60
Tiverton 16–22
Tiverton Castle 16–17
Tiverton Town Hall 20
Tome Stone, Barnstaple 50
Topsham 8
Tor Royal, Princetown 76
Torbay 110–16
Torquay 113–16
Torquay Museum 116
Torre Abbey, Torquay 113–14, *114*
Totnes 99–104, 120
Totnes Museum 102
Towan Head, Newquay 166
Tower Hall, Plympton 140
Town Hill, Totnes 101
Town Mill, Buckfastleigh 86
Trebetherick 163
Trematon Castle, Saltash 130–1
Trengrouse Way, Helston 200
Tresavean Mine, Gwennap 173, 185
Tresco, Scilly Isles 188–9
Tresungers farm, St Endellion 176
Trevaunance Cove 168
Trewinnard Coach, Royal Cornwall
    Museum 248
Trippet Stones, Bodmin Moor 239
Troy Town Farm, Scilly Isles 189
Truro 228, 232, 233–6
Truro Cathedral *227*, 234–5
Truro port 211
Tuckers Hall, Exeter 7–8
Tuckingmill 171
Tudor Lodge, Plympton 144
Tunnels Beaches, Ilfracombe 48
Turk's Head pub, Exeter 13
Turks Head Tavern 145
Two Moors Way, Lynmouth 42

Valley of the Rocks, Lynton 44–5
Vernon Place, Falmouth 225

Veryan 225
Victoria Park, Bideford 53
Victoria Tower, Truro Cathedral 235

Walsingham Place, Truro 233
Warfleet Creek, Dartmouth 96
Warleggan 241–2
Warren Cottage, Polperro 225
Weare Giffard 59–60
Weare Giffard Hall 59
Wellington Hotel, Boscastle 158
Wendron 203
West Gate, Exeter 5
West Looe 226
West Lyn River 42, 43
West Okemont River 68
West Street, Ashburton 82
Westward Ho! 54–5
Wheal Coates Mine, St Agnes 168
Wheal Roots Mine, Wendron 203
White Hart Hotel, Exeter 7
White Hart Hotel, Launceston 229
White Lady Waterfall, Lydford
    Gorge 74
Widecombe Fair 69, 74
Widecombe in the Moor 75–6
Widemouth Bay 175
Wild Futures Monkey Sanctuary,
    Looe 226
Winnianton Farm, Gunwalloe 207
Winnianton Manor, Gunwalloe 206–7
Woodbeer Court, Plymtree 26
Woody Bay 60
Woody Bay Station 60
Woolbrook Cottage, Sidmouth 31
Wynards Almshouse, Exeter 7

Yeolm Bridge 249
Yeolmbridge 249
Yes Tor, Dartmoor 66

Zennor 183
Zennor Quoit 201

ACKNOWLEDGEMENTS

My thanks to the team at Ebury, Publishing Director Elizabeth Bond for her support of the series, Editor Fionn Hargreaves for her organisational skills and guidance, Editorial Manager Jessica Anderson for her help and advice, and copyeditor Katie Fisher and proofreader David Campbell for a job well done.

Thanks also to my agent Ros, always there for us.